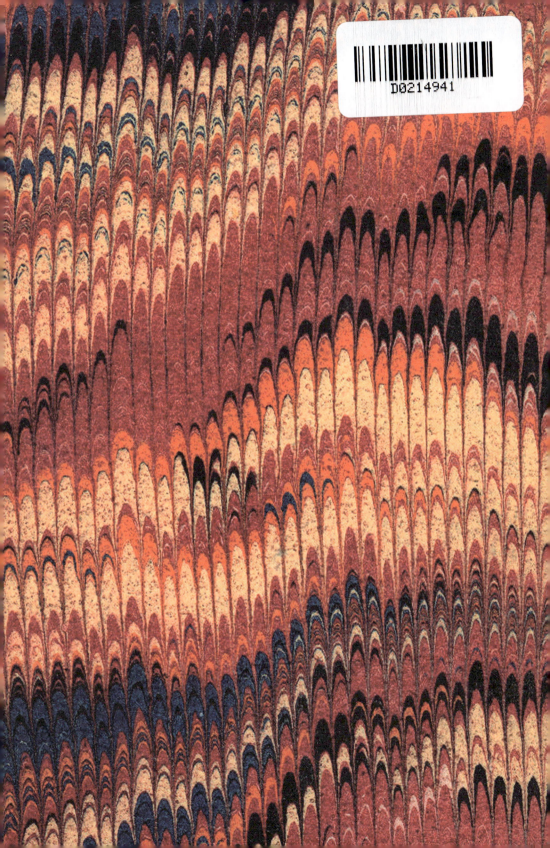

Mark Atherton is Lecturer in English Language and Literature at Regent's Park College, Oxford. He is the author of *Teach Yourself Old English/Anglo Saxon* and contributed to *A Companion to J R R Tolkien* (edited by Stuart Lee, forthcoming).

'C S Lewis wrote of his friend and academic colleague J R R Tolkien praising his "unique insight at once into the language of poetry and into the poetry of language". Generations of readers have responded to the power, precision, and delicacy of J R R Tolkien's linguistic imagination. This absorbing new study of *The Hobbit* brings a philologist's eye to that work's creation, structure, and expression, positioning it within the broader development of Tolkien's professional thinking about philology and the evolving mythography of his creative writings. Mark Atherton, himself what Tolkien calls "a scholar of gramarye", imaginatively shows how Tolkien's academic interests in philology, linguistic-aesthetic and in reconstructive philology spilled over into the crucible of his own mythography, and was catalysed by the alchemy of his own reading in myths and contemporary fairy stories by writers such as William Morris, Edward Thomas, Francis Thompson and Robert Graves. This book gives them new ways of appreciating the interplay between his narratives and the linguistic enchantment of their imaginative world. Atherton's insights bring to mind Tolkien's own comment: "How those old words smite one out of the dark antiquity!"'

Vincent Gillespie,
**J R R Tolkien Professor of English Literature and Language,
University of Oxford**

'*There and Back Again* is essential reading for all Tolkien fans – and also for anyone interested more broadly in medievalism, or the ways in which later writers have responded to the culture of the Middle Ages. Mark Atherton is that ideal combination: a reader and critic deeply appreciative of Tolkien's literary artistry, his imaginative scope and his linguistic invention, who is also, like Tolkien himself, a distinguished scholar of medieval language and literature. In this highly readable and accessible study, Atherton brings his own scholarship to bear on Tolkien's sources for *The Hobbit*, and in the process illuminates the whole of Tolkien's remarkable oeuvre.'

Heather O'Donoghue,
Vigfusson Rausing Reader in Ancient Icelandic Literature &
Antiquities, University of Oxford

'Mark Atherton's treatment of one of the most famous books of the twentieth century is timely and welcome. On the face of it, *The Hobbit* appears an engaging fantasy adventure for young readers; but, as it later transpired, Mr Bilbo Baggins' exploits "there and back again" were simply a prelude to the apocalyptic drama that was to unfold in *The Lord the Rings*. One reason for the enduring appeal of both of these works is that J R R Tolkien imbued his tales of a fictional realm with resonances of ancient themes and universal truths. In this detailed exploration, Mark Atherton provides the reader with a comprehensive understanding of the many origins, influences and inspirations – biographical, historical, geographical and literary – that, combined with a unique imagination, resulted in the crafting of a new mythology.'

Brian Sibley,
author of *The Lord of the Rings: The Making of the Movie Trilogy*
and of *Peter Jackson: A Film-maker's Journey*

MARK ATHERTON

THERE AND BACK AGAIN

J R R TOLKIEN AND THE ORIGINS OF THE HOBBIT

I.B. TAURIS

LONDON · NEW YORK

Published in 2012 by I.B.Tauris & Co Ltd
6 Salem Road, London W2 4BU
175 Fifth Avenue, New York NY 10010
www.ibtauris.com

Distributed in the United States and Canada Exclusively by Palgrave Macmillan
175 Fifth Avenue, New York NY 10010

ISBN   978 1 78076 246 3

A full CIP record for this book is available from the British Library
A full CIP record is available from the Library of Congress

Library of Congress Catalog Card Number: available

Designed and typeset by 4word Ltd, Bristol
Printed and bound in Sweden by ScandBook AB

Contents

Illustrations

Abbreviations

EDD	Joseph Wright, *The English Dialect Dictionary*, 6 vols (London: Henry Frowde, 1898–1905)
FR	J.R.R. Tolkien, *The Fellowship of the Ring*, Part I of *LOTR* (London: George Allen & Unwin, 1954)
LOTR	J.R.R. Tolkien, *The Lord of the Rings*; the novel consists of three volumes (*FR*, *TT* and *RK*) and six books (because the *LOTR* exists in many printed editions, citations are by book and chapter rather than by page)
NED	*New English Dictionary* (the older preferred title for the multi-volume *Oxford English Dictionary*)
OE	Old English
OF	Old French
ON	Old Norse
RK	J.R.R. Tolkien, *The Return of the King*, Part III of *LOTR* (London: George Allen & Unwin, 1955)
SGGK	*Sir Gawain and the Green Knight*
TCBS	Tea Club, Barrovian Society
TT	J.R.R. Tolkien, *The Two Towers*, Part II of *LOTR* (London: George Allen & Unwin, 1954)

Acknowledgements

THE ORIGINAL IDEA for this book came from Kate Kirkpatrick. The first draft was read with enthusiasm by Maria Artamanova, Richard Lawes, Daniel Thomas and Erik Tonning. With the 'kindness of summer', Julie Dyson went through the whole of the final draft, providing wise commentary and spotting errors along the way. Alexander Carroll has been a fine sounding board: he saw both first and final versions and offered useful suggestions. Many other people have since given encouragement or comment; they include Douglas A. Anderson, John Garth, Tony Harris, Joanna Harrison, Stuart Lee and Paul Sullivan. I am grateful for interest shown by colleagues such as Paul Fiddes, Julian Thompson and Lynn Robson at Regent's Park College, Oxford. For photographs I would like to thank Julie Dyson, Kazutomo Karasawa, Samuel Robertson and Ryan Simpson, for illustrations Steve Lunn, Sophie Millns and Rosalind Mills, and I am specially grateful to Fergus Parnaby, who – quite late in the day – provided pictures to order. Many thanks also to Michael Gabriel for his thoughtful and perceptive comments.

The editorial support from Alex Wright at I.B. Tauris Publishers has been invaluable and much appreciated.

Fig. 1a   Dragon circle

PART ONE
Shaping the plot

J.R.R. TOLKIEN OFTEN regarded his moments of creative inspiration as epiphanies that came to him unexpectedly during moments of concentration, when his mind was elsewhere, engaged in the intricacies of philological scholarship or carrying out his duties as a university teacher. The making of *The Hobbit* is no exception; it fits the pattern neatly. According to how Tolkien remembered it, he was marking secondary school examination papers some time in 1930 in order to earn extra money to supplement his university income – although he held the prestigious professorship of Anglo-Saxon at Oxford University he nevertheless had four children to bring up and educate. The marking was not his favourite task, and to help keep his sanity, as he saw it, he had a habit of doodling on the examination scripts, which of course was quite possible to do, since the scripts were never returned to the candidates themselves. In a moment of distraction or boredom, then, he wrote the following much-quoted sentence on a spare page of examination paper:

In a hole in the ground there lived a hobbit.[1]

This account is one of a number of different and even slightly contradictory reports as to how *The Hobbit* first came into being. John D. Rateliff has discussed these in full, and the conclusion seems to be that although Tolkien did not finish writing *The Hobbit* until 1933 and did not publish it until 1937, it began life as a spoken tale told to his children.[2] Tolkien was an enthusiastic and actively involved father, and in the mid- to late 1920s, with his four children to occupy and entertain, he began to tell stories to them. For material he used an eclectic mix: scenes from his own childhood, events in the daily lives of his children, his reading of both general fiction and children's literature. To this he added his private interest in mythology and in the writing of poetry, and his professional concern with 'the literature of the middle ages, philology, the history of stories, words, and languages'.[3] All this derived – as will be seen in the course of this book – from his work as a university professor of English language and literature.

In the first part of this book the emphasis will be on the plot, theme and setting of *The Hobbit*. The plot is a quest, well summed up by Tolkien's subtitle 'there and back again', though the narrative mostly covers the going *there* and only briefly touches on the coming *back*. It will be argued that it begins as a children's story, in the manner of an oral tale told by a narrator to a listening audience. At this stage it is also a comedy, written in a lively humorous style. But that style shifts markedly as the journey reaches its end, and it veers towards the serious and tragic. At the centre of the narrative is the twofold purpose or goal of the quest: first to recover a treasure, a goldhoard and a marvellous jewel; and then to overcome a danger, in the form of the guardian of the treasure, a sophisticated and malicious red-golden dragon. Both the goldhoard and the dragon are archetypes. They correspond quite closely to many fundamental myths in European literature and help to explain the appeal that this story has held on the imagination of its readers. The theme of the novel is closely tied to the quest; the desire for red gold and white gemstone becomes symbolic of the lust for wealth of Thorin, one of the principal characters, who becomes at the end a kind of tragic hero.

The setting of the story forms the other major theme of this novel. England is re-imagined as a western land on the edge of a large and unexplored continent. The protagonist Bilbo Baggins harks back to his little England on many occasions on his journey and it becomes the measure or perspective by which he judges all the events that happen to him on his quest through the Wild. In some ways the novel can be seen as a fantasy of travel literature; a reworking of the classic pattern of the intrepid traveller moving from his comfortable home and discovering the wide world beyond his door. As Laurence Durrell once suggested in an essay on the sense of place, good travel writers and novelists know how to tune in to the *rapport* of a location. What makes 'big' books is as much to do with their site as with their characters and incidents:

When they are well and truly anchored in nature they usually become classics. One can detect this quality of 'bigness' in most books which are so sited from *Huckleberry Finn* to *The Grapes of Wrath*. They are tuned in to the sense of place.[4]

Tolkien is a writer very finely attuned to landscape, nature and setting. The subtitle of *The Hobbit* 'there and back again' encapsulates not only the plot but also the twofold nature of the setting: the *there*, the goal of the journey is the Mountain, and mountains in fact dominate the journey throughout; the *back again* is the valley, whether the valley of the Water, where the hobbit has his home, or its otherworldly equivalent in the magical valley of Rivendell to which Bilbo Baggins also returns at the end of his travels. The journey there and back also suggests life-experience, a gaining in stature or wisdom. In this story Bilbo's experience of the Mountain changes him, but at the same time he also changes and transforms the Mountain. As the end of the novel suggests, Bilbo is only a little fellow in a wide world, but he still has a hand in making the prophecies come true.

Fig. 1b   The Misty Mountains in summer

Chapter One

'We must away ere break of day'

I N 'AN UNEXPECTED Party', the first chapter of *The Hobbit*, the respectable well-to-do Mr Bilbo Baggins finds himself entertaining a whole troop of vagrants who turn up for afternoon tea unexpectedly. The previous day he had made the mistake of inviting one of them, an old family friend, little suspecting that he would bring twelve of his companions with him, many of whom arrive early, in dribs and drabs, in ones or twos, demanding food and drink. And their talk scares him. It is all about 'mines and gold and troubles with the goblins, and the depredations of dragons'; and soon the plans are being made, for they 'must away ere break of day'. Night falls and eventually the outlandish visitors – they are in fact dwarves – are put up in the spare bedrooms and on chairs and sofas. Ironically the hobbit oversleeps (his long lie-in is a running joke, for he often oversleeps), and his guests are gone. But they have left a formal note of thanks in which they set their meeting for 11am at the Green Dragon Inn, Bywater. Bilbo barely makes the appointment in time. Against his better judgement he has agreed to join the expedition, and to leave his comfortable situation far behind him.

Childhood memories and the setting of *The Hobbit*

The respectable village that forms the setting of *The Hobbit* goes way back to Tolkien's childhood. For the first few years of his life after the family returned from South Africa, Tolkien lived in what was then part of

Worcestershire, in the small country hamlet of Sarehole, at 5 Gracewell, the end house in a row of brick cottages, near what was at the time the village of Moseley, in other words close to, but far enough away from, the teeming industrial city of Birmingham. According to his biographer Humphrey Carpenter, Ronald Tolkien was 'just at the age when his imagination was opening out' on his arrival at Sarehole with his mother Mabel and his younger brother Hilary in 1896. In an interview given seventy years later in 1966, Tolkien was to describe his country home in this period as a 'kind of paradise', and with good reason. Robert Blackham's *The Roots of Tolkien's Middle-earth* provides in loving detail a nostalgic photo-gallery of this area of Warwickshire/Worcestershire and Birmingham at the time when the Tolkiens lived there.[5] The period photographs conjure up this lost era: the architecture of the cottages, the water-mill, the old sand-and-gravel pit, the trees, the countryside and the people. A picture in the *Tolkien Family Album* of the main thoroughfare to Moseley village shows an unmetalled road, a hedgerow and field to the left, a fenced wheat-field to the right; in the distance the half-timbered houses of Gracewell peep through the trees.[6]

If one examines a colour painting *The Hill: Hobbiton-across-the-Water* that Tolkien made in 1937–8 for the first American edition of *The Hobbit*, the analogues and similarities immediately become apparent.[7] The picture shows the Water (i.e. the name of the river), with the wooden bridge and the yellow road winding up to the Hill, into which the house Bag End has been built. On the left as a traveller crosses the bridge is a white-painted wooden signpost (marked WEST in one direction and HILL in the other), the sort of signpost that is still to be found in outlying English country districts, although most are now manufactured in painted steel. On the right-hand side of the bridge is the Mill, a three-storey building resembling a church tower and nave done in large yellow ashlar-stones and with a red-tiled roof. Behind the Mill is another road going from left to right lined on the riverside by a redbrick wall, presumably intended to keep people from straying down to the dangerous waterwheel and the mill-race. The dwelling house on the other side of the road is a large building, complete with a white-washed outhouse and a water-butt to collect rainwater from the roof. The garden is wooden-fenced on one side, with a hen hutch in the middle of the lawn and a worked plot for vegetables and cut flowers.

From the bridge the main road winds up through farmland to the Hill; it is a wide but unmarked yellow track, the same colour as the ploughed earth of many of the cultivated fields. On the left a wooden fence protects an orchard and a large prosperous-looking walled farmhouse with main house and outbuildings in the form of a quadrangle. Behind it are the stooks of the August hayfield, a green pasture bounded by a hedge; further back up the hillside are the round doors of some hobbit dwellings, the roundness of the doors being the only 'alien' feature in view, while in front of each house there is an unfenced strip of land for pasture and/or crops, a medieval or even Anglo-Saxon effect. Hobbits live in a world that resembles an idyllic version of England in about the year 1890; an ahistorical English countryside – one that never underwent the notorious enclosures of the early 1800s that so taxed rural workers and was captured in, say, the writings of the poet John Clare. It is an ordered, 'respectable' society with a municipal organisation (signposts), and some basic industrial production (baked tiles), but otherwise basically a pre-industrial modern world. In brief it is anachronistic, a vestige of rural England.

Tolkien uses the favourite trick of English language nomenclature: turning a concrete noun into a name simply by capitalising its initial letter. So in *The Hobbit* Bilbo lives on the Hill, and at the beginning of his journey he walks down the track past the great Mill to the river, the Water, then travels up the road alongside the Water to meet the dwarves at the Green Dragon Inn, at the village of Bywater (*The Hobbit*, chapter 2). At first as they travel they pass though 'respectable' hobbit country, with good roads and places to stay, and an occasional 'dwarf or a farmer ambling by on business'. When Bilbo moves out of his familiar home country, however, the toponymy becomes unfamiliar and imprecise, all part of an otherwise unrecorded region of the Lone-lands (again capitalised as a name) in which no one lives, there are no inns and the roads are poor (*The Hobbit*, chapter 2). A respite is granted at Rivendell (chapter 3), with its sounds of running water rising from rock, the scent of trees, and 'a light on the valley side across the water' – here the phrase 'the water' could very easily have been capitalised to turn it into a place-name, though Tolkien resists the temptation. On their journey back, they at last return to 'the country where Bilbo had been born and bred, where the shapes of the land and the trees were as well known to him as his hands and his toes'; eventually he sees 'his own Hill' in the distance, and 'they crossed the bridge and passed the mill by the river and came right back to Bilbo's own door' ('The Last Stage', *The Hobbit*, chapter 19).

Sarehole was a threatened idyll, and it lasted only four years, for in 1900 the family moved to Birmingham. And Sarehole itself was anyway far too close to the city. In 1911 it was annexed to Warwickshire (it had originally been part of Worcestershire), and in the present day it has become part of the Hall Green suburb of Birmingham, in what is now, after the county reorganisation of 1974, the West Midlands. For Tolkien, however, Worcestershire was to remain the notional heartland. It was from the small town of Evesham in this county that his mother's family the Suffields, had originated, and Tolkien felt closely the pull of family tradition and rooted-ness, even if most of the Suffields now lived in Birmingham. Throughout their childhood, the two boys had close contact with their relatives, particu-larly with their mother's side of the family.

One character in particular is John Suffield (1833–1930), the Tolkien brothers' sprightly maternal grandfather, who had managed his own pros-perous drapery business in Birmingham until it had gone bankrupt; he then worked as a travelling salesman, and lived a highly active life to a ripe old age. He was a skilled draughtsman and calligrapher (his ancestors had been engravers), able to write the entire Lord's Prayer in fine copperplate script on an area of paper the size of a sixpenny coin. Both his daughter Mabel and grandson Ronald inherited this calligraphic trait. His portrait in the *Family Album* (p. 14) shows an old man in a buttoned coat, with a long white beard, sharp nose and bright eyes. In John Suffield there is something of the Old Took, the adventurous patriarch referred to in the opening pages of *The Hobbit*, and ancestor of both Bilbo (on his mother's side) and Frodo, a family legend among the adventurous Tooks, though the respectable Bagginses look on his exploits with suspicion. As Carpenter points up the similarities, there is on the one hand Bilbo Baggins, son of 'the famous Belladonna Took, one of the three remarkable daughters of the Old Took, head of the hobbits who lived across The Water' (*The Hobbit*, chapter 1), and on the other hand John Ronald Reuel Tolkien, 'son of the enterprising Mabel Suffield, herself one of the three remarkable daughters of old John Suffield'.[8]

As for the name Bag End, this Tolkien owed to a house on an estate farmed by his enterprising aunt Jane Neave, his mother's sister. Jane Suffield, a trained teacher, was one of the first women to study science,[9] receiving her degree from Mason College (later the University of Birmingham). She was close to her sister Mabel and acted as a go-between passing messages from Mabel to Arthur Tolkien before her father John Suffield gave his permis-sion for the marriage. Married in the early 1900s to Edwin Neave, Jane had the misfortune to be widowed in 1909, but she was able to recover her life, and her career followed various turns. In 1911 she was among several of the family, including Ronald Tolkien, who undertook an adventurous mountaineering holiday in the Swiss Alps organised by the Brookes-Smith family (see chapter 9). From 1912 to 1914 Jane Neave appears to have lived in Aberdeen working in a college, and it seems likely that Tolkien visited her there. By 1914 she was active as a market gardener with her nephew Hilary Tolkien, and based at Phoenix Farm at the village of Gedling near Nottingham. In the 1920s she lived on a farm that sported the unprepossessing name of 'Bag End', located at Dormston near Inkberrow in Worcestershire. It is here of course that Tolkien must have found the name for the Baggins property in his fiction. Like her nephew Hilary, who also became a fruit farmer, Jane ended up living back in the home territory of Evesham and its environs: staying in a caravan on Hilary's land and then later moving to Wales to live with her cousin Frank Suffield. Ronald visited her on many occasions, particularly in his school and university years. He wrote his poem about the sea while visiting her at Aberdeen in 1912 (see chapter 8) and his important poem on Eärendel was composed at Phoenix Farm in 1914 (see chapter 13). In later life Jane Neave was instrumental in persuading her nephew to publish his poetry anthology *The Adventures of Tom Bombadil*; these poems appeared in 1962, shortly before her death in her ninety-second year. Evidently Jane was a sort of literary mentor or encourager to her nephew Ronald.[10]

It is fair to say that Tolkien re-created his late Victorian childhood paradise when he invented Bag End and Hobbiton. After he had published *The Lord of the Rings* (*LOTR*), he found it disconcerting that readers and reviewers assumed that Bilbo's home in Hobbiton was somehow an analogue of the residential suburb in north Oxford in which he and his family then lived, a region of large Victorian houses built in the nineteenth century to accommodate Oxford dons and their families. In reaction to such opinions, Tolkien wrote in 1955 to his publisher Allen & Unwin that Hobbiton is essentially a Warwickshire village from the time of Queen Victoria's Diamond Jubilee, nothing at all like the 'characterless straggle' of north Oxford, 'which has not even a postal existence'.[11] The latter fact (about postal existence) remains true to this very day, and although perceptions may well have changed as to the depressing character of north Oxford, the old medieval city two miles down the road is what captures the attention of the present-day visitor. It is indeed significant that Tolkien compared his then surroundings unfavourably with those of his early childhood.

Comic novels

When Tolkien became a story-teller for his own children, he turned first of all to humorous tales, especially animal fables: stories that had an animal as protagonist, or tales that featured talking animals among the main characters. These include *The Father Christmas Letters*, with one main character called Karhu or Polar Bear; *Roverandom*, the adventures of a dog; the early oral version of *Farmer Giles of Ham*, which also has the dog Garm as one of its main characters; *The Adventures of Tom Bombadil*, a story which, to judge by the poem of 1934, contained an episode with talking badgers. Against this background of animal stories told to children, we have *The Hobbit*, which, in terms of the way novels usually begin by setting a scene or getting the action moving, actually starts twice. The first page begins, rather like an animal story, with a creature in a hole, and then, a few paragraphs later, the story kick-starts again, this time rather more conventionally for a novel, with Gandalf's unexpected visit – indeed, the title of the first chapter is 'An Unexpected Party'. The double-barrelled opening offers a number of interesting comparisons with stories that Tolkien had been reading at the time, either for his own pleasure or for the enjoyment of his children.

The first opening is the famous one already cited, found now in dictionaries of quotations, about the hole in the ground. There is a balance to the rhythm and phrasing of these two opening sentences, which certainly accounts for their appeal. There is also a rhetoric of expectation and contradiction. The hobbit may live in a hole but it is not a nasty, dirty wet one nor a dry, bare, sandy one but a hobbit hole, 'and that means comfort': the assertion helps to keep the attention of reader and, given the oral origins of this story, of listener. The choice of colloquial phrases suggests an audience of children accustomed to the language of story-telling: the fact, as the narrator goes on to declare, that the hole has a '*perfectly* round' door with a '*shiny* yellow brass' doorknob or that the entrance hall has '*lots and lots* of pegs' for hats and coats because 'the hobbit was fond of visitors', the expressions here italicised being found more often in speech than in formal writing.

Since Tolkien certainly knew and admired Kenneth Grahame's writings, a likely inspiration for the opening scene of *The Hobbit* is the first paragraph of Kenneth Grahame's *The Wind in the Willows*:

> The Mole had been working very hard all morning, spring-cleaning his little
> home. First with brooms, then with dusters; then on ladders and steps and

chairs, with a brush and a pail of whitewash […] Spring was moving in the air above and in the earth below and around him, penetrating even his dark and lowly little house with its spirit of divine discontent and longing. It was small wonder, then, that he suddenly flung down his brush on the floor, said 'Bother!' and 'O blow!' and also 'hang spring-cleaning!' and bolted out of the house without even waiting to put on his coat.[12]

The industrious mole keeping a tidy burrow that resembles a late Victorian or Edwardian gentleman's bachelor dwelling: all of this is highly reminiscent of the houseproud Mr Bilbo Baggins. And the mole's exit in a hurry is not unlike Bilbo's precipitous departure from Bag End without any money, or even a pocket handkerchief, 'as fast as his furry feet could carry him' down the Hill, past the Mill and along the river to Bywater. In both stories, there is the same tension between on the one side the settled home life and on the other the pull of adventure.

But Grahame's animals are treated in part realistically. At the same time as being an anthropomorphised animal, the Mole is also really a mole, with certain characteristics – such as his scrabbling and scratching to dig his way up to the surface at the arrival of spring – that remind the reader of what moles really are like. Similarly, at first sight, the hobbit with his furry feet has been wrongly equated with a rabbit, not only by uncomprehending literary critics but even by characters in the story itself, such as the eagle who carries Bilbo to the Carrock, or one of the trolls, who wonders for a moment whether he has caught a rabbit when he apprehends Bilbo attempting to pick his pocket in the 'Roast Mutton' chapter of *The Hobbit*. In short, even though hobbits belong to the human genus, they nevertheless share some affinities with characters in animal stories and fables.

We are plain quiet folk and have no use for adventures. Nasty, disturbing uncomfortable things. Make you late for dinner!

Fig. 1c   No adventures

The word *hobbit* itself appears to be Tolkien's invention.[13] It is possible but unlikely that he saw the word in a nineteenth-century folklore treatise known as the Denham Tracts. This text gives a long list of natural and supernatural creatures; the relevant part gives the following *pot pourri*: 'boggleboes, bogies, redmen, portunes, grants, hobbits, hobgoblins'.[14] These diverse beings do not have much in common, except the element *hob-* in *hobbit* and *hobgoblin*. The *Oxford English Dictionary* (*OED*) distinguishes two basic meanings for *hob*. The first is a generic name for 'a rustic or clown', in which *hob* comes from Hob, a by-name for Rob, just as Hodge and Hick derive from Roger and Richard. It is to be expected of course that the first name Hob occurs in the Shire in *LOTR* (e.g. Hob Hayward the gatekeeper in book VI, chapter 8, 'The Scouring of the Shire'). The second sense listed in the *OED* is 'Robin Goodfellow or Puck; a hobgoblin, sprite, elf', and the first citation for the history of the word is from the medieval Townley plays of about the year 1500; in its Middle English spelling it reads 'Whi, who is that hob ouer the wall? We! who was that that piped so small?' A *hob* is a mischievous sprite-like creature with pan-pipes, rather like Tinfang Warble in *The Book of Lost Tales*, or perhaps Tom Bombadil in *LOTR*; such beings will be discussed further below (chapters 5, 6, 16). The *hob* of folklore is not exactly a hobbit, but perhaps the germ of an idea was planted here in Tolkien's mind.

At first sight rather surprisingly, Tolkien admitted a possible influence on *The Hobbit* from the contemporary American novelist Sinclair Lewis's similarly leporine-sounding *Babbitt*, which was published in 1922 and sold well throughout the 1920s and beyond. As also happened later with the word *hobbit*, the word *babbitt* entered the language: both words are listed for instance in the *Concise Oxford Dictionary*. And as literary historian James M. Hutchisson shows, the word was used widely and creatively: Sinclair Lewis himself wrote in August 1921 of how he was 'Babbitting away furiously'; the British sociologist C.E.M. Joad published a study of American society in 1926 entitled *The Babbitt Warren*; and the American writer H.L. Mencken popularised the term 'Babbittry'.[15] Tolkien himself echoed this in his use of the word 'hobbitry' when discussing critically, in his letters, whether the sections of *LOTR* focussing on hobbits and the Shire were unduly long and distracting from the main narrative of the War of the Ring.

Any surprise one might feel at Tolkien's interest in *Babbitt* is legitimate, for the plot of the story was surely alien to his concerns. George F. Babbitt is a businessman living in the medium-sized American city of Zenith, where, as the ironically worded first sentence declares, 'The towers of Zenith aspired above the morning mist: austere towers of steel and cement and limestone'.[16] Nothing could seem more different to Tolkien's opening scene. The surprise I think lies in the nature of the novel *Babbitt*, the epitome of the American 'great realist novel', intended as a satire on the conventionality of Midwestern urban society. The realist technique based on close sociological research is heavily laid on, with numerous personal and social details such as waking, washing and dressing in the opening sequence of the story. This is the kind of literature one might expect a former member of the TCBS – Tolkien's rather purist literary set from his school days in Birmingham – to dislike and avoid. The TCBS, or 'Tea Club, Barrovian Society', was a kind of literary club, a circle of like-minded school friends, who met through the committee of the school library and organised illicit tea-parties inside the school library and at the tea shop in Barrow's stores (hence the name Barrovian Society), where they read and discussed their literary work together.[17] In some ways the TCBS prefigures the much more famous Inklings literary circle of which Tolkien was a key member while he was a professor of English philology at Oxford University.

Two folk-tale elements in Sinclair Lewis's novel are used ironically in the initial setting of the scene, and they perhaps caught Tolkien's attention. First, there is the mention of 'giants' in the description of the factory whistles heard across the city:

> The whistles rolled out in greeting a chorus cheerful as the April dawn; the song of labor in a city built – it seemed – for giants.

The protagonist – who is pointedly called 'unromantic' – is an anti-hero, and Sinclair Lewis is at pains to emphasise that there is 'nothing of the giant in the aspect of the man who was beginning to awaken on the sleeping-porch of a Dutch Colonial house in [...] Floral Heights'. This novel is evidently a satire, a far cry from the preoccupation with the Anglo-Saxon *eald enta geweorc* (the ancient work of giants) in Tolkien's writing. Second, there is the mention of a 'fairy child', but only in the context of a recurrent dream that comes to Babbitt every morning as he wakens to the rattle and bang of the morning milk-truck and the slam of the basement door:

> He seemed prosperous, extremely married and unromantic; and altogether unromantic appeared this sleeping-porch, which looked on one sizable elm, two respectable grass-plots, a cement driveway, and a corrugated iron garage.

Yet Babbitt was again dreaming of the fairy child, a dream more romantic than scarlet pagodas by a silver sea.

For years the fairy child had come to him. Where others saw but Georgie Babbitt, she discerned gallant youth. She waited for him, in the darkness beyond mysterious groves. When at last he could slip away from the crowded house he darted to her. His wife, his clamouring friends, sought to follow, but he escaped, the girl fleet beside him, and they crouched together on a shadowy hillside. She was so slim, so white, so eager!

There is of course very little that is reminiscent of Tolkien here, except perhaps the notion of *escape*, repeated a number of times on this page and the next, for essentially escape is the theme of Sinclair Lewis's novel, a conventional man's failed attempt to escape the trammels of his confined existence – the escape leads him from domesticity to an affair and from safe conservatism to a brief flirtation with radical socialism.

For Tolkien – as he terms it in his contemporary *On Fairy-stories* lecture – escape is one of the features of the fairy-story alongside recovery and consolation. And by *escape* he seems to mean a kind of protest against the mechanical and mechanistic straitjacket that modern society has imposed on itself in the name of progress. Here then is an instance of thematic affinities between Tolkien and a modern realist writer, despite the fact that their whole method and outlook are so very different. But even on the question of style some points of contact do exist, for both Tolkien and Sinclair Lewis are clearly comic writers. The following ironic passage on Bilbo Baggins's conventionality brings this out well; if Baggins were changed to Babbitt and 'The Hill' to 'Floral Heights' the extract would fit quite well into Sinclair Lewis's novel:

> The Bagginses have lived in the neighbourhood of The Hill for time out of mind, and people considered them very respectable, not only because most of them were rich, but because they never had any adventures or did anything unexpected: you could tell what a Baggins would say on any question without the bother of asking him. This is a story of how a Baggins had an adventure, and found himself doing and saying things altogether unexpected.

In a very different social world, Babbitt also has his adventure, and the novel tells of his journey there and back again. By the end of the novel, Babbitt has at least acquired greater self-awareness, and he is unexpectedly liberal towards his son's aspirations to make his own way in the world rather than follow family tradition and expectations. The sense of being larger and wiser after many experiences surely lies behind Bilbo's loss of 'reputation' in the community after his return from abroad.

A similar theme runs through a children's novel that the Tolkien household knew well and admired, E.A. Wyke-Smith's *The Marvellous Land of Snergs*, with its main character Gorbo, 'the gem of dunderheads', who nevertheless ably helps his companions to survive their adventures.[18] The consultant mining engineer Edward Augustus Wyke-Smith had begun composing fiction by telling stories to his grandchildren; he published his *Marvellous Land of Snergs* with copious illustrations by George Morrow in 1927. Tolkien was aware of it as a model for his own illustrated *Hobbit*, and he later described it to W.H. Auden as an unconscious source-book, which his children enjoyed hearing just as much as his own story about the hobbit.[19] There are numerous similarities in the two plots and in certain minor themes and motifs: the Snergs are equivalent to the complacent hobbits since they are fond of feasting and rather set in their ways, while the escaped children Joe and Sylvia seem to have the resourcefulness of Tolkien's dwarves, even down to their ability to mimic bird-calls.[20] In some scenes, for example in the Forest Land, Wyke-Smith's descriptive style recalls that of Tolkien:

> In parts where the trees were not very thick the grass was all dappled with spots of sun, and sometimes there were great shafts of light through the trees to make a guide for them, for all they had to do so far was to go as fast as they could in the direction of the sun. (p. 29)
>
> But it was getting dark; the sky was now hidden by a roof of matted leaves, and on all sides and above them the thick smooth branches twisted and crossed and locked together. (p. 50)

There is the same attention to the perils of the wild and the need for Gorbo, the foolish Snerg, to devise ways of evading the dangers; fortunately for Joe and Sylvia, he slowly becomes less gullible and less eager to please, more suspicious and more resourceful, and he rescues them from the supposedly friendly Golithos the ogre:

> It will probably occur to the thoughtful reader at this point that a change had come over the character of Gorbo. A sense of responsibility, mingled with self-reproach, had brought forth qualities hitherto unsuspected... . (p. 84)

Above all it is the change in the Snerg's character as the tale progresses that demonstrates the debt that Tolkien owed to this now little-known children's story.

Finally, a similar pattern of departure and return informs the plot of a very popular children's story, or set of stories, by the writer Hugh Lofting. The Hobbit-like plot of Hugh Lofting's *Doctor Dolittle* (published in 1922) is summarised by its lengthy subtitle *Being the History of his peculiar life at home, and astonishing adventures in foreign parts*. It begins as follows:

> Once upon a time, many years ago – when our grandfathers were little children – there was a doctor; and his name was Dolittle – John Dolittle, M.D. 'M.D.' means that he was a proper doctor and knew a whole lot.
>   He lived in a little town called Puddleby-on-the-Marsh.[21]

Puddleby is respectable, like Floral Heights or the Hill, and its citizens do not take kindly to eccentrics, such as a doctor who keeps animals in the drawing room that also serves as a waiting room for his patients; the comically eccentric Dolittle drives first his housekeeper away and then all his patients. According to John Rateliff, Lofting based his fictional town on his own native Berkshire, and imagined a setting in early Victorian England, rather like Tolkien's locating of Hobbiton in the England of the Golden Jubilee.[22] As to the place-name Puddleby, the element *on-the-Marsh* recalls the real place Morton-on-the-Marsh, whereas the *-by* suffix is Danish, and would belong better in the Danelaw of the east Midlands or Yorkshire. Apart from the obvious play on the idea of wet ground, there may be a further linguistic joke in the Puddle element, since various Dorsetshire villages with the place-name element Piddle were renamed Puddle in the nineteenth century on the occasion of Queen Victoria's visit, just in case their unrespectable names proved offensive to her royal ears.

Unlike Tolkien in *The Hobbit*, Lofting eschews verbal description of setting or place. Instead, however, he illustrates the story with line drawings at regular intervals, and it is here that some further similarities can be discerned in the figures of Dolittle and Baggins. An illustration on p. 17 of the first edition 'And she never came to see him any more' pictures the moment when a patient walks out of Dolittle's parlour, because of a hedgehog on the sofa, never to return. The small squat figure of Dolittle with his round paunch, top hat and dress coat is very hobbit-like; he is seen in profile on the left looking down the long sitting room at the retreating figure of the lady. A proud ancestral portrait on the wall adds to the effect, as do the low-slung chairs, and general air of respectability gone awry. It is tempting to speculate that Tolkien recalled the composition of the picture when he described the hobbit's dwelling and drew his own illustration of *The Hall at Bag End, Residence of B. Baggins Esquire* – with its image of Bilbo in profile, the round coffee table and low chair, the fire-place and oak panelling and portraits – which appears in classic editions of *The Hobbit*.

Lofting has a plain simple style, peppered with didactic interpolations such as the above explanation of the initials M.D. The narrative moves at a great pace as the bumbling doctor first loses all his clients, then learns the language of the animals through the Helper figure of his pet parrot, and finally goes on a medical mission to rescue sick monkeys in Africa. He returns with a kind of treasure, a rare beast known as the pushmi-pullyu, with which he earns a great fortune at the circus, before retiring to his sleepy town once more:

> And one fine day, when the hollyhocks were in full bloom, he came back to Puddleby a rich man, to live in the little house with the big garden. (p. 182)

Clearly this is another case of a story of there-and-back-again, and the emphasis on the language of animals that is associated with Dolittle is surely another influence on Tolkien, to which further reference will be made below.

'By some curious chance one morning long ago in the quiet of the world'

The second beginning to *The Hobbit* actually reworks the opening formula, reintroduces the protagonist looking out of his doorway after breakfast, and at last sets the narrative in motion. In some ways this is a typical folk-tale start with its temporal adverbial 'one morning long ago', although the clause 'when there was less noise and more green' perhaps recalls the opening of Lofting's *Doctor Dolittle*. But unlike 'In a hole in the ground there lived a hobbit', this is at the same time a more novelistic beginning: it sets the scene in a subordinate clause 'when ... Bilbo Baggins was standing at his door' – which tells us in detail what the protagonist was doing – and then reveals the punchline in the delayed main clause 'Gandalf came by'.

In jauntily familiar language with the exclamation 'Gandalf!' and with direct address to the child reader 'if you had only heard...', and collo-quial vocabulary such as the verb *sprouted up* in 'adventures sprouted up all over the place wherever he went', Tolkien goes on to set a tone, constantly reminding his readers that this is a tale with an adult teller and a distinctive wit, speaking to an audience of listening children. The first conversation between Bilbo and Gandalf, a witty exchange on the pragmatic meaning of the social greeting 'good morning', is worthy of Lewis Carroll in *Alice through the Looking Glass*, and that children's novel was certainly one of the ingredients that also went into the mix. The dialogue between Bilbo and his visitor follows on from the description of Gandalf with its many adjectives of size, quality and colour: 'little old man', 'tall pointed blue hat', 'long grey cloak'.[23] Interestingly this description echoes another, written by Tolkien broadly in the same period, concerning a 'bad old man', with a 'ragged old coat', 'old pipe', 'old green hat'. It comes in fact from the story *Roverandom*, in which another wizard of more suspect nature than Gandalf comes prowling up the garden path and sets an adventure in motion.

Roverandom

Like the author Hugh Lofting, who wrote letters home to his children from the front during the First World War, and like Kenneth Grahame telling his stories of the adventurous Toad to his young son Alistair, then rewriting them later as *The Wind in the Willows*, Tolkien began his *Roverandom* – and a few years later also *The Hobbit* – as a tale told to his children. The plot of *Roverandom* is picaresque: the dog Rover, later renamed Roverandom, is lost on the beach and has various magical adventures on the moon and under the sea before he returns to his family. The occasion for telling the story was the need to console his sons for the loss of a toy dog, and to keep them calm during a storm. In August 1925, Tolkien and his wife Edith were celebrating his appointment as Rawlinson and Bosworth Professor of Anglo-Saxon at Oxford University; up to this point he had been a Reader at Leeds University since 1920 and a Professor since 1924. As his duties at Oxford did not begin until October, they left Leeds for a holiday at Filey on the Yorkshire coast with their three children John, aged nearly eight, Michael, nearly five, and Christopher, aged one (their daughter Priscilla was born in 1929). It was a typical seaside holiday, and they stayed in a cottage on the cliffs overlooking the sea.

On the night of Saturday 5 September 1927, however, there was a great storm on the coast: 'the water heaved and shook and bent people's houses and spoilt their repose for miles and miles around';[24] the abnormally high tide caused a lot of damage and Michael's toy dog, which he had left on the beach, was now irretrievably lost. Two years later, on a holiday at Lyme Regis in Dorset (which he had visited as a boy), Tolkien seems to have retold the story and then written it up; he also drew three pictures related to it: *House Where 'Rover' Began his Adventure as a Toy*, a picture similar in many respects to his painting of Bag End in *The Hobbit*, and with an inscription to his son Michael; *The White Dragon Pursues Roverandom & the Moondog* inscribed to his son John, with some affinities to pictures of Smaug flying round the Lonely Mountain; and *The Gardens of the Merking's Palace*, a unique and rather rich and exotic underwater seascape. He also at the same time painted some impressive illustrations to his ongoing mythology, including *Halls of Manwë on the Mountains of the World above Faerie* and *Taur-na-Fúin*, the tangled pine forest where Beleg first met Flindling the fugitive.[25] A similar picture was used without the two elves as an illustration of Mirkwood in the first impression of *The Hobbit*, in 1937 (in chapter 8, 'Flies and Spiders').[26]

The published version of *Roverandom* retains the colloquial style and tone, beginning with the conventional 'once upon a time there was a little dog, and his name was Rover'. Even more so than *The Hobbit*, there are frequent comments addressed to the young reader, such as 'he would have known better', that evaluate the events or, in this particular passage, anticipate what is about to take place:

> He was very small, and very young, or he would have known better; and he was very happy playing in the garden in the sunshine with a yellow ball, or he would never have done what he did.[27]

In fact, the child reader has to persevere and even turn the page – to discover what it was that Rover actually did: namely to bite a patch out of the visiting wizard's trousers, whereupon as punishment he is turned into a tiny toy dog, and later tidied away and put on sale as a second-hand toy in a shop window.

The plot progresses quickly, in sudden leaps and bounds, and there is a sense almost of the surreal, that anything can happen in this mingling of the mundane and the marvellous. For this kind of story (and the same could be asserted of his *Father Christmas Letters*) Tolkien borrows freely and happily from all sorts of sources and texts, including mythology (Celtic, Nordic and his own) and various classics of children's literature. There is a freedom and playfulness in all the borrowing, despite the bizarre plot.

For example, Rover reaches the moon in his first adventure through the agency of another wizard, the sand-sorcerer, a strange obstreperous creature who sticks his ugly head out of the sand and castigates the dog for barking and disturbing his sleep (p. 13). The sand-sorcerer then declares his name to be Psamathos Psamathides, the head of all the Psamathists, and as he utters these names he pronounces every letter, including the plosive 'p', sending a cloud of sand through his nose that half-buries Rover the dog. Without scruples, Tolkien lifts the figure of Psamathos almost unchanged straight out of Edith Nesbit's *Five Children and It*.[28] Here the sand-fairy has eyes on stalks, bat-like ears, a spider's tubby body covered in fur and monkey's feet, and is scornful and angry at the ignorance of the five children who discover it:

'You don't know?' it said. 'Well, I knew the world had changed – but – well, really – do you mean to tell me seriously you don't know a Psammead when you see one?'

'A Sammyadd? That's Greek to me.'

'So it is to everyone,' said the creature sharply. 'Well, in plain English, then, a Sand-fairy. Don't you know a Sand-Fairy when you see one?'

It looked so grieved and hurt that Jane hastened to say, 'Of course I see you are, *now*. It's quite plain now one comes to look at you.'

'You came to look at me several sentences ago,' it said crossly, beginning to curl up again in the sand.

Nesbit playfully presents a linguistically oriented creature who thinks in terms of sentences as units of time, and she makes language puns on the phrase 'that's Greek to me' and the fact that the etymology of *psammead* is Greek *psammos* plus the suffix *-ad*, as in *dryad*; incidentally she also indicates the pronunciation of *Psammead* as 'Sammyadd' in Anthea's bemused reply.[29] In his borrowing of the figure, Tolkien the philologist takes the word derivation yet further with his suffixes *-ides* (son of) and *-ist* (expert), and he plays on the well-known prescription in the first edition of the *OED* that words beginning with *ps-* should be pronounced by academics with a clear 'p' consonant.[30] Where Nesbit's Psammead pronounces a modern and colloquial 's', Tolkien's Psamathos uses an old-fashioned, if not pedantic, 'ps'. Of course there are no grotesques of this kind in *The Hobbit*, with the exception of Gollum, and even he, it turns out in the sequel, is a kind of degenerate hobbit.[31]

What, surprisingly, *Roverandom* and *The Hobbit* have in common is the same mythology and cosmology, for both are set in the world of Tolkien's *Book of Lost Tales* and *The Silmarillion*, which he had begun in 1916–17, with an admixture of Norse or medieval lore and legend as an added extra. For example, the eccentric figure of the Man in the Moon in *Roverandom* has some affinities with the aged elf who stows away aboard the vessel of the Moon in *Lost Tales*, and also with the figure of fun in the poem 'The Man in the Moon Came Down Too Soon', which Tolkien published in *A Northern Venture* in 1923 and then again in *The Adventures of Tom Bombadil* in 1962.

When Roverandom rides to the moon on the back of the seagull Mew they fly over the edge of the flat world and there is a moment of cosmic vertigo for the little dog, and also for the involved reader, as they see the waterfalls cascading over the edge of the earth and down into the darkness of the abyss below. This is the cosmology of *The Silmarillion*, and arguably also of many medieval maps, which portray the world as a disc surrounded by the circle of the Great Ocean (although some scholars in medieval times were aware of the Antipodes and knew that the earth was a globe). At the end of *Roverandom*, the giant sea-serpent that encircles the earth in Norse myth makes a brief and dangerous if also comic appearance. The myths sit a little uneasily with a story set in a modern world, but the playful spirit of this surreal wonder-tale or children's adventure mostly absorbs them quite easily.

The Norse element in *The Hobbit*

In earlier drafts of *The Hobbit* the connection with the modern world was more explicit: there was mention of the Gobi Desert, the Hindu Kush and Shetland ponies. The Norse influences remain many and various, but, unlike *Roverandom*, the world in which *The Hobbit* is set is a northern world situated in the past, where Norse elements fit much more easily. A well-known case of borrowing is the names of the dwarves who make up the expedition and who gather so unexpectedly at Bilbo's house in the first chapter of the story. These come straight from the *Voluspa* in the Norse anthology of myth and poetry known as the *Elder Edda*.[32] A similar list is to be seen in the *Gylfaginning* in the *Prose Edda* by the thirteenth-century Icelandic writer Snorri Sturluson, who writes, in Faulkes's translation:

Thus it says in *Voluspa*:

> Then went all the powers to their judgement seats, most holy gods, and deliberated upon this, that a troop of dwarfs should be created from bloody surf and from Blain's bones. There man-forms many were made, dwarfs in the earth as Durin said.

And the names of these dwarfs, says the prophetess, are these:

> Nyi, Nidri, Nordri, Sudri, Austri, Vestri, Akthiolf, Dvalin, Nar, Nain, Niping, Dain, Bifur, Bafur, Bombor, Nori, Ori, Onar, Oin, Modvitnir, Vig and Gandalf, Vindalf, Thorin, Fili, Kili, Fundin, Vali, Thror, Throin, Thekk, Lit, Vitr, Nyr, Nyrad, Rekk, Radsvinn.[33]

It will be apparent that Tolkien selected from this list a set of names for his dwarves in *The Hobbit*, incidentally changing the standard English plural *dwarfs* to *dwarves* for linguistic-aesthetic reasons.

Tolkien even tried to match dwarf name to character, as well as allowing his dwarves to travel in groups of related names. The first to knock at Bilbo's door for the 'Unexpected Party' of chapter 1 are Dwalin and his older brother Balin of the white beard; then the two young dwarves Fili and Kili, also brothers; then Dori, Nori, Ori; then Oin and Gloin; while Bifur, Bofur and Bombur appear last of all along with Thorin, the important dwarf. The arrival at the trolls' camp in chapter 2 is carried out in the same order of appearance; it is clear that Tolkien relishes the repetition and the roll-call of the names, and he expects his audience to enjoy the ritual too. Naturally, any brothers or other relatives have names that rhyme on their vowels or alliterate on their initial consonants. An added twist is that most of the names also have meanings: thus in Snorri's *Edda* the name Nyi is New Moon, and Nordri, Sudri, Austri and Vestri in Snorri's list signify north, south, east and west respectively. Tolkien perhaps chose names appropriate to character or looks: so Dvalin means Dawdler, Fili and Kili are Trunky and Creeky, while Bifur, Bofur and Bombur are translated by Ursula Dronke as the alliteratively connected names Trembler, Trumbler (a blend, perhaps, of 'trembler' and 'tumbler') and Tubby.[34] Thorin of course is Darer, which certainly fits his rather risky venture. In Norse myth the dwarfs are children of the earth, and Tolkien followed suit: one of the dwarves in the story of Túrin is Mîm the fatherless, which indicates a similar origin (see chapter 4 for further discussion). However, Tolkien seems to change his conception of the dwarves over time, making them more personable, more

human, and by the time he wrote *The Hobbit* they appear to be an amal-
gam of Norse myth and German fairy tale. In *Sneewittchen* (*Snowwhite*), for
example, the dwarfs are miners who go out to work each day 'hacking and
digging out precious metal' and return to their little house, in which 'every-
thing was tiny, but more dainty and neat than you can imagine'.[35] The same
kind of domesticity is seen in *The Hobbit* in the visiting dwarves' demands
for afternoon tea: some call for tea with seed-cake (if Bilbo has any), some
demand ale, some porter (a dark beer popular in Victorian England), one
requires coffee (an anachronism, of course, like the tea), while Gandalf and
Thorin take a little red wine.

It is fair to say that the penchant in *Roverandom* for bizarre figures and
surreal events is not transferred to the slightly later *Hobbit*, which is much
more grounded in the coherent world of Tolkien's mythology, with this
added mix of Norse mythology and the Grimms' *Household Tales*. And
despite the word-play on *hobbit–babbitt–rabbit* that was discussed above, the
protagonist of *The Hobbit* belongs to a race of people and is most definitely
not a talking animal like the dog in *Roverandom* or in *Farmer Giles of Ham*.

Fig. 1d   Ents

Chapter Two

Fairy-stories and animal fables

'A Short Rest'

IN *THE HOBBIT* a recurring motif – and part of its often deliberately humorous perspective – is the perils and discomforts of the journey that the respectable protagonist is forced to endure. Bilbo Baggins constantly harks back in his thoughts to the comforts of his own home, the sitting room by the fire and the kettle on the boil for a pot of tea. His daydreams of his comfortable home contrast sharply with the other recurring motif, the 'adventure', in which events good and bad literally 'come to' him: this is the etymology of 'ad-vent' in the originally medieval expression *adventure* or *aventure*, which Tolkien in his *Middle English Vocabulary* explained as 'chance, (notable) occurrence, feat'.[1] In addition, as a story of a quest *There-and-Back-Again*, both *The Hobbit* and the later *LOTR* also contain many scenes of arrival and departure in which the hero experiences 'a short rest' from the adventure, as well as assistance and comfort, and sustenance for the journey onwards. Rivendell, where stands the Last Homely House West of the Mountains, is the classic setting for the first of such scenes of arrival in *The Hobbit*.

To add interest to the plot of *The Hobbit*, the place of rest is anticipated well in advance – for Bilbo it is a comforting thought that he has a goal to look forward to – but nevertheless the longed-for respite is often difficult to achieve. Moreover, the travellers have to work hard for their reward, since Rivendell is a secret location hidden in the silent wasteland of heather and crumbling rock that lies between the Trollshaws and the Misty Mountains. As its name hints, Rivendell is a valley 'riven' into the landscape, and not easy to find. Gradually the travellers make their way through the dreary hill country towards the great mountains that appear to be marching down to meet them on their journey. As is to be expected, it takes all the skills of the wizard Gandalf to guide them safely past the unexpected valleys, the sudden gullies and the dangerous marshes that can swallow a pony and its baggage without a trace. 'Here it is at last!' is his cry as they come upon the valley so unexpectedly that his horse almost stumbles down the long steep slope.

By some kind of law of paradox, as the travellers descend the zig-zag path so their spirits rise accordingly: they reach the tree-line in their descent and the drowsy smell of pine trees gradually fades as they drop still further and the trees become beech and oak. Evening is falling, and a comfortable feeling starts to come over them, and they reach a clearing in the woodland not far from the stream, just as the green of the grass is turning grey in the gathering dusk. Bilbo's next remark is striking and unusual: 'It smells like elves!' As he looks up at the bright blue stars he hears a burst of a song, akin perhaps to Gerard Manley Hopkins's evocative poem 'The Starlight Night', which talks of the *diamond delves* and the *elves' eyes* and begins as follows:[2]

> Look at the stars! look, look up at the skies!
> O look at all the fire-folk sitting in the air!

The opening of Tolkien's poem – the burst of song just mentioned – is far more mundane:

> O! What are you doing,
> And where are you going?

The first four rhymes here are *doing/shoeing* and *going/flowing*; and the narrator comments ironically that it may not be to your taste. Probably few readers of *The Hobbit* would disagree. The elves in this scene sing nonsense verse, and it is not very palatable nonsense verse.

'The Longaevi'

For a more sober introduction to the beings that Bilbo meets in the woodland glades of Rivendell, a better place to start would be 'The Longaevi' chapter in a book on the medieval worldview by Tolkien's colleague

C.S. Lewis. *The Discarded Image* is Lewis's spirited survey of the background to medieval literature, in which he explores what he calls the Model, the systematic cosmology, geography and philosophy that medieval writers of many kinds subscribed to. Within this Model, there was just about room for belief in alternative beings, creatures who introduced an element of chaos into the highly ordered, almost over-organised medieval worldview. Following late Roman writings that were widely read in the Middle Ages, Lewis calls these beings the *Longaevi* (the long-lived ones), described by the writer Martianus Capella in his Late Classical terms as 'dancing companies of *Longaevi* who haunt woods, glades, and groves, and lakes and springs and brooks, whose names are Pans, Fauns … Satyrs, Silvans, Nymphs'.[3]

An interest in these *Longaevi* lasted all the way through the Middle Ages and into the early Modern period. Lewis cites instances in the poetry of Milton. Here for instance is a passage from the end of book I of *Paradise Lost* (lines 781–8):

> […] or faerie elves,
> Whose midnight revels, by a forest side
> Or fountain some belated peasant sees,
> Or dreams he sees, while overhead the moon
> Sits arbitress, and nearer to the earth
> Wheels her pale course: they on their mirth and dance
> Intent, with jocund music charm his ear;
> At once with joy and fear his heart rebounds.

The peasant who is charmed and afraid is not unlike Bilbo, who feels a similar blend of love and awe; and though he is tempted to stay longer in this forest side and fountain to hear more of the revels, in the end he passes on to his more conventional board and lodging in the great house.

The explanation for the singing elves of Rivendell is perhaps to be found in *The Coming of the Valar*, the third story of *The Book of Lost Tales*, in its description of the various gods or Valar; here it is stated that Aulë and his consort Yavanna, gods of nature and creativity, are accompanied by other, lesser beings, variously called fays or 'sprites of trees and woods, of dale and forest and mountain-side',[4] who hide in the waving grass and the standing crops and sing their songs at daybreak and dusk. These beings are not the same as the Eldar or Noldor who love the world with devotion; the sprites are older than the world and laugh at it playfully, since they had a hand in its creation. Pan (though of course Tolkien would eschew the name) and probably Tom Bombadil, who will be discussed further in chapter 5, also belong in this company. As to their source, one possibility is the popular Catholic writer Francis Thompson (1859–1907), a poet and critic, whom Tolkien admired; his poem 'Sister Songs' describes a vision of dancing sprites in a woodland glade.[5] In *The Fellowship of the Ring* (*FR*) the elves of Rivendell are Eldar, including the lords Gildor and Glorfindel, but in *The Hobbit* the Rivendell music-makers seem much closer to sprites than to the high elves of Tolkien's later fiction.

Tolkien's Andrew Lang lecture

Tolkien gave his famous Andrew Lang lecture *On Fairy-stories* at St Andrews in 1939, and he worked on the topic in the same period as the publication of *The Hobbit*. He began with a definition, that fairy-stories deal with *Faërie*, the otherworld, and the encounter of human beings with that world. He then proceeded to elaborate his definition with finer shades and nuances, and at times it appears that he is writing also about certain kinds of fantasy and romance as well as the genre of the folk-tale or *Märchen*.

As his theme develops, he takes great care to distinguish the various kinds of marvellous tale that do not fall under the head of fairy-stories: so he excludes travellers' tales, especially the Lilliputian satires of Jonathan Swift or the exploits of Baron Munchausen, or even stories of space or time travel; dream-visions or dreams are also excluded, since events imagined in one's sleep are not of the same quality as 'the realization' – in other words, the making real, 'of imagined wonder'.[6]

The other genre Tolkien excludes from *Faërie* is the animal fable, though he is careful to emphasise that he enjoys reading such stories. Animal fables are narratives in which animals feature as heroes and heroines and human beings hardly appear, or stories in which the animal characters are a 'device of the satirist or preacher' used to convey a moral or didactic message. Examples he gives include the medieval *Reynard the Fox* and Chaucer's *The Nun's Priest's Tale* from *The Canterbury Tales*; more modern examples would be the American *Brer Rabbit* or even the children's story *The Three Little Pigs*.

The problem as Tolkien sees it is one of overlap, that sometimes fairy-tale and animal fable overlap, for one of the great themes and attractions of the world of *Faërie* – Tolkien terms it one of the 'primal desires' of *Faërie* – is 'the magical understanding by men of the proper language of birds and beasts and trees'. This important theme has been touched on already, and it will appear again below in discussions of his mythology, his poetry and his fiction: one might consider also the ents or tree-men, who appear in *LOTR* but not in *The Hobbit*, or the animals and trees with which Tom Bombadil communicates in stories and poems associated with him (which already existed in the period when *The Hobbit* was composed and written). As we will see in chapter 3, the attractive power of the dragon lies in his animal-like ferocity and human-like intelligence coupled with the ability to use human language. Another talking creature not so far mentioned is the giant eagle, another heraldic and marvellous being who is also gifted with speech; in addition, *The Hobbit* contains the figure of Beorn, huge black-haired man by day, huge black bear by night, a shape-changer who has various Norse parallels. A talking dragon, a talking eagle, a bear-man, and even an intelligent raven – none of these appear out of place as part of the world of Tolkien's sub-creation. By contrast the brief cameo of the talking fox in the early part of *LOTR* seems to jar; it is almost as if he has wandered into the tale from a story of Reynard the Fox.[7] This is the moot point; since Tolkien admired the beast fable he may have found its influence difficult to resist. Practice does not always follow theory consistently.

A few further cases of overlap between beast fable and fantasy are likewise difficult to judge. For instance, are Beatrix Potter's stories beast fable or fairy-tale? Tolkien considers the question in a footnote to his lecture, and decides that some of Potter's fiction, notably *The Tailor of Gloucester*, does cross the borderline from fable to tale. Here the classic example already discussed is *The Wind in the Willows*; Tolkien states that it is beast fable, though not all would agree with him. In the present book it will be argued that Grahame's novel is indeed a form of fantasy; that it influenced Tolkien not only in his conception of *The Hobbit* but also in his sense of the numinous, to use a favourite expression of Tolkien's Oxford colleague C.S. Lewis, particularly in the episode of divine epiphany 'The Piper at the Gates of Dawn', a vision of Pan on the river which may well have had an effect on Tolkien's story of Tuor in his *Silmarillion*.

If we exclude his animal-stories purposefully intended for children, such as *Roverandom* or *The Father Christmas Letters*, there remains in fact one story from Tolkien's early fiction that does seem to cross the line in the other direction, from fairy-tale to animal fable. This is *The Tale of Tinúviel*, part of the then unpublished *Book of Lost Tales* (essentially the earliest version of *The Silmarillion*) that Tolkien wrote in the latter stages of the First World

Fig. 2a   Pan

War. The beast fable element in this early version is surprising, since in its basic form the narrative is one of the keys to *The Silmarillion*; it is an enduring myth of the beauty and power of nature, the skills of the jeweller or artificer, and the lust for power and beauty that can topple great kings at the height of their glory. C.S. Lewis was tremendously impressed with it when he read the poetic version of the story that Tolkien wrote at intervals in the period from 1925 to 1930. And it is clear that he was still working on the poem in the early phases of his writing of *The Hobbit*: in the manuscript (though not in the published version) the two main characters of the tale, Beren and his beloved Lúthien, are mentioned by name. The wizard tells the dwarves that Beren and Lúthien destroyed the power of the Necromancer (i.e. Sauron), who fled in vampire form to Mirkwood, where he eventually rebuilt his tower.[8] It is this threat from the Necromancer in his tower that draws Gandalf away from Thorin's expedition at a crucial moment, leaving the travellers unguided on the final leg of their journey through the forest and on to the Lonely Mountain. At first, then, Tolkien intended to use the story of Beren and Lúthien as a prequel to the events of *The Hobbit*, and it will be argued later that King Tinwelint in the original version of the tale of Beren and Lúthien closely resembles the Elvenking of Mirkwood. In the end, however, Tolkien changed his mind. Instead the story of the two lovers is set in ages past, leaving nevertheless a vestigial influence on *The Hobbit*, and the story features again more prominently as background to *LOTR*.

The Tale of Tinúviel

'Gil-galad was an Elven king/ Of him the harpers sadly sing'. So begins a short ballad sung by the hobbit Sam Gamgee, servant to Frodo, the central character of J.R.R. Tolkien's *LOTR*, as he and his friends make their way towards the distant hill of Amon Sûl where they hope to find Gandalf, their friend and adviser, waiting to meet them. On the run from strange hostile riders on black horses, the four friends have taken up with a wayward but resourceful woodman or Ranger by the name of Strider, whom they have met six days earlier in their journey at the inn at Bree. 'And who was Gil-galad?' asks Merry, one of the travellers. Strider does not reply, and in fact the ordinary reader of the novel never finds out. It is only the enterprising reader prepared to take on the wider writings of J.R.R. Tolkien's *History of Middle-earth* or *The Silmarillion* who will obtain a full answer to that

question. Merry repeats his question later that evening, but Strider is in
no mood for such baleful tales, and he commands them to talk of other,
brighter things.

Like the personal name Gil-galad, a hero of ages past, so the place name
Amon Sûl conjures up the glories of an ancient kingdom now crumbled
into ruin. Its present name, in the common tongue of the time of the narrative (represented by English in the novel), is Weathertop. Like many such
phenomena in Tolkien's writing its name speaks its nature: a tall round hill
with views all about the wide, wild countryside that surrounds it. On the
crown of the hill, where a ring of fallen stones is all that remains of the great
watch-tower that stood there, the legendary Elendil once bided the arrival of
Gil-galad from out of the west. Here Frodo and his companions also sit and
wait. But Gandalf on this occasion does not appear, and the four hobbits
are left to face off the enemy in the dark, with an unknown stranger as their
only support. Strider's mood becomes a little less severe as night falls, and to
pass the time he chants ballads and stories, and the tale he tells echoes in the
dark and resonates with the travellers' own predicament, for 'the dark seems
to press round so close', as Sam puts it.

Despite his earlier misgivings about mention of the land of the enemy,
and his unwillingness to speak of Gil-galad, Strider tells the tale of Tinúviel,
the Nightingale, which he says will lift up their hearts. He begins with a
song then summarises the rest of the story, for it is a long tale, 'of which the
end is not known', a tale shrouded it would seem in the mystery of life. At
once the mode of the narrative shifts. From modern adventure novel, the
narrative shifts to ballad and from ballad to wonder tale, and from tale to
myth: a story of love and loyalty; a quest in which the hero undertakes an
impossible task; a raid on the fortress of Angband and the recovery of one
of the fabled Silmaril jewels from the crown of the Enemy; a myth of death
overcome and immortality overcome (Lúthien is a woman of the elvish race,
while Beren is a mortal man). As the story unfolds, we see its effect on the
listeners: the companions watch closely the 'strange eager face' of the teller, lit
by the glow of the fire as the stars brighten in the dark sky above them. Like
the Romantics before him (the Wordsworth of the *Lyrical Ballads* and the
Coleridge of the *Ancient Mariner* spring to mind), Tolkien achieves a strange
admixture of setting and telling, an atmosphere which will then be broken as
the moon rises and the dark figures of the enemy close in on the camp.

Of the song only nine stanzas are heard and, as to the tale itself, the reader
is merely given a summary of salient facts; less than a page of the novel is

devoted to it. And probably rightly so: in the context of a long and tightly plotted novel there is a need to keep the action moving swiftly and clearly. Instead, as T.A. Shippey has pointed out in various studies of Tolkien's achievement, we are given hints, vistas, glimmerings of further events which, though they lie in the background, nevertheless remain real and authentic, and give it depth.[9] In the episode by the campfire on Weathertop the main function of the story-telling, the narrating of the tale of Beren and Lúthien, is to provide that sense of depth; at the same time it contributes to the tension and atmosphere of the scene, the emphasis being placed here on the act of narration rather than on the content of the narrative. For a longer version of the story, readers of *LOTR*, first published in 1954, had to wait many years until the appearance of *The Silmarillion*, edited by J.R.R. Tolkien's son Christopher in 1977, while the first, rather different version of the story, *The Tale of Tinúviel*, was published in *The Book of Lost Tales II* in 1984.

In fact, the story of Beren and Lúthien was close to Tolkien's heart, and remained so for all of his life, for it was the product of his time at school in Birmingham, his experience of travel abroad, and the development of his studies at Oxford in the period just before the First World War. 'First Love' and its failure, the rather desperate theme of a short novel by Turgenev, was almost the fate of Tolkien's youthful affection for Edith Bratt, a couple of years his senior and a young working woman, whom he met in 1908 while he was still a pupil at King Edward's School in Birmingham. Also an orphan, she was staying in the same boarding house. Tolkien's guardian was outraged when he heard of their friendship and tried to suppress it. The couple were forbidden to see each other, and Tolkien obeyed his guardian's wishes until he came of age at 21, when he re-established contact; Edith broke off a new attachment and the couple became engaged. They eventually married shortly before Ronald enlisted to fight in the war; this was a difficult time, since Edith lived in many different locations in the period before his active service, when Tolkien was transferred from one training camp to the next, and then again after his contraction of trench fever in the Somme, when he was moved from one military posting to the next within the country.

During a period in Yorkshire at Roos, on one of his days of leave, the couple were out together on a country walk, when Edith suddenly danced beneath some tall hemlock plants. In his account Tolkien uses the word hemlock in its older meaning, to refer to non-poisonous plants of the Umbelliferae family such as *Queen Ann's Lace* or *cow-parsley*, neither of which was a suitable word for his purposes because of their anachronistic connotations.[10] The plants he has in mind are taller than cow-parsley and can grow up to seven feet in height in Britain. At the sight of Edith's dance, Ronald Tolkien was amazed and captivated and he transformed this moment into one of the key scenes in his *Tale of Tinúviel*. Here his feeling for nature finds early expression in his depiction of Tinúviel's dance through the shady woodland glade with its white mist of hemlock flowers (note the presence also of the elm trees, which will be discussed in chapter 6).[11]

A fugitive traveller or wanderer – a recurring figure in Tolkien's fiction – passes unharmed through the terrors of the Iron Mountains, for the region is overrun by the forces of Morgoth. His name is Beren, son of Egnor the forester. By chance he finds his way into the woodland king-dom of Tinwelint, king of Artanor (later named Doriath). Here he sees the king's daughter Tinúviel dancing barefoot in the woods among the white hemlocks, but her companion Dairon spots the stranger's face peer-ing through the elm-leaves and calls on Tinúviel to escape. She drops down beneath the tall flowers with their spreading leaves and stays still, but Beren looks everywhere, and by chance his hand strays onto her slender arm as he searches beneath the leaves. He instantly falls in love, and the tender touch of her arm makes him more eager than ever to find her.[12] He takes to following Tinúviel on her woodland walks and watching her dance, until one day he summons up the courage to speak to her. Tinúviel, who has been aware of her admirer for some time, decides impulsively to take him with her into the cavern that serves her father as a royal palace.

Of course in the later versions of the story there is added a whole other dimension: the theme of forbidden love between mortal and immortal. But here in this as yet undeveloped version of the narrative the outsider Beren is merely of a lesser kindred than the great family of King Tinwelint. Protected by the magic circle of Gwendeling the Queen, who is of the children of the gods, the woodland elves feel themselves separate and superior to the renegade Noldoli, to whom Beren belongs. These Noldoli are felt to be untrustworthy, for they have the reputation of being the thralls of the evil Morgoth. The king sees Beren as 'this wild Elf of the shadows' with false designs on his daughter, and he treats Beren's wish to marry his daughter as an uncouth jest. If he will bring him a Silmaril from the Crown of Melko, on that day he will marry his daughter, the king declares, and the demand is like one of those impossible conditions in an English folksong: 'Tell her to make me a cambric shirt, without any seams or needlework, and then she'll be a true love of mine.'[13] Which is as good as saying she will never marry him. But Beren takes up the impossible challenge and bursts his way out of the hall in his anger and determination.

Nevertheless, Beren is totally unprepared for his venture into the Wild. He is captured by orcs while searching for food and taken before the throne of Melko (Morgoth). But the dark lord does not mete out the dreadful punishment one might expect, for Beren claims to be a hunter who could be of service to him. Melko in his twisted way orders him to be delivered into the power of his lieutenant Tevildo to work in the kitchens of his castle. So far so bad; this is what we might expect in tales of this sort, and Tevildo functions in the same way as Thû, Melko's chief captain, later called the Necromancer in *The Hobbit* and Sauron in *LOTR*.

In the next scene, however, the tone shifts surprisingly and rather abruptly in the direction of beast fable, though the change is uneven and inconsistent. Tevildo it turns out is in fact the Prince of Cats, a kind of wicked spirit inhabiting the body of a cat-like creature similar to a panther. This Tevildo is served by a whole menagerie of feral cats who have been transformed magically into similar panther-like creatures. And his rule inspires fear. One is reminded perhaps of Shere Khan in Kipling's *Jungle Book*. But, rather comically, Tevildo's purr is described as like the roll of drums and his growl like thunder, and his bloodcurdling yell causes small animals and birds to freeze to the spot or fall down lifeless at the very sound. There are moments in Beren's imprisonment and Tinúviel's subsequent rescue of him that also verge on the comic, though it is hard to see whether the humour is intentional. For example, when Tinúviel comes to rescue Beren she finds her way into the castle by flattering the gatekeeper, an old cat she finds lying in the sun on one of the lower terraces of the castle. And when Beren hears her voice while at work in the kitchen in his surprise he drops all the pots and pans with a great bang and clatter. And again, when the hunting dog Huan helps Tinúviel in her rescue attempt, he chases the cat Tevildo and his captain up the nearest tall and smooth tree, where they hiss down their curses at him.

In the end of course the panthers are transformed back into the small cats that once they were, 'and that tribe has fled before the dogs ever since' (p. 29). Though at times in the scenes of fighting or of magic the writing is as effective as that of Kipling in his *Jungle Book*, here the most apt comparion would be with one of Kipling's *Just So Tales*, beast fables written to amuse and entertain children, with titles such as 'How the Leopard got his Spots' or 'How the Elephant got his Trunk'. In brief, I think that

Tolkien's first attempt at telling this story, with its menagerie of talking cats and dogs, was not the most successful of his *Lost Tales*.

The hall of Beorn

Though the *Tale of Tinúviel* in the form just described had long been entirely abandoned by 1930, Tolkien could not shake off all the influences of beast fable and animal story from his writing of *The Hobbit*. As we have seen there are parallels with Mole in *The Wind in the Willows*, and with Doctor Dolittle at the beginning and end of the story, in the there-and-back-again motif. But unlike *Roverandom*, in which mythic legend and children's animal story clash to deliberate comic effect, *The Hobbit* manages on the whole to assimilate all the disparate influences into a unified whole. One exception, it could be argued, is chapter 7 of *The Hobbit*, the lodging at Beorn's hall. Beorn and Beren are just possibly related names, and both are in fact shape-shifters: in *The Silmarillion* Beren is transformed for a while into a werewolf as a disguise, while Beorn regularly turns at night into a large black bear. The idea derives from the legend of Bothvar Bjarki, the bear-man who fights for King Hrolf in the Old Norse *Hrolf Kraki's Saga*,[14] just as Beorn fights to devastating effect in the Battle of the Five Armies. Linked to the idea of shape-changing is the name itself, for Beorn derives from Old English *beorn*, a word used in heroic poems to mean 'warrior' but deriving ultimately from a word meaning 'bear', for Tolkien often used Old English as a source of names and concepts (see chapter 13).

At times the Beorn episode in *The Hobbit* can be seen as a meeting place of two rather incompatible styles of writing: on the one hand the world of children's story and animal fable; on the other that of heroic saga and Norse-style myth. Both styles of writing can include lighter and more serious registers, both can be humorous in their own way, but the attempt to mix the two types of humour may well be unsuccessful. The problem lies in the theme of the man who talks to animals. It comes as a surprise, at least to some readers, that Beorn is a vegetarian, who drinks milk and eats bread with butter and clotted cream (with admittedly the expected honey that great bears proverbially love). Even more contrary to expectation, however, is the array of servants who bring in the food: four white ponies and several grey hunting dogs. Here the realism of presentation is seriously at

Fig. 2b   Beorn in battle

risk. Whereas Tolkien's description of a dragon retains throughout an air of conviction and authenticity, as will be argued in chapter 3, the same claim can hardly be made for Beorn's animal servants. The ponies and dogs, we are led to believe, have the ability to carry lighted torches in their mouths, walk on their hind feet and place them in brackets round the hearth; they can set up boards on trestles and even wait on tables equipped with plates, jugs, and bowls of mead. What is more, Beorn speaks to his servants in 'a queer language like animal noises turned into talk'. All this sits uneasily with the otherwise convincing depiction of Beorn's character as Norse-berserker and shape-changer that is given elsewhere in the chapter. Quite simply, the domestic Beorn is too much of a Doctor Dolittle.

Otherwise, Beorn's hall comes straight out of heroic literature. The hall itself is Anglo-Saxon or Norse in function and layout, with its wooden mead-benches and trestle tables and hearth fire set in the middle of the hall, and smoke-hole or louver high up in the rafters above the cross-beams. Appropriately, Tolkien drew an illustration of Beorn's hall, for which the source has been discovered in a similar illustration in *An Introduction to Old Norse* by his Leeds University friend and colleague E.V. Gordon; appropriately enough the picture illustrates the story of Bothvar Bjarki from *Hrolf Kraki's Saga*.[15] The presentation of Beorn as a fierce and reluctant host is well done, with Gandalf introducing the guests gradually while involving his host more and more in the interesting news that these guests have to tell. There is intentional humour here, and it works well, for it is compatible with the theme and setting. Apart from the Dolittle theme, then, the scene at Beorn's hall would fit just right with another significant motif in Tolkien's work, the notion of the guest and the law of hospitality; its origins will be explored in part II of this book.

Chapter Three

'A green great dragon'

A T THE AGE of seven, heavily under the influence of the *Red Fairy Book* by the Victorian writer and mythographer Andrew Lang, Ronald Tolkien started to write a story about a dragon, and in adult life he recalled that moment in a letter to the poet W.H. Auden: 'I remember nothing about it except a philological fact.'[1] Where Ronald had written 'a green great dragon', his mother corrected the phrase to 'a great green dragon'. The young Tolkien wondered why, and from that time on he became absorbed in language, and did not attempt another story for many years. It is interesting that his mother, Mabel Tolkien, questioned the grammar but did not dispute the existence of dragons with her young son. We will return shortly to the 'philological facts' of the case, but for now we will stick with the biography, with the young Ronald Tolkien's first solo venture into the world of fiction.

'A desire for more acquaintance'

It was his mother who had taught him to read and write, instilling in him a love of fine handwriting and calligraphy that remained with him all his life. He developed various calligraphic hands; later in his teenage years he would invent alphabets; later still as a young man he experimented with phonetic notation. From his mother also the young Ronald Tolkien learned to draw and paint. He became interested in botany, and particularly loved trees. Landscapes, seascapes, ports and beaches figure in his early sketches and watercolours.

His most prominent skills were linguistic; his mother taught him German and etymology and he developed an aptitude for Latin and some ability in French, though he preferred the older of those two languages.[2] He read deeply and widely. Reportedly, young Ronald read the tale collections of Andrew Lang, in particular *The Red Fairy Book*. His abiding love and *desire* (the word recurs in several contexts in his writing) became the Old Norse legend of Sigurd and the dragon Fáfnir, a tale which Lang retells in this anthology. As Tolkien pointed out in his later reworking of this story, the poem *The Legend of Sigurd and Gudrún*, the Norse poets were particularly skilled at their verse forms, and their language was well suited to the atmosphere and ideas of the story, but even in modern English translation the stories have the power to move and instil in the young reader 'a desire for more acquaintance'.[3]

Other tales in Lang's collection may have become part of the 'leaf-mould': *The Red Fairy Book* for instance also retells the Norwegian tale of the Master Thief, about a young man who falls in with a band of robbers and surprises them with his abilities, a theme reminiscent of Bilbo and the band of dwarves in *The Hobbit*. *The Red Fairy Book* also reworks the Grimms' tale of Rapunzel, the young woman imprisoned in a tower who uses her hair as a rope ladder, a story that may well have influenced Tolkien's later stories and poems about Beren and Lúthien in *The Silmarillion*. But the immediate effect of such reading was to instil in Ronald Tolkien a fascination with dragons, even with the very idea of 'dragonness' or *draconitas*, an abstract term deriving from Latin *draco* (dragon) that Tolkien was to use in his famous lecture on *Beowulf and the Critics*.[4] The fact is that a dragon can seem real even if it does not, or should not, exist in the empirical world of the senses.

Although the young Tolkien's reading included *Treasure Island*, which he apparently disliked, and *Alice in Wonderland*, which he enjoyed, the real stimulus to his imagination was Andrew Lang's *The Red Fairy Book*. It seems appropriate to speculate on the boy's developing mind, to inquire into why Lang's version of Sigurd and Fáfnir so fascinated young Ronald, and one is tempted to conclude that the *verbal* description of the dragon in the story captured his fancy. Certainly Lang's text is well written, a fast-paced narrative style that preserves the main features of the original Old Norse narratives of the Volsungs, which Tolkien was to read in his teenage years. In the early part of this legend, Sigurd the fatherless child grows up and takes on a quest to recover the lost treasure of his foster-father Regin that is guarded by Fáfnir, a man who has been magically transformed by avarice and greed into a merciless dragon. The details of this myth or legend would influence his own *Tale of Túrin*, which he wrote and rewrote in various styles throughout his career, and also his *Legend of Sigurd and Gudrún* of the 1920s or 1930s.

But the descriptive writing in Lang's tale, in the *Völsungasaga* and in Tolkien's *Legend*, is notably sparse, limited to significant details. For example, it is implied in the tale that dragons' underbellies are soft, which is why Sigurd hides in a pit on the dragon's route so that he can attack the dragon from below with his sword. Another detail in all three versions is the mention of the ground shaking and the venom spraying from Fáfnir's mouth as he approaches the waiting Sigurd. This element in the story is notably missing in the retelling of the tale published by Edward Thomas in 1912. It appears that Thomas was more interested in the dramatic confrontations of the characters – there is a scene where the dying Fáfnir speaks with Sigurd, but there is no description of the dragon itself, or of his approach to the waiting Sigurd.[5] By contrast, the passage below is what Tolkien eventually made of the scene in his verse paraphrase, a dramatic piece that seeks to capture the terse style and tension of the original Norse verse. When reading this aloud for the rhythm, emphasis should be placed on the alliterating words (which begin with the same letter or sound), as in *deep* and *dark*, *hollow* and *hillside*, *long* and *lurked*, and so on:

> In deep hollow
> on the dark hillside
> long there lurked he;
> the land trembled.
> Forth came Fáfnir,
> fire his breathing;
> down the mountain rushed
> mists of poison.[6]

As a boy, Tolkien most probably first read these details in Lang's 'The Story of Sigurd', in *The Red Fairy Book*:

> There he waited, and presently the earth began to shake with the weight of the Dragon as he crawled to the water. And a cloud of venom flew before him as he snorted and roared, so that it would have been death to stand before him.[7]

Lang is clearly taking his text from the Old Icelandic sources, but I think it is reasonable to argue that the description is not enough in itself to kindle the desire for dragons, the intense fascination that Tolkien clearly felt.

Illustrated dragons

If it was not the verbal descriptions as such that captivated our young reader, this is not the end of our investigation, for there is another medium to be considered, namely pictorial art. To judge from his later preoccupations, Tolkien enjoyed picturing dragons visually, as a number of sketches and paintings from the 1920s demonstrate. There is an image of a coiled dragon in one, and a warrior with winged helmet and sword faces the onslaught of a winged dragon in another. A caption citing the much-admired Old English heroic poem *Beowulf* points to the source, or at least to the point of departure for Tolkien's art in this period.[8]

Andrew Lang's *The Red Fairy Book* is well supplied with black and white prints and these, it must be assumed, helped to stimulate the young Tolkien's imagination. Of the two illustrations of Fáfnir the dragon, one is a particularly striking and detailed portrait of a dragon by the artist Lancelot Speed (1860–1931), now reproduced in an article by Rachel Hart.[9] It shows a rocky cliff face, made of up-tilted sedimentary strata, which covers the whole background of the picture. From a cavernous fissure top left, the front torso of the great lizard Fáfnir emerges, the right limb with claw stretching forward and down and the left limb bent, its claw nails gripping the cliff face. The long coiled neck extends down to the bottom of the picture; looming in the foreground is the ugly horned head of this (apparently Chinese-style) dragon, the eyes searching ahead, almost but not quite looking eye-to-eye at the viewer or reader of the book. Smoke rises from his nostrils and billows up the right-hand side of the picture, while at the very bottom on a rocky ledge are the skulls of his human victims. Interestingly, as Rachel Hart points out, the latter detail – the human skulls – is found also in the same position in Tolkien's own, later illustration of the dragon Smaug sitting on his treasure, which he prepared for the publication of *The Hobbit* in the late 1930s.[10]

Tolkien perhaps recalled the Fáfnir picture when he painted *Glorund Sets Forth to Seek Túrin* in September 1927, an illustration for the story of Túrin – the name matching the *Turambar and the Foalókë* version of the story of 1917–18, now published in *The Book of Lost Tales*. In the watercolour of 1927, which unlike the Fáfnir picture is also a landscape, the reddish-gold, almost yellow dragon emerges from a cave set in a river valley; behind are vast snow-capped mountains and sky that recall Japanese views of mountains (Tolkien is recorded as owning Japanese prints as an undergraduate in Oxford). Clearly the style and treatment of the theme are very different to those of the illustrator of the *Red Fairy Book*, but the dragon's greenish mask-like face resembles Lang's Fáfnir, along with the outstretched front limbs and claws. In this way, then, Lang became the catalyst for Tolkien's earliest foray into the world of fiction at the age of seven.

For Tolkien as a young boy in Warwickshire, the discovery of the dragon Fáfnir was an enriching literary experience: he later wrote in *On Fairy-stories* that he 'desired dragons with a profound desire'; they were the key at that time to his interest in myth, legend and fantasy.[11] The fascination did not leave him even as a teenager: on a trip to Lyme Regis on the Dorset coast in 1906 he found a fossil jawbone, which he playfully imagined was the jawbone of a dragon.[12] His desire for dragons, however, was tempered with caution; he did not, so he said, wish to have a dragon intruding into his neighbourhood, into his 'relatively safe world' where he could read the stories without worry or fear, but the world was a richer and more beautiful one for there being a Fáfnir in it.

At school in Birmingham, Tolkien later came across another dragon narrative in the Anglo-Saxon poem *Beowulf*, where the dragon is described as follows (lines 2275–7):

> Its way is to go looking for a temple in the earth where, old in winters, it keeps watch over heathen gold; it is none the better for that.[13]

In his professional life Tolkien became an expert on the poem and its language, and wrote a pioneering essay on the symbolism of the poem as a work of literature.[14] The dragon was a particular fascination, and many details of the *Beowulf* episode were used to good effect in *The Hobbit*. So, for example, a solitary outlaw finds the dragon's treasure hoard and steals a cup from it; the *Beowulf* dragon appears to have an acute sense of smell and discovers traces of the theft; in its anger the dragon flies out to the nearest human settlement and destroys it with flames; Beowulf the aged king goes out to deal with the threat and falls in the fighting.[15] Arguably all of these details from *Beowulf* found their way into *The Hobbit*.

The dragon in *The Hobbit*

Throughout *The Hobbit*, the chief narrative perspective is Bilbo's, the outsider from 'the quiet Western Land'; Bilbo is the focaliser: the reader sees the world of dwarves, trolls and dragons through Bilbo's unheroic eyes and shares his naïve and sensible reactions and responses. As a bachelor, Bilbo lives a comfortable and sheltered existence on the money he has inherited from his parents: into this complacent world intrudes the *adventure* in the form of Gandalf, and Thorin Oakenshield and his twelve companions, who whisk him away on their expedition that forms the narrative of the book. Being descended on his mother's side from the adventurous Took family, he is susceptible to the *desire of the dwarves* when – as chapter 1 'An Unexpected Party' reports – *something Tookish woke inside him* as he listens to their song and music. A running joke in the story is the tussle between the two sides of his character: the complacent Baggins and the adventurous Took.

As far as the discovery of *draconitas* is concerned, the key passage is Bilbo's first stealthy visit to the dragon Smaug's cave down the long narrow passageway through the hillside ('Inside Information', *The Hobbit*, chapter 12). In the role of burglar, a role that has been imposed on him but has begun to suit him (particularly after his acquisition of the ring of invisibility), Bilbo bids farewell to his companions and sets off, though with great trepidation, down the tunnel. At the end is the great dungeon-chamber where the dragon is sleeping on his treasure. The narrative proceeds in fits and starts, since Bilbo half-knows what to expect. At first he wishes himself elsewhere or dreaming; then he sees the red glow ahead in the tunnel, then he hears the strange gurgling sound, which turns out be the snoring of 'some vast animal'. At this point he stops dead in his tracks; the fear is upon him, and only with a great effort of will does he continue to the end of the tunnel. Here the narrator switches briefly to the historic present tense and invites the reader to picture how the hobbit's little head 'peeps out' into the vastness of the chamber.

A new section of the chapter now begins, marked visually, as in the rest of the book, by a blank line in the text. Immediately the narration switches back to the past tense *lay* as we see with Bilbo's fascinated eye how the vast red-golden dragon lay sleeping on top of his stolen treasure and weaponry. The countless piles of treasure are emphasised, and a new paragraph reiterates the same scene (note the repetitions of the verb *lay*), but with new details added, such as his folded wings and his long pale underbelly encrusted with bits of gold and gemstone to form a kind of protective cover. But what Tolkien also seeks to convey here is the wonder – nicely captured by the dialect word *staggerment* – and the *desire of the dwarves* that Bilbo Baggins feels on seeing for the first time the glory of the dragon and glory of the dragon's wealth. Since the day many years before, when the child

Fig. 3a   'A green great dragon'

Ronald Tolkien had written 'green great dragon' in his story book, it is clear from this passage that the adult writer had learned his lesson and remembered his philological facts about the placing of adjectives of size, colour and shape. In point of fact Smaug is a *great red* dragon, here termed 'a vast red-golden dragon', and he boasts a 'huge coiled tail' and a 'long pale belly'.

A philological fact

As Tolkien the scholar must later have known, the actual rules about the ordering of modifiers before a noun in English are explained in the linguist Henry Sweet's *New English Grammar* of 1898:

> When a noun has more than one modifier, the general principle is that the one most closely connected with it in meaning comes next to it, as in *the three wise men*, where *wise men* is equivalent to the single word *sages*. Qualifiers come before such groups, the one that is most special in meaning (*three*) coming next to it. Hence there is a gradation of increased specialization from the beginning to the end of such a group (*the, three, wise*).[16]

Sweet goes on to consider how the rule might work for a series of adjectives denoting size and grades of colour, such as *a tall black man* or *bright blue sky*, and he concludes that his general principle of a gradation of increased specialisation still applies. The ordering of adjectives therefore follows fixed rules and expected patterns. These a writer like Tolkien can exploit to his advantage, as he does in *The Hobbit* (chapter 1), in the passage on Bilbo's first introduction to an old man with a staff, a 'tall pointed blue hat', a 'long grey cloak', a 'long white beard' and 'immense black boots'. The verbal description with its reiteration of adjectives in fixed patterns is clearly intended to signify one thing only, that the figure described is a wizard.

Given his later mastery of the *philological fact*, what was it that caused the young Tolkien's wonderment at the impossibility of the collocation 'green great dragon'? Presumably, following Sweet's rule of *increasing specialisation*, the collocation would only work if *great-dragon* was a specialised class in itself, equivalent (say) to the single word *firedrake*, which Tolkien uses in his tale of *Túrin Turambar* that he wrote in 1919, and which he knew in its Old English equivalent *fyr-draca* from his study of *Beowulf*. In which case there could conceivably be green or golden firedrakes, or even the red and white ones of Welsh mythology that he mentions in his story *Roverandom*. Already we are speculating on the nature and classification of dragons according to what many years later Tolkien was to call a *mythical grammar*.

Mythical grammar

In his Andrew Lang lecture delivered at the University of St Andrews in 1939, Tolkien at one point discussed the human mind and its powers of generalisation and abstraction, its ability not only to distinguish the concept *green grass* from other concepts but also the ability to perceive that it is *green* as well as being *grass*. In Tolkien's view, the adjective is an immensely power-ful tool of human language, for like a spell or incantation it can transform things. As an example he considers a set of adjectives: *light, heavy, grey, yellow, still, swift*. Human ingenuity can invent such words and at the same time conceive of the magic that would turn a heavy stone into, say, a light feather, or – to use Tolkien's alchemical example – transform *grey lead* into *yellow gold*.[17]

In the mythical grammar, the colour that is normally applied to the sky can be reapplied creatively to something else, so we can have a *blue moon*;

the same goes for the colour of leaves or wool which can be made silver or gold, and burning fire can be given to the cold-blooded reptile, transforming him into a dragon. This is the capacity of myth and fantasy, to harness the power of the adjective for creative purposes, such as the construction of a mythical world in which a *green sun* is a distinct reality. The science fiction writer H.G. Wells created such a world in his 'The Plattner Story', as Flieger and Anderson point out, but Tolkien never attempted such a construction, though he did work creatively with dragon adjectives in some of his mythological writing of the 1910s in order to 'put hot fire in the belly of the worm'.

Glorund, a worm, a firedrake (or *foalókë* in the Gnomish language), takes centre stage in the story of *Turambar and the Foalókë* (in *Lost Tales II*): this remarkably loathsome creature is the epitome of malice; if anything his character is even more depraved than that of his model the Norse Fáfnir. Like Smaug in *The Hobbit*, Glorund devastates a kingdom, the caves of Rodothlim, gathering a host of orcs to guard his conquest and accumulating a hoard of treasure from the spoils of war. The very sound of Glorund's approach is terrifying, while his evil stench becomes overpowering as he crawls relentlessly to the attack. Conversations with this dragon are fatal, misleading and deceitful. One glance from his eyes and people are mesmerised by the dragon-sickness and barely able to move, and if he fixes his stare upon them they fall in a swoon or wander off in a daze, forgetful of who they are or where they come from. Such is the fate of Nienori after she meets Glorund; the loss of memory she suffers leads to her forgetting her name and lineage, to the meeting with her own long-lost brother; to their tragic marriage and eventual suicide when at the second encounter with the dragon her memory returns, and falling into despair she plunges into the raging torrent and is lost.

The value of a dragon

Dragons white, red and gold feature prominently in Tolkien's writings on Middle-earth as real and very dangerous creatures, coldly calculating and fiercely intelligent. In point of fact, however, a real-life green dragon never appears, at least not in Middle-earth as such, although there exist the two illustrations of a green dragon in Tolkien's pictures associated with *Beowulf*. As we have seen, the dragon Glorund in *Turambar*, the predecessor of 'Glaurung the Gold-worm of Angband' in the *Tale of Túrin*, is golden, and

Smaug in *The Hobbit* is a 'vast red-golden dragon', and both are to be taken seriously in terms of the world in which they live.

In Tolkien's lighter verse and fiction, however, dragons can be vehicles for humour, if still highly dangerous. Humorous dragon fights occur in traditional mummers' plays,[18] and Tolkien perhaps came across the lighter touch also in the story 'Miss Cubbidge and the Dragon of Romance' in *The Book of Wonder* (1912) by the fantasy writer Lord Dunsany, whose most famous novel is probably *The King of Elfland's Daughter* (1924).[19] There is also the story 'The Reluctant Dragon' (1898) by Kenneth Grahame, author of *The Wind in the Willows*, and various dragons feature in *The Book of Dragons* (1901) by Edith Nesbit and in the fantastical Arabian Nights adventure *The Land of Green Ginger* (1937) by Noel Langley.[20] A dragon also comes to life in the short story 'Winter Music' (1911) by the writer Edward Thomas (1878–1917). Before becoming a poet in the last three years of his life Thomas was a prolific writer of literary criticism and biography, natural history, travel narratives and fiction, as well as being the author of two books of myths and legends in *Celtic Tales* (1911) and *Norse Tales* (1912). The dragon's flight at the end of 'Winter Music' is a memorable moment:

> Once more he peered into the thicket where he had slept, but his flowers were gone and the leaves lay on the earth instead of moving against the sky. He mounted the knoll once more and looked round. He listened. The hoot of an owl wandered like a dream of the hunters among the mountains to the moon. The dragon slowly unfurled his wings and launched himself above the waves of the tree-tops and rising in tranquil circles vanished beyond the moon.[21]

Clearly, Edward Thomas has the same devoted interest in the English landscape and its place-names, folklore and legends that is to be found also in Tolkien's writings.

In Tolkien's medievalist parody and satire *Farmer Giles of Ham*, first drafted in the same period as *The Hobbit*, the reluctant protagonist and equivalent of Bilbo Baggins is Giles the farmer of the Middle Kingdom (the Midlands). Giles inadvertently gains the reputation of being a hero superior to all the knights of the realm, who are singularly useless in defeating monstrous invaders whether in the shape of giant or dragon. By a process of common-sense and good luck he gains a special sword (like Bilbo's Sting) which he is able to use to subdue the hungry dragon that has invaded the country. And acting like a true farmer and trader 'chaffering and arguing like folk at a fair' he forces the dragon to deliver its treasure, on its

Fig. 3b   Trees and cloud

back, to his farmhouse home in the Middle Kingdom. A darker kind of humour is met in 'The Dragon's Visit', one of Tolkien's six satirical 'Bimble Bay' poems, written in 1928 (i.e. just before the inception of *The Hobbit*), but not published until 1937.[22] In the 'Tales and Songs of Bimble Bay' the author, identified as K. Bagpuize, clearly a pseudonym based on the Oxfordshire village of Kingston Bagpuize, satirises English holiday resorts, criticising their waste and pollution, as well as their philistinism.[23] This is the target for the satire in 'The Dragon's Visit', a kind of unheroic version of the story of Smaug's attack on the town of Dale in *The Hobbit*, in which the dragon only attacks after extreme provocation from the townspeople. As the dragon flies away undefeated he expresses his surprise that people do not have the wit to admire a dragon's song or colour; 'the world is getting duller', he thinks, and this is exactly Tolkien's point.

Similarly, in the workaday existence of 'respectable' Hobbiton and Bywater, no one is prepared to believe the prodigal Bilbo's talk of dragons:

> He wrote a book about it, of course, but even those who had read it never took that seriously. It is no good talking to hobbits about dragons: they either disbelieve you, or feel uncomfortable; and in either case tend to avoid you afterwards.[24]

In *LOTR*, the existence of dragons is a matter of debate over a beer at the inn, simply the subject of an argument in a public house. The Shire is in fact well supplied with inns, where its rustic inhabitants discuss current affairs and gossip, or philosophise on more abstruse issues. Old Hamfast Gamgee for one is a regular in The Ivy Bush, and we first meet him in *The Fellowship of the Ring* (*LOTR*, book I, chapter 1) chiding the miller Sandyman, whom we are told he does not particularly like, for spreading gossip about Bilbo Baggins and his nephew Frodo and the 'outlandish folk' who visit them. In a parallel scene in the next chapter we see Hamfast's son Samwise supping ale at *The Green Dragon* and arguing with the miller's son Ted Sandyman, like his father a rather unsympathetic character, about the existence or otherwise of dragons and 'tree-men' (perhaps the ents who appear later in the story). Sam says he knows someone who has seen one of the tree-men on the moors, but the unpleasant Ted pours scorn on the story, to the general amusement of the other drinkers in the inn, and he scores a point against the hapless Sam by declaring that there is only one dragon in Bywater and that is the green one in which they are sitting.

The Green Dragon is a name on the sign of the inn at Bywater, just like The Ivy Bush on the Bywater Road or The Golden Perch at Stock, or The Prancing Pony in Bree. Ironically – and here is an example of Tolkien's philological humour with a serious point – green dragons do not exist in the world of *The Hobbit* and *LOTR* (only gold ones and red ones). The green dragon, then, is a fantasy within a fantasy.

This discussion about dragons and the truth in the old stories may have had its real-life equivalent, though accounts differ over the details. Certainly dragons must have been discussed in the various academic circles to which Tolkien belonged. In particular there were the Inklings, a group of like-minded intellectuals that included Tolkien, his colleague and fellow-author C.S. Lewis, and the novelist Charles Williams, among others.[25] The group met regularly in Oxford in the 1930s, at various public houses and college rooms, in order to discuss each other's writings and make constructive criticism on unfinished projects. In some ways the group is reminiscent of the earlier TCBS of Tolkien's schooldays or the Viking Club of Tolkien's period of work at Leeds. The original Inklings were a group of Oxford university students: again one might think of the Exeter College Essay Club to which Tolkien belonged as an undergraduate before the war and to which he gave papers in the 1920s.

Fig. 3c   The Eagle and Child, St Giles, Oxford, the Inklings' meeting place

Without a doubt the centre of the circle was C.S. Lewis, a lecturer in English literature whose interests in the medieval period chimed with those of Tolkien, although in his scholarly writing Lewis was less of a philologist and more obviously a literary critic. Lewis was one of the first readers of both *The Silmarillion* and *The Hobbit* in their unpublished forms, and he read and commented on the draft versions of *LOTR* as they gradually appeared. Lewis was based at Magdalen College while Tolkien was at Pembroke College, and the two men first met at English faculty administrative meetings at Oxford in the late 1920s (a longer account of their first meetings and discussions may be read in Humphrey Carpenter's study *The Inklings*). It is a fact of collegiate life in Oxford University that lecturers tend to see the fellows of their own college (who teach other subjects) more frequently than the colleagues of their faculty (who are members of other colleges). When they eventually met, Lewis regarded Tolkien as belonging to the other 'wing' of department politics,[26] but they soon struck up a friendship based on their common interests and enthusiasms. One of his works that Tolkien then lent Lewis to read and critique was his long narrative poem *The Lay of Leithian*, a retelling in verse of his story of Beren and Lúthien. Lewis himself later wrote science fiction and fantasy that was influenced by Tolkien's work or used the same medieval writings as inspiration; these include *The Voyage of the Dawn Treader* in which, rather like Fáfnir, a greedy human being finds himself transformed into a treasure-hoarding dragon.

In one of his poems, Lewis told the story that he and Tolkien were discussing dragons in a Berkshire country pub, when one of the locals intervened with the rather breathtaking claim that he had seen one himself. Here is the text, in a normalised spelling:

> We were talking of dragons, Tolkien and I
> In a Berkshire bar. The big workman
> Who had sat silent and sucked his pipe
> all the evening, from his empty mug
> With gleaming eye glanced towards us;
> 'I seen 'em myself', he said fiercely.[27]

There are shades of the Inn of the Prancing Pony at Bree in this poem, written in an alliterative metre. Tolkien by contrast remembered a different occasion, a similar debate in an Oxford college Senior Common Room, when out of the blue one of the distinguished scholars, a venerable authority in theology, suddenly blurted out that he had himself seen a dragon, and – when pressed as to where – replied that he had seen it on the Mount of Olives, though he was unwilling to pursue the topic any further.[28]

The theological point about dragons is one that Tolkien was well aware of. Even in *The Hobbit*, which avoids religious imagery, there is a hint that the dragon is a token of greed in the notion of the dragon-sickness. The symbolism of evil is also present, though not at all overt. In the famous conversation with Smaug, Bilbo has the temerity to try to goad the dragon, whom he addresses as 'Smaug the unassessably wealthy', with threats of revenge, at which the dragon merely laughs loudly and falls into a boast in which he compares his armour to shields, while his teeth are swords, his claws spears and his wings a hurricane.[29] The dragon's roar is terrible, but his enumeration of the various parts of his body is familiar, and the style falls readily into rhythmical two-beat phrases that also seem familiar. The familiarity of the language is biblical, as Rateliff points out.[30] The description of Smaug perhaps echoes for example that of the great Leviathan in the Old Testament, here given in a standard Roman Catholic translation:

> His teeth are terrible round about. His body is like molten shields, shut close up with scales pressing upon one another. [...] His breath kindleth coals: and a flame cometh forth out of his mouth. In his neck strength shall dwell: and want goeth before his face. [...] His heart shall be as hard as a stone, and as firm as a smith's anvil. [...] When a sword shall lay at him, it shall not be able to hold, nor a spear, nor a breastplate.[31]

If Tolkien deliberately alluded to biblical dragons then he clearly took care not to make the allusion too obvious. Nevertheless, it fits with statements at the end of his treatise *On Fairy-stories* that myths and legends contain truths or glimpses of truth that are fulfilled by the one true story of the Christian faith. Tolkien may have observed this approach to myth in the work of the nineteenth-century philologists and folk-tale collectors Wilhelm and Jacob Grimm; a recent study of their work comes to the conclusion that they thought of fairy-tales as 'remnants of ancient faith expressed in poetry'.[32] Certainly, Tolkien shared this view of myth with a number of his contemporaries, and his conviction exerted an immense influence on his friend and colleague C.S. Lewis.[33]

Lewis provided yet another perspective on the topic of dragons, in a discussion of realism in literature, where he made the useful and perceptive distinction between realism of content and realism of presentation.[34] When people speak of realism generally they usually mean the empirical observation of 'real life' in, say, the depiction of Dublin in the year 1904 in the fiction of James Joyce (to take an example from this period). In *Dubliners*, Joyce presents believable characters in a believable manner: this is realism of both content and presentation; in *Finnegans Wake*, on the other hand (written in the 1920s), the content is realistic but the presentation is playfully subversive. By contrast it is certainly possible in a work of the imagination for the content to be unrealistic, for instance a fantasy about dragons, but nevertheless for it to present the dragon in a realistic manner so that the creature comes across as believable. Lewis's example of presentational realism here is one that Tolkien certainly knew well – the depiction in the Old English heroic poem *Beowulf* of the dragon snuffling along the rock as it wakes and gradually realising by its acute sense of smell that someone has visited its lair while it has been asleep. This is only a brief touch, but it secures the creature in the tangible world (personally, Tolkien would have liked to have had more such details in the presentation of the dragon in *Beowulf*). The Beowulfian approach to decription of the worm – occasional realistic touches – is seen in the *Tale of Turambar and the Foalókë* in Tolkien's *The Book of Lost Tales*. Here the dragon 'came from its lair and sliding down the bank lay across the stream, as often was his wont'.[35] This is the kind of dragon Tolkien first encountered in the story of Sigurd and the dragon Fáfnir in Lang's *The Red Fairy Book* and then later in the Old Norse *Völsungasaga*. The well-observed detail was something he made good use of in his detailed presentation of the dragon in *The Hobbit*.

As to the truth contained in the old tales this is a hard nut to crack, to use a well-known metaphor, but that is the whole purpose of stories and narratives: they have to be worked at before they release their kernels, and these have to be read and digested before they unclose their symbolic import. Sam Gamgee, in *The Green Dragon* in the Shire, loses his argument about the truth of fireside-tales and dragons to Ted Sandyman, the miller's son. Ironically, Ted Sandyman is the bogey, later in league with the enemy Saruman and part of the band of thugs that take over the Shire at the end of the novel in an ecological nightmare of propaganda and enforced mechanisation. In the debate in *The Green Dragon* it is easy for the hardline realist to score points in discussion. And Sam is after all only Samwise, son of Hamfast, another philological joke, a play on the Old English words *sam-wis* meaning 'half-educated' and *ham-fæst*, 'stay-at-home'. Like the young Tolkien learning his adjectives in 1898, Sam would have to gain in experience and wisdom before he could successfully justify the value and appeal of a 'green great dragon'.

Chapter Four

'The Heart of the Mountain'

'The Hoard'

O NE OF THE keys to understanding a major theme of *The Hobbit* is a short poetic narrative known as 'The Hoard', written during Tolkien's period at Leeds University in the early 1920s. It was first published as *Iumonna gold galdre bewunden* (i.e. 'the gold of men of former times, wrapped in enchantment', line 3052 from the poem *Beowulf*) in January 1923 in the Leeds magazine *The Gryphon*. The gold referred to in this line is dragon's gold, and essentially this is a poem about a dragon's attack; it was reprinted in 1937 in the same Oxford University magazine that had also printed 'The Dragon's Visit' only a month before. This was the year of publication of *The Hobbit*, and its author was very much preoccupied with the theme of dragons. Later, 'The Hoard' was published in Tolkien's verse collection *The Adventures of Tom Bombadil* (1962).

Tolkien's 'The Hoard' is a moral tale of an enchanted treasure that does its successive owners great harm. In each case, the attraction of the gold becomes a pleasure, then a desire, then an obsession that leaves the owner witless, defenceless and open to attack from those who wish to possess the gold for themselves. The tale unfolds in five sections or stanzas. It begins in a first age of the earth when silver and gold were plentiful and the elves created much fine metalwork, until a shadow rolled over them. Greed possessed them, and induced them to pile up their wealth 'in dark holes'. The second stanza tells of one such dark cave, where a dwarf, a skilled craftsman, sits working the precious metal into coins and rings. His greed is captured in the telling phrase that 'his fingers clave' to the gold and silver that he touched, 'and he thought to buy the power of kings'. But old age dims his senses, so that he does not see or hear the dragon enter his cave, until it is too late, and the dragon destroys him with his fiery breath. In the third stanza the perspective shifts forward in time to the dragon, now guardian of the hoard, but the fateful cycle repeats itself. An obsessive desire to 'snuff and lick' the gold and silver has taken over this dragon in his senility as he counts every 'least ring beneath the shadow of his black wing'. Like the dwarf, his predecessor, he is too old to hear the newcomer's arrival: the bright young warrior who kills him and takes the treasure for himself, only to find that the same fate befalls him too. In his old age, now a venerable white-bearded king, he cannot resist the glamour of the elvish gold, and all he can think about is his chest of stored treasure, hidden away underground. But his rule becomes unjust, his thanes neglect their duties and his kingdom declines, until one day the battle horns of his enemy are heard sounding before his gate, his halls are burned, and the king dies in the fighting. So now, left undiscovered in the hidden cave where it belongs, the gold awaits a better time: grass grows on the mound above it, the sheep graze, the larks rise and the wind blows from the shore.[1] Night will keep the old hoard; it is, as the original subtitle of the 1923 publication suggested, 'the gold of men of former times, wrapped in enchantment'.

The immediate source for this phrase is line 3052, already cited, from the Old English narrative poem *Beowulf*, which reads 'Iumonna gold galdre bewunden'. The significant word here is *galdor* from *galan* 'to sing, chant', which has similar connotations to the noun *enchantment* with its root syllable *chant*. The context is the protagonist Beowulf's final fight as an aged king against the dragon that is threatening his kingdom. The theft of the gold cup from the dragon's hoard in *Beowulf* is the key (and as already pointed out, this theft clearly influenced the conception of the plot of *The Hobbit*). In the poem the finder is an outlaw on the run from his master, lord of the hall. Finding the treasure-hall presumably by chance the outlaw risks his life to enter the old cave, steal the plated cup (*fæted wæge*, line 2282) and take it to his master as a peace offering. His master gazes for the first time on the 'fira fyrngeweorc' (the ancient works of men) (line 2286), the treasure that a few lines earlier in the poem has been called 'hæthen gold' (heathen gold) (line 2276). There is something amiss with this treasure, though Beowulf does not realise it; his last wish after his fight with the dragon is to gaze upon the treasure, which he calls 'ær-wela' (ancient wealth) and 'swegle searo-gimmas' (bright and curious gems in Clark Hall's translation), but the term 'searo' is ambivalent, perhaps with connotations of cunning and artifice. The faithful Wiglaf hurries to the barrow to fetch as much as he can. There follows a scene (lines 2752–66), which Tolkien recalled in *The Hobbit*, where Wiglaf goes under the barrow's vault and surveys the marvels, the glittering gold lying on the ground, the drinking-cups and weapons. But as the poet observes:

> Treasure, gold in the earth, may easily get the better of any man, conceal it who will.[2]

The treasure in *Beowulf* has magic attached to it, as later passages also affirm.

There are obvious parallels here in stories connected with the Silmarils in *The Silmarillion*,[3] for these three jewels exert a morally debilitating influence on those who own them. Though originally designed and crafted with good intentions, each time they are stolen with violence, more and more evil accrues to them. And the sons of their maker – the craftsman Fëanor – have sworn an oath that no one shall own them but they. The Silmarils prefigure in many ways Tolkien's most famous creation, the story of the Ring of Power that exerts such a destructive fascination on its successive owners, from Isildur to Gollum to Frodo. As various experts on Tolkien have shown, the Ring (written with an initial capital in *LOTR*) gives its owner great power, but only at a price: addiction to that power, a desire to wield that power with good intentions but disastrous results.

In *LOTR* the Ring is treacherous – like an addictive drug it can destroy its user; it can suddenly abandon its owner almost as though it had a will of its own. So, for example, in the distant past it fell from Isildur's finger as he swam the river, leaving him open and visible to the darts of the enemy; found in the river by Dëagol, it immediately betrayed him to the murderous clutches of his supposed friend Smëagol. In turn, Smëagol became a friendless wretch, driven from his homeland as a suspected thief in the night. Now a monstrous if disturbed and conscience-haunted cannibal, Smëagol becomes a dual personality, his dark and dominant side being the character Gollum. And according to what Gandalf says in *LOTR* the Ring then betrays Gollum, falling from his finger in a dark passage under the mountain so that it can be found by the next outsider to pass that way, in this case Bilbo. All these aspects of the Ring belong to *LOTR*, where

Fig. 4a Leader of men: the warrior Wiglaf

Tolkien brought new ideas to bear on its significance, but in the earlier prequel *The Hobbit*, the magic ring (with a lower-case initial letter) is much more benevolent. So much so in fact that in 1947, preparing the second edition of *The Hobbit*, Tolkien felt compelled to rewrite chapter 5, 'Riddles in the Dark', to re-emphasise the nature of the Ring with a capital 'R' as he now conceived it. In the first edition Gollum is even willing to give away his magic ring freely when he loses the riddle match.[4] The rewritten chapter prepares well for *LOTR*, which came out in 1954–5, but does not change the essence of the ring in the rest of *The Hobbit*. Throughout his journey Bilbo wears the ring at will without repercussions, and it exerts no pull on people who see it; for example, the dwarves feel no desire to steal it or use it once they find out about its existence – in stark contrast to Boromir's attempt to take the Ring by force in *LOTR*, where neutral *ring* has become malevolent *Ring*.

In *The Hobbit* – as in the poem 'The Hoard' – it is the dwarvish love of enchanted gold and the related 'dragon-sickness', the desire for the dragon's treasure-hoard rather than desire for the Ring, that form the moral centre of the novel. And this desire, as we saw in the previous chapter, provides the major motive for the quest in the first place. Gandalf the wizard promises to find a 'burglar' to accompany Thorin Oakenshield and his dwarves on their venture. For reasons at this stage known only to himself, though Tolkien's later writings tell us more about his motivations, Gandalf's choice falls on the bourgeois hobbit Bilbo Baggins, who insists on a formal written contract. Their legitimate goal to recover stolen treasure later becomes an obsession in the mind of Thorin, particularly with his loss of the Arkenstone jewel, the symbol of his desire, and ultimately the cause of strife between the dwarves on the one hand and the men of Esgaroth and the elves of Mirkwood on the other. Unknown to Thorin it is Bilbo who has taken the Arkenstone and kept it for himself as his one-fourteenth share in the hoard, as payment – according to his contract – for his services as a burglar. Only the arrival of a common enemy in the shape of the goblin army leads to a reconciliation. The warring forces now join together to resist the invasion. Disaster is averted, though not for all: Thorin and his bodyguard fall in the fighting. Happily, Bilbo is reconciled with the dying Thorin; the fabled Arkenstone is laid on Thorin's breast in his burial mound, and all mourn his loss.

A poem on the same theme as 'The Hoard' is included in the first chapter of *The Hobbit*: the song of the dwarves, 'Far Over Misty Mountains

Cold', which they sing as they pore over the map in Bilbo's parlour at Bag End and plot and plan their expedition to the Lonely Mountain. A little later in the discussions, after he has recovered from his panic, Bilbo claims not to have understood the song, and in his best business-like manner he declares that he would like to hear it all plain and clear. Rather reluctantly, Thorin explains in everyday language the various events that have led up to his expedition: his grandfather Thror's kingdom under the Mountain, the trade with Dale, the prosperity and wealth, the dragon's attack. But it is worth reading through the text once again in 'An Unexpected Party' in *The Hobbit*, for the song reveals rather more than Thorin was prepared to say in so many words in his prosaic account.

Basically the song describes the treasure, and the dragon's theft of the treasure. It begins, of course, with the refrain 'we must away', the urge to begin this expedition. But to do what? The purpose of the expedition according to Thorin is to recover his inheritance, but according to the song it is to seek 'pale enchanted gold'. Why is the gold 'enchanted'? One reason is the magic that the dwarvish goldsmiths used to entrap the light of sun and moon within their artefacts, 'silver necklaces' and 'twisted wire' as they are described in the fourth stanza. (The notion of twisted wire is one met in *Beowulf*; it is a poetic phrase describing the fine filigree goldwork that is used, for instance, on Anglo-Saxon brooches and sword pommels. Examples of this fine and intricate metalwork can be seen in the Alfred Jewel, which Tolkien must have seen in the Ashmolean Museum in Oxford, while in the British Museum in London there are the artefacts of the Taplow Hoard, or indeed the splendid Sutton Hoo Treasure discovered in a burial mound in the 1930s, or the Staffordshire Hoard, found only recently by a metal detector, long after *The Hobbit* was written.)

Noteworthy of course is the effect of the dwarves' song on Bilbo's sensibilities, an intense 'desire for more acquaintance' – in other words, the dragon-fascination or, in its negative aspect, the 'dragon-sickness' (see chapter 3). Tolkien calls it 'glamour', the spell that is cast by the knowledge of letters or *grammar* (the derivative word *glamour* had an old pedigree before the age of Hollywood). He also calls it 'bewilderment', the action of being *be-wildered*; that is, led astray into the wilderness, whether the literal 'wild' or the metaphorical wilderness of the moral world, or even both in the case of the Master of Lake-town at the end of *The Hobbit*. This form of enchantment can induce madness and greed and even murderous thoughts in the minds of those affected by it.

The Necklace of the Dwarves

Above all, Thorin's song hints at many aspects of the *Silmarillion* mythology. Stanzas three and four speak of a king of the elves in ancient times, who commissioned the dwarvish goldsmiths to produce their masterpieces of finely made silver carcanets – jewelled collars or necklaces. The reference here must be to the story *The Nauglafring* (*The Necklace of the Dwarves*), the fullest account of which is given in chapter 4 in part II of *The Book of Lost Tales*. This story is another narrative that is well worth taking the time and trouble to get to know. It can be read as a short story in one sitting, and its plot can be easily grasped, even by those who do not know the earlier stories of Túrin and Beren that are connected with it.

The setting for the story is the caves at Artanor, home of Tinwelint, king of the Wood-elves, the father of Lúthien, the same king who set Beren the near-impossible task of recovering the Silmaril from the crown of the evil Morgoth in Angband. Beyond Tinwelint's wildest dreams, Beren succeeds in the task, and (in a very unexpected manner) delivers the jewel. Tinwelint also features prominently in the story *Turambar and the Foalókë*, or Túrin and the Dragon, since it is he who gives refuge to Túrin before he becomes an outlaw. Here, Tinwelint is portrayed as a king with a 'need and desire of treasury': hence no doubt his earlier longing to own a Silmaril. His desire for gold is a principal motivation; it is one major reason why he sends his warriors to aid Mavwen (Túrin's mother) in her abortive attack on the dragon's lair in *Turambar and the Foalókë*.[5] His payment would have been half the gold of the hoard.

This is the background to the story *The Necklace of the Dwarves*. For those who already know the story, it is worth reviewing the details for their relevance to the themes and plot and characters of *The Hobbit*. The following discussion will therefore take the form of a summary, which – while it cannot replace the enjoyment of reading the original itself – will help to point up the connections with the plot and action of *The Hobbit*. Above all the focus is on Tinwelint, the king who will be renamed Thingol in the later (and much abbreviated) version of the story in *The Simarillion*. Unlike Thingol, Tinwelint is less refined, more rustic, the king of a 'wild and woodland clan', whose crown is a simple wreath of red flowers. His followers are mostly Ilkorindi, 'eerie they were and strange beings', who – unlike the Noldor – never went to Valinor, never saw the trees of the Sun and the Moon, never lived in the city of Kôr; they have little knowledge of light or music, therefore, 'save it be dark songs and chantings of a rugged wonder that faded in the wooded places or echoed in deep caves'.[6]

The teller of this tale, Ailios by name, in the frame-tale setting of Lindo's Hall in *The Book of Lost Tales*, begins by recalling what occurred at the end of the narrative of Túrin and the Dragon, *Turambar and the Foalókë*, when Úrin the Steadfast (Túrin's father) was released from captivity. During that captivity Morgoth had contrived for him a kind of second sight, which allowed him to see what was happening in the outer world, but only events that Morgoth wished him to see, and the interpretation of those events was distorted by the lense of Morgoth's hatred. So Úrin becomes convinced that Tinwelint betrayed and rejected his son Túrin and failed to assist his wife Mavwen. Planning revenge, Úrin takes up with a band of renegade elves and outlaws. They make their way to the caves of Rodothlim where Glorund the dragon had been living before he was slain by Túrin.

But the outlaws find the caves deserted and abandoned apart from 'an old misshapen dwarf' called Mîm (there is a clear parallel to the dragon-slaying in *The Hobbit* here, for when the armies of Laketown and Mirkwood arrive at the Mountain they find the dragon's hoard guarded by Thorin and his companions). A strange character whose origin is obscure, Mîm is similar to the dwarves of *The Legend of Sigurd and Gudrun* such as Andvari or Regin. And, as in the poem 'The Hoard', the dwarf Mîm is described as sitting on a pile of treasure and muttering black spells to himself. The sorcery serves a necessary purpose: it wards off the 'evil of the drakes of Melko' from the treasure, and it binds the treasure to Mîm as his possession or even as part of his will and personality. Despite this warning, Úrin is adamant that the treasure is not Mîm's to keep for himself, and Úrin claims it in the name of his son, who after all was the only man strong enough to attack the dragon and kill it. As they seize the treasure Mîm opposes them with terrible and evil curses; these are not spelled out in full, though they were perhaps on the lines of the dark curse of Andvari in the Sigurd story, here given in the version by Edward Thomas (1912):

> This treasure shall be the death of two brothers. It shall make feuds among eight kings. Nobody shall have joy of it.[7]

In response, Úrin is moved to sudden anger (rather like the irascible behaviour of his son Túrin earlier in the *Tales*) and strikes Mîm a mortal wound with his sword.

Fig. 4b   Warriors with axe and sword

But the dying dwarf prophesises disaster for all who use or handle this treasure, which is now doubly accursed, by both dragon and dwarf. Shuddering at the horrible curse, Úrin nevertheless orders them to carry the gold to the caves of King Tinwelint and cast it before his feet. His purpose is to shame Tinwelint for what he sees as his cowardice and treachery, and perhaps also to leave Tinwelint to deal with the afflicted gold as best he may.

It is here in the scene before the king's high-seat that the story *The Necklace of the Dwarves* begins, with this dramatic confrontation between king and grizzled warrior, after which Úrin takes his final leave. Tinwelint gazes sadly after the fate-stricken man, and as he does so the spells of Mîm woven about the piles of gold (the phrase *galdre bewunden* fits neatly here) begin to affect all those present, including even Tinwelint himself.

Scarcely has Úrin left the hall before his outlaw band start to demur, laying claim to a share in the treasure that they have carried for so many miles. Though Tinwelint agrees to grant them a share of the gold, as much as they can carry in either hand, it is now the turn of the king's men to object. In the subsequent battle that breaks out, there is great bloodshed on both sides, and eventually all Úrin's heavily outnumbered followers are killed fighting over the gold.

'Thus did the curse of Mîm begin to take its course', Ailios the narrator comments. On the king's orders, a burial mound is then built after this skirmish and given the name Cûm an-Idrisaith, the Mound of Avarice. The name suggests that Tinwelint is aware of the morally harmful effects of the treasure, and is struggling in vain to resist the avarice that it engenders. His far-seeing wife Gwenniel (in *The Silmarillion* she is Melian the Maia, of the same order of being as Gandalf) senses the strength of the enchanted gold even more so than others. She warns him that it is now trebly cursed: by the dragon, by the recent killing of the outlaws, and by the baleful influence of Mîm's curses. The king accepts her advice, and plans to have the gold cast into the river that flows past the gates of his city. But unable to 'shake off its spell' he begins to weaken in his resolve, for, rather like Beowulf at the end of the Anglo-Saxon poem, he intends first to gaze on it in all its splendour for one final time. First he has the gold washed clean of the blood spilled over it during the fighting, but this of course exacerbates its attractiveness. He cannot give it up.

Hesitating now with the gold of the dragon's hoard actually before his gaze, Tinwelint is approached by Ufedhin, a prosperous and wealthy Noldo, dressed in rich clothing trimmed with fine gold, who is skilled in metalwork. Ufedhin has spent time visiting the dwarves, who are renowned as goldsmiths, and he wants to preserve the gold. The scene nicely portrays the greed and longing of the king, who looks first at Ufedhin's rich clothes, and then back again at the gold and wealth that he himself is planning to destroy. And he changes his mind. Ufedhin successfully persuades the king not to throw away the raw gold uselessly, but to have it sent to the Nauglath – the dwarves – so that it can be fashioned into beautiful objects. But the *glamour* of the gold now has its effect. Tinwelint is full of distrust. He has Ufedhin restrained from the journey and held hostage until the Nauglath return with the worked gold.

The Woodland king in *The Hobbit* is clearly based at least to a certain extent on the model of Tinwelint, although by the end of the book he turns out more positively and reveals, rather unexpectedly, a fair-minded generosity. In chapters 8 and 9, 'Flies and Spiders' and 'Barrels out of Bond', we see where and how this Elvenking lives, in a great cave with many adjoining passages and lesser caves. The great cave serves as a 'strong place for his treasure', and this desire for treasure is his weakness, just as it is for Tinwelint. The Elvenking does own some treasure, but he is eager for more, especially as his people live and hunt in the open woods, and do not work metals or jewels, nor do they devote themselves to trade or agriculture. In the earlier draft of *The Hobbit*, they are very simply equipped and weap-oned, 'chiefly with clubs, and bows, and arrows pointed with bone or stone'. In this respect they are akin also to the elves of folklore from the eighteenth century back to the Anglo-Saxon period, who are traditionally regarded as archers, not always benevolent ones; the prehistoric flint arrow-heads found in ploughed fields were interpreted as 'elf-shot' or in Scotland as *elf-arrow-heids*. The traveller Thomas Pennant, for instance, reported on these beliefs in 1769:

> *Elf-shots*, i.e. the stone arrow-heads of the original inhabitants of this island, are supposed to be weapons shot by Fairis at cattle, to which are attributed any disorders they have: in order to effect a cure, the cow is to be touched by an elf-shot, or made to drink the water in which one has been dipped.[8]

The woodland elves in the first version of *The Hobbit* then are truly wild, like those 'eerie ... and strange beings' of *The Nauglafring*.

Furthermore, in the illustration appended to chapter 9 of *The Hobbit* we see the bridge crossing the river that runs before the gates of the cave, very similar to Tinwelint's Artanor. As to the Elvenking's appearance, this is described in the scene where he receives the dwarves, who have been taken prisoner in the Forest, in his great hall on a chair of carven wood, wearing as a crown a wreath of berries and red leaves and bearing in his hand an oaken staff. The king has already had Thorin confined 'in one of the inmost caves with strong wooden doors' for refusing to reveal the purpose of his journey. He now questions the resentful dwarves, and puts them all in separate cells until they learn some manners.

The scene is reminiscent of the equivalent episode of arrival in *The Nauglafring* when the dwarves come 'over the bridge and before the chair of Tinwelint'. Here they display the reworked gold, fashioned now into cups and goblets, bowls with interlaced handles, horns and flagons, 'all the appurtenances of a kingly feast', along with 'cunningly adorned' bracelets and collars and crowns. The king is highly pleased now, but even more mistrustful, and will not release the other half of the goldhoard. He confines his guests to house arrest: they are allowed to rest and feast, but the gates and doors are all guarded and they are obliged to continue their craftsman-ship and smithying 'in a deep place of Tinwelint's abode which he caused to be set apart for their uses'. Hiding their resentment the smiths set about their tasks. Eventually, pleased with their handiwork, the king is persuaded to grant Ufedhin's next request, namely that the dwarves be given leave to shape a fine necklace, the finest carcanet that has ever been seen, to provide a suitable setting for the Silmaril, by far the greatest artefact in Tinwelint's treasury.

Treachery is now brewing on both sides, but it is Tinwelint, 'bewildered by the golden spell and the curse of Mîm', who fans the flames of conflict as he summons the craftsmen once again before him, asking them to name their reward. Ufedhin scornfully asks for nothing, since, so he says, he was merely accepting the *guestkindliness* of the king. Now as we will see in chapter 7 below, *guestkindliness* is a sacred duty in Middle-earth, and never has it been more abused than it is in this narrative. Tinwelint practically refuses to pay the craftsmen for their labours. As for the dwarves, they also break the rules: their demands for payment, and in effect for compensation, are simply outrageous, for as well as riches beyond measure each also demands an elvish maiden to take back with him to his bower. Tinwelint, affronted, has them flogged. From this moment, the violence spirals down into tragedy: the later return of the vengeful dwarves with a vast army, the fall of Tinwelint's kingdom, his own death, and the theft of the necklace. The result is an enmity between dwarves and elves that will last for many ages.

In *The Hobbit*, the story of the dispute, apparently the same dispute, is briefly summarised: the elves, so says the narrator, accused the dwarves of stealing their treasure, while the dwarves 'gave a different account, and said that they only took what was their due' after the elvenking had employed them to shape his raw gold for them but then refused them their pay. The reason is, as the narrator goes on to say, that the elvenking has a weakness for treasure. At this point in the narration, the elvenking of *The Hobbit* seems practically identical to Tinwelint of *The Lost Tales*. Certainly, from the way the story is told in *The Hobbit*, it seems as if this elf-king is the one who was actually involved in the old dispute with the dwarvish goldsmiths. If so the story has been changed (as is often the case in Tolkien's developing legends), for the elf-king is still alive. What is clear, however, is that this feud took place in the past, and we are told that Thorin's family were not involved in the old quarrel, but it nevertheless lies behind the Woodland king's harsh treatment of the dwarves when he finds them wandering at will in his forest kingdom.[9] Unlike Tinwelint in *The Nauglafring*, however, the Woodland king remains in the end little affected by the enchantment or desire of the gold.

Fig. 4c   Sweet chestnut in Oxfordshire woodland

The change of tone in *The Hobbit*

As Tolkien's friend and colleague C.S. Lewis shrewdly observed when he first read *The Hobbit*, it begins like a children's story but ends like a tragic Norse saga. There is enough material in chapter 1 above to prove the truth of the first half of this statement. And one is almost inclined to agree with the second half as well. What critics have noticed is the marked shift in tone that takes place towards the end of the novel.[10] While the narrative perspective is still that of an omniscient narrator, who at times is party to information that no other character in the novel could possibly have – he knows the dreams of Smaug for instance – the narrator falls more and more into the background as the plot rises to a climax. There are fewer exclamations, fewer statements of the order 'out jumped the goblins', fewer addresses to the listening audience, fewer humorous asides or exaggerations, such as the anecdote in chapter 1 of how the goblin Golfimbul contributed to the invention of golf.

The later tone is more neutral, but at times, as befits an account of feuds and battles, it is deadly serious. It would be difficult to state precisely where the change occurs. There is humour, for instance, in the exchange between Smaug and Bilbo, but it arises from the verbal fencing of the two personalities involved. The wit is expressed in the words of the two characters rather than in the intervening words of the narrator. The journey through Mirkwood, for instance, has some disturbing moments for many readers, particularly when Thorin is peremptorily seized and bound and locked in a dungeon deep in the king's stronghold. The incident is a sign of what is to come. The seriousness of theme and tone centres now on the character of Thorin, the leader of the dwarves, as he abruptly falls under the glamour of 'the hoard'.

At first this is a gradual process. It goes back, as we have seen, to the song 'Far Over Misty Mountains Cold' in the very first chapter, when Thorin strikes up his harp. The sudden, sweet music of the song awakens Bilbo's Tookish longing for travel and adventure, and simultaneously an empathy for *the desire of the hearts of dwarves*, the *glamour* being defined here in positive terms as 'the love of beautiful things made by hands and by cunning and by magic running through him'. The definition is a rich one, celebrating the practice of the craftsman, the ingenuity of the designer, the strength of feeling that is invested in the work. It could almost be a manifesto for medieval craftsmanship as envisaged by William Morris and the pre-Raphaelite brotherhood, for in some indefinable way the emotion runs by magic through the hands of the workman into the object. The telling phrase comes next, since this 'magic running through him' is also 'a fierce and jealous love'. Such is the feeling that Thorin's music conveys.

The phrase 'fierce and jealous love' is eminently suited to Thorin's character, even in chapter 1 of *The Hobbit*. The first sight of him as a figure of fun soon changes: from lying flat on his face on the doormat when Bilbo pulls open the door too quickly he is soon standing on his own dignity. In appropriate tones he tells the history of Smaug's attack on his grandfather's kingdom and the escape and exile of his family, he emphasises their need to earn their living even if it meant 'black-smith work or even coalmining', and he indicates the success of their monetary endeavours as he strokes the gold chain around his neck. Thorin is an important dwarf, as the narrator states quite early on. And when he speaks at solemn moments Thorin demonstrates his importance by rather long-winded and pompous speeches in which there are enumerations, rhetorical embellishments and complex syntax. Another occasion when he employs what might be called his 'self-important style of speaking' is the *solemn moment* when Bilbo sets off for the very first time down the passageway into the Lonely Mountain to see what he can obtain from under the wings of the sleeping dragon. At other times, however, Thorin is direct and authoritative: 'where are you going?' he demands loudly of Bilbo when he tries to slip away during the early planning after the song. A terser, fiercer side to Thorin's way of speaking comes out in his confrontation with the Elvenking. Here he is simply angry, at being the victim of their spell in the forest, at being arrested as a vagrant, at being accused of attacking the elves when he was simply petitioning them for food.

By contrast, an equally terse but grander direct style emerges when he reaches Laketown and announces himself to the startled guards. Here, Thorin is minimalist but dignified, allowing the facts of the matter to speak for themselves. The men of the Laketown accept him for what he is. And while their minstrels are heard singing of 'the king beneath the mountains', there is talk and prophecy of the 'rivers running with gold'; in fact, this is the first mention of a motif that now recurs at regular moments and finds its partial fulfilment on the very last page of the novel. And as the Laketown tailors fit him out in fine cloth appropriate to his status and standing, the warm reception awakens Thorin's pride: he even walks differently, as if he has already regained his kingdom.

Pride comes before a fall, it is tempting to add, and indeed in the later story, *The Quest of Erebor*, this is Gandalf's view of what happened to Thorin: 'Pride and greed overcame him … he fell at the end of the journey.'[11] Moreover, in chapter 12 of *The Hobbit*, 'Inside Information', we are presented with a reminder that dwarves, within the world of Middle-earth, are 'not heroes, but calculating folk' and some are treacherous, while others, such as Thorin and company, are decent 'if you don't expect too much'. The narrator's warning is timely. A page later Bilbo is staring in 'staggerment' at the great hoard, with 'the desire of the dwarves' now a palpable reality before his very eyes. And two pages later Bilbo has stolen the golden cup from the dragon's hoard and is receiving the excited praise and effusive congratulations of the dwarves, on the ledge at the side-entrance to the Mountain. But again, only a few pages later, Bilbo is actually speaking to the dragon on his second venture into the heart of the Mountain. And the dragon is sowing seeds of doubt, not altogether unjustified, in Bilbo's mind about the terms of his contract and its lack of provision for cartage and delivery of the treasure. How, the dragon asks in his ironic way, did the burglar expect that his share of the fortune was going to be delivered back to his home? Did he really expect the men of Laketown or the elves of Mirkwood to allow it? The dragon Smaug is an overwhelming *personality*: the word is a rare usage in Tolkien's writing, as T.A. Shippey has shown, because in many ways as a psychological term it is anachronistic in a medieval or pre-medieval world-view.[12] However, as was suggested in chapter 3, Smaug is like Glorund: with a power of persuasion and insinuation that is difficult to resist; and Bilbo is 'in grievous danger of coming under the dragon-spell' as happened to Niniel in the tragic story of *Túrin and the Dragon*.

In fact, of course Bilbo resists the dragon-spell, and (though the narrator does not make too much of it) it is important to note that Bilbo has the moral courage to raise the issue with the dwarves to their faces (at the end of chapter 12). Thorin resumes his 'self-important style' in his reply, which is full of rhetorical repetition and verbal qualifiers: 'we knew ... and we know still', 'I assure you we are more than grateful', 'I am sorry if you are worried', 'I admit the difficulties are great', 'believe me or not as you like'. At this stage the narrator remains as it were silent and does not inform us whether Thorin's words have persuaded Bilbo. The conversation now shifts to the Arkenstone that Thorin is so desperate to recover: a great white gemstone that shines 'like snow under the stars, like rain upon the Moon'. It is now Bilbo's turn to be silent. Probably he has become a little more cautious, and perhaps in his own way he is also becoming 'calculating'. Certainly he remains practical: the enchanted desire has fallen from him and he is listening for the returning dragon, a measure that saves all their lives at this point in the story.

'Not at Home', the thirteenth chapter, when the hobbit and the dwarves explore the now abandoned treasure chamber, sees a new and keener focus

on the glamour of the hoard. Once again the enchantment exerts its hold
on Bilbo. We recall that in chapter 12 on his first descent into the hall, and
on his amazed sight of the dragon, he felt '*drawn* almost against his will'
to leave the shadow of the doorway and approach the treasure (my italics).
There is something mysterious here. The past participle *drawn* is agentive in
the sense that it implies an *agent* – someone or something is drawing him
towards it. Is it the dragon-magic or is it the enchantment of the treasure
that draws him? I am inclined to think the latter, for the past participle
drawn appears again later. In chapter 13, with the dragon 'not at home',
Bilbo again proceeds into the hall, this time with the dwarves waiting in the
passage behind him. From their perspective as they watch they see Bilbo as a
small dark figure with a dancing torch in his hand, making his way across the
vast hall toward the mound of treasure. They see him climbing the mound,
and they see him stoop momentarily. The narrator now tells us why. The
perspective shifts to Bilbo, and we see the scene again through his eyes: we
learn that even as he was climbing the mound, the gleam of the Arkenstone
had been shining and 'had *drawn* his feet towards it'. And as Bilbo stands
above the radiant jewel looking down on it the same verb occurs yet again:
'Suddenly Bilbo's arm went towards it *drawn* by its enchantment.' It is as
though Bilbo has lost control of his own actions; the will of the Arkenstone

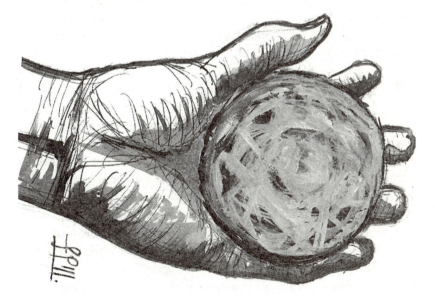

Fig. 4d   Arkenstone in hand

entices him, encourages him to take it. He soon realises what he has done, but he does not repent or confess; an element of calculation has come into his behaviour.

Again the narrator issues a warning about the fire of dwarvish hearts, for when they are rekindled by treasure all about them, they are apt to become bold or even fierce. Thorin is becoming bewitched by the treasure, always looking from side to side for something he cannot find. Later when he is informed by the raven messenger Roäc that the men of Laketown are seeking compensation for their ruined town and that it will cost him dear in gold, he reacts angrily to the news, calling the townsmen violent thieves (chapter 15). And when the vanguard reaches the dwarves' wall he simply repeats his accusation to their faces. The other dwarves are troubled at this falling out among friends, but Thorin only scowls. He is becoming unreasonable.

A scene of parley now ensues. This is the kind of scene that Tolkien excels at, as a number of studies have shown with regard to *LOTR*.[13] Here in the prequel, the dialogue is equally impressive, and looks back to similar dramatic conflicts in *The Book of Lost Tales*. It is such moments of drama that the Icelandic saga writers also excelled in, and, as C.S. Lewis observed, Tolkien is clearly writing here with that model in mind. The sagas, written in Iceland in the thirteenth century, use a plain prose style and realistic dialogue to portray men and women bound by promises and duties and self-interest, and forced into feuds and violence against their own better judgement. Such a pattern is repeated here in Tolkien's *The Hobbit*. On the one side is Bard, the grim-voiced killer of the dragon, hence the actual liberator of the treasure, who is heir of Girion of Dale, hence also owner of part of the treasure. On the other side is Thorin, heir of Thror, king of the Mountain, but already fallen heavily under the spell of the gold. Bard is fair in his intentions but unfortunately makes the mistake of making his three claims in the wrong order. Thorin homes in on the last and weakest of the three, the claim for compensation for the town of Dale, and ignores completely Bard's other two points. And when the messenger returns with a demand for one-twelfth portion of the treasure, Thorin shoots an arrow into his shield. Unreason prevails, and violence is about to be loosed.

It takes the outsider Bilbo to find a resolution through his newly won ability to be calculating and to make use of the Arkenstone. He becomes, as the title of chapter 16 tells us, a 'thief in the night', the proverbially unexpected newcomer. *Thief in the night* is also of course a biblical expression; there is a hint of symbolism here in Bilbo's attempt to redeem the situation.

But he almost fails, and almost loses his life. For the lust of the treasure is heavy on Thorin; he vows vengeance on anyone who finds the Arkenstone and keeps it for himself. On his discovery of what Bilbo had done he would have thrown him from the wall of the fortification down onto the rocks below but for the intervention of Gandalf.

In word at least, Thorin agrees to 'redeem the Arkenstone, the treasure of my house' as he calls it, in exchange for one-fourteenth share of the hoard (Bilbo's portion as agreed in his contract). But as in the conflict of *The Necklace of the Dwarves*, treachery is brewing. By now 'the bewilderment of the treasure' is upon him and his moral decline has begun: he is planning to withhold the payment of Bilbo's share and recapture the Arkenstone with the help of Dain and his newly-arrived allies. Only the turn of events prevents his purpose. Luck or good fortune come to his rescue and rehabilitation.

The meaning of the Arkenstone

The Arkenstone thus fulfils the function that the silmarils assume in *The Silmarillion*; it is a source of enchantment, the focus of men's desires and self-interests, a symbol of power in the political games that the various peoples of the story have to play. Like the Ring of *LOTR* it has a will of its own, it draws people to it, but it affects them in different ways. Thorin is drawn to avarice and desire, Bilbo on the other hand uses its power in an attempt at reconciliation which, at least partly, succeeds. It is tempting to see the Arkenstone as a kind of silmaril (Old English *eorclanstan*) prefiguring the function of the Ring in the larger novel *LOTR*.[14]

But there are differences between the Ring of Power as portrayed in *LOTR* and the Arkenstone of *The Hobbit*, and these are worth teasing out in more detail. In general, many artefacts in Tolkien's world can be summed up in the above-cited maxim 'the love of beautiful things made by hands and by cunning and by magic running through him'. This fits very well the two swords that Elrond identifes as blades of Gondolin made for the goblin wars – these glow in the dark in the presence of their goblin enemies. The rule is that the artisan or maker invests the artefact he has made with his desires, will and emotions; this is more than just a psychological projection, for the artefact really does take on the projected human attributes and powers. The sword Orcrist really does feel antipathy to goblins. The necklace of the dwarves can be understood in a similar way; fashioned by the imprisoned dwarvish goldsmiths it assumes something of their indignation and resentment. Likewise, the Silmarils are bound up with the personality of their maker Fëanor and his descendants, and when his last two descendants Maglor and Maidhros prove unworthy, the Silmarils finally reject them. The Ring by contrast has no power to reject evil-doers, for its nature is bound up with the lust for power that has been projected into it by its architect and artisan Sauron.

This brings us to the ultimate and very significant difference between the Ring and the Arkenstone. The Ring comes from Mordor, where it was forged by the smiths, whereas the Arkenstone comes from Erebor, where the dwarves discovered it 'beneath the roots of the Mountain'. It is worth recalling once again the initial description that Thorin gives of this gemstone: 'The Arkenstone! The Arkenstone! … It was like a globe with a thousand faces; it shone like silver in the firelight, like water in the sun, like snow under the stars, like rain upon the Moon.' The imagery all derives from natural phenomena: fire, water, snow and rain; and this is the crux: the Arkenstone is a natural phenomenon, it is not a necklace or silmaril or ring forged by an artisan.

It is in fact the Heart of the Mountain. The capitalised word Heart is, as usual in this novel, a proper noun, a name, and the word may be more than simply a metaphor. In the roughly contemporaneous Andrew Lang lecture on fairy-tales, Tolkien discussed 'the very widespread folk-tale notion' that the soul or life of a person or creature can reside in a separable heart, which can be hidden 'in a bag or under a stone or in an egg'.[15] The latter phrase 'in an egg' alludes to the Grimms' story *Die Kristallkugel* (*The Crystal Ball*), which Tolkien mentions in his lecture. At the end of this story the hero uses the crystal ball that he has recovered from the egg of a magical bird to break the power of a sorcerer and drive him from the kingdom of the Castle of the Golden Sun; the same crystal is used to restore the bewitched princess and the hero's two brothers.[16] Another example Tolkien cites is *The Giant's Heart* by George MacDonald.[17]

All this prompts speculation on whether to a certain extent the Mountain is also imbued with personality. Certainly this is true of Caradhos in *LOTR*, who seems to be a mountain spirit hostile to the travellers that attempt to cross over him. And in *The Hobbit* the language of the narrative projects a certain emotional state onto the Mountain that is the goal of the journey. For Bilbo the Mountain seems to frown at him as he approaches it (chapter 10); a little later it towers 'grim and tall before them' (chapter 11). Elswehere,

Fig. 4e   A lonely mountain (Bynak Mor, Strathnethy)

there are faintly suggestive expressions like the 'face' of the Mountain, the 'roots' of the Mountain, that hint at its animate nature. If the soul of a man or giant can reside elsewhere then why not also the soul or heart of a mountain? Landscape and character are closely connected, as they are at Rivendell. The Arkenstone is localised; it represents the desire of the hearts of dwarves. It draws a well-intentioned person to it, and this finder uses the Arkenstone to restore the world under the Mountain. The Arkenstone is the Heart of the Mountain, and in this sense the Mountain is the ultimate character in the *dramatis personae* of *The Hobbit*.

Chapter Five

Return to Bag End

'The Last Stage'

THE FINAL STAGE of Bilbo Baggins's journey begins as he leaves Rivendell for a second time, travelling west towards his home, only to be met by dark clouds, and rain driving into his face. As he wryly observes, his back is now to legends and he is going home. But the May weather brightens, and he arrives back 'in the middle of an auction'. The satire on English provincial life forms 'The Last Stage' of *The Hobbit*. 'Mr Baggins' now causes 'quite a disturbance' on his unexpected return to Bag End. Given all that Bilbo has been through: encounters with monstrous enemies, riddles in the dark, pursuit by wolves, rescue by giant eagles, river rafting, a conversation with a dragon, 'horror in the halls of stone', fierce wrangles over his share in the takings, a terrible battle – given all these harrowing events, the phrase 'quite a disturbance' can only be comic. The attitude is ironic: not so much the view of the narrator as that of the inhabitants of Hobbiton. Indeed, Bilbo's cousins the Sackville-Bagginses are already measuring up the house prior to their moving in with their furniture, and most of Mr Baggins's possessions have already been sold either for 'next to nothing' or 'going for a song' at this 'auction'. The word has another significance in Yorkshire dialect (a subject of interest to Tolkien since his Leeds days): basically, as Shippey points out amusingly, *auction* means a terrible mess or chaos.[1] The puns, wordplay and philological jokes come thick and fast at this lighter moment in the narrative.

All this is the 'great commotion' that Bilbo meets when he arrives at his own door after his big adventure. Ironically, for the reader, Bilbo, now quite an accomplished poet (it is only one of many changes in his character), immediately falls back into his old attitudes: he is appalled that people, whether respectable or not, are simply going in and out of the house, many 'not even wiping their feet on the mat'. But this throwback to his old self is not set to last long. Bilbo has in fact changed almost beyond recognition, and the Sackville-Bagginses at first simply refuse to accept him as genuine.

Rather like his literary creation Bilbo, Tolkien himself had changed since he first wrote *The Hobbit* in the early 1930s. He now rather regretted the 'children's story' angle, as is immediately apparent in the change of style that can be observed towards the end of *The Hobbit* itself. That book was however a resolute success, and almost immediately Tolkien was prevailed upon to begin the sequel. But famously *The Lord of the Rings* 'grew in the telling' and was not published until 1954–5. By that time Tolkien had issued the second edition of *The Hobbit* (1947), in which he rewrote one of the chapters and made other changes to bring it into line with the themes and plot of the as yet unpublished sequel. *The Hobbit* therefore also 'grew in the telling' and, although in one sense it is a separate and autonomous novel, in another sense it is closely dependent on its larger and better-known relative.

This point needs to be borne in mind when reading *The Hobbit* – we come to it very often with our knowledge of *LOTR* already firmly in our minds. We know what happens next, and sometimes we remember details from *LOTR* and project them back onto the prequel. Everyone knows, for example, that the story of Bilbo Baggins begins and ends in the Shire, but in fact *The Hobbit* never makes use of this actual place-name. The first chapter informs us that 'the Bagginses have lived in the neighbourhood of The Hill for time out of mind'; in the eleventh chapter Bilbo sits 'On the Doorstep' of the dragon's cave, thinking of 'the quiet Western Land and the Hill and his hobbit-hole under it'; this is the familiar 'country where Bilbo had been born and bred', as the final chapter reminds us. But in the early 1930s when the story was being written, that country or region did not have a name other than Western Land.

Even when Tolkien began the draft sequel, the name still did not exist. The opening of the draft version of December 1937, printed in *The Return of the Shadow*, begins with Bilbo son of Bungo making preparations for his seventieth birthday celebrations. This causes some stir in the neighbourhood, since he had once briefly been famous among the local population of Hobbiton and Bywater due to his sudden disappearance one April 30th and equally sudden reappearance on June 22nd of the following year. Bilbo wrote 'a nonsensical account' to account for himself but then appeared to settle back down into normal life again.[2] There is mention in this draft of the 'neighbourhood' and the restored 'confidence of the district' (confidence, that is to say, in Bilbo's restored normality); a little later it is stated that some guests invited to Bilbo's party come from the 'other side of the shire', the lower-case *shire* being a description and not yet a name. When the opening chapter was redrafted in the following year, mention was made of 'the shaken confidence of the *countryside*' (my italics). Tolkien was rethinking, and when it came to describing the guests at Bilbo's party in the second draft, the word 'Shire' now appeared with an initial capital for the first time.

Tolkien thus invented the Shire early on in the process of writing the sequel to *The Hobbit*. A desire for authenticity and an attention to detail now became characteristic of Tolkien's method. He began to elaborate the names of places in his newly re-invented Shire; he extended its borders, devised new places and created new characters to live in those places, such as the dialect-speaking Farmer Maggot. At times characters also appeared in the new work that had already existed at the time of the writing of *The Hobbit*: here the best example is the figure of Tom Bombadil. And as *LOTR* neared completion, Tolkien began more and more to rethink some of the original concepts of *The Hobbit*, above all the nature of the ring and the character of Bilbo. In 1947 he famously rewrote the chapter 'Riddles in the Dark'; in 1955, as *LOTR* was published, he wrote 'The Quest Of Erebor', in which a whole new perspective on the narrative of *The Hobbit* is revealed for the first time. Gradually the sequel was taking over, and reshaping the earlier story.

The final rewriting of 1960 was never finished; it could possibly have changed the whole concept and tone of the original, if the new material had been included. Here for instance is the opening sequence as Tolkien rewrote it for the 1960 edition:

> In a hole in the ground there lived a hobbit. Not a nasty wet hole, filled with worms and an oozy smell, nor a dry hole, bare and sandy, with nothing in it to sit down on or to eat: it was a hobbit-hole, and that means comfort.[3]

Tolkien has done some fine-tuning. The premodifying adjectives are reduced in number: 'a nasty, dirty, wet hole' becomes 'a nasty wet hole', while 'nor yet a dry, bare, sandy hole' becomes 'nor a dry hole, bare and sandy'. The effect is to moderate the style, to make it more like a piece of writing than a story-telling at tea-time, to make it more like a conventional novel for adult readers. Further changes reinforce this impression in the description of the hobbit-hole that now follows: the schoolboy jargon of 'it had a perfectly round door' becomes 'it had a round door' and the colloquial *shiny* of 'shiny yellow brass knob' is removed, as is the rather childlike phrase *lots and lots* 'of pegs for hats and coats'. Basically, Tolkien was reworking the children's story in the style of *LOTR*.

The shaping of the Shire

When Tolkien returned to the fictional world of *The Hobbit* in December 1937 he must have realised that its toponymy, or system of place-names, was too simple and unhistorical for the needs of his sequel. He must have seen that the simple capitalisation of concrete nouns (which we noted in chapter 1 as characteristic of *The Hobbit*) was no longer adequate. He needed names which followed the shape and contours of the landscape but also sounded older and more firmly established.

His solution was to use Old English place-name elements and adapt these for his own needs, usually on the model of the compound names that divide into two elements, such as Shire-burn or Green-way. Basically, as his etymological studies informed him (he was one of the first members of the Place-Name Society when it was founded in the 1920s), the majority of the place-names of England have topographical roots. This fact has long been recognised: the original English settlers in early Anglo-Saxon England named their homes according to various landscape categories. This at least seems to have been Tolkien's preferred theory. In one of his first academic reviews, published in 1924 when he was Professor of English in Leeds, he was highly critical of the place-name specialist Eilert Ekwall's theory that place-names ending in *-ing* mostly derive from personal names, so that for example Hastings derives from a man called Hasta, and Wenning, a tributary of the Lune in Lancashire, derives from a personal name Wenna.[4] Instead, while granting that the personal-name explanation is clearly correct in some cases, Tolkien argues for a 'derivative from *wann*, dark, and primarily the name of the stream'.[5]

As studies show, English places are frequently named after rivers, springs, pools and lakes; after marshes, moors and flood-plains; after river crossings and landing places; after roads and tracks; after valleys, hills, slopes and ridges; after trees, forests, woods and clearings; and finally also after ploughland and pasture. Tolkien followed suit in his invention of new place-names for the Shire. Examples with Tolkienian echoes are many. Here are some English water-related place-names: Milbourne, meaning the same as Millbrook (water mills were in use in England from the ninth century), Shireburn and Shirebourne, Frogmore meaning 'frog pond', Marish from Old English *merisc* (marsh), Bridgenorth and Bridgend. For roads and tracks there are Fosseway, Greenway, Ridgeway. Other relevant place-names analysed by Margaret Gelling include names with the element *wood-* such as Woodborough and Woodbury, meaning 'fort in a wood', Woodstock and Woodton, meaning 'settlement in a wood', or the self-evident names Woodburn, Woodcroft, Woodhouse and Woodhall.[6] The latter appears for the first time in Tolkien's writing in *The Return of the Shadow*: Woodhall is the special location (to be discussed in chapter 6) where the hobbits are given their first taste of hospitality on their travels. Greenhill is another obvious speaking-name, whereas Buckland is more of a wordplay: in Tolkien's Shire it signifies the region run by the Brandybuck clan beyond the river Brandywine, whereas in Old English terms (and the name is surprisingly common in modern England) it is a locality reflecting the common Anglo-Saxon institution of *boc-land* – that is, an estate granted by a *boc*, literally a 'book', a royal diploma or charter, a document in which the extent of the property in question (the so-called 'charter bounds') is described so fully and precisely in Old English that even today it is sometimes still possible to beat the bounds of the old estate according to relatively stable and still existing landmarks such as large rocks, streams and ditches.

For the philologist attuned to the origin and history of words, as Tolkien certainly was, English place-names are rooted in the geography of the countryside, and it is clear that Tolkien imagines the people of the Shire as analogous to the Anglo-Saxons, as settlers in a region who closely observed the features of its topography and named them accordingly. The word 'Shire', Old English *scir* (the letters 'sc' in Old English are pronounced 'sh'), is after all an Anglo-Saxon institution, which came into being during the period when England became a unified country under the West Saxon royal dynasty during the tenth century. As he came to write *LOTR* in 1938 as a sequel to his newly published novel *The Hobbit*, Tolkien filled out the topographical details and developed a much more elaborate nomenclature, with a map on which all the places could be traced. Often details appear for their

Fig. 5a   Sarehole Mill pond

own sake on the map, whether or not they are mentioned in the published text of *LOTR* itself. Using the map in the *The Fellowship of the Ring* (*FR*), readers can trace precisely the journey of Frodo, Sam and Pippin across the Shire and beyond, whereas in *The Hobbit*, Bilbo's journey is summarised much more succinctly, and some of the topographical details are lacking. In his later years Tolkien was bothered by this discrepancy between *The Hobbit* and *LOTR*, and when in the 1960s the opportunity arose to issue a third edition, Tolkien compiled an itinerary showing how the topography of the two novels could be made compatible. In the new version, had he ever completed it, Bilbo and the dwarves would have stayed at Bree, camped near Weathertop and crossed the Ford of Bruinen; none of these places are of course mentioned in *The Hobbit* in its original conception.

Black and White Ogre Country

Tolkien of course had his Warwickshire home village in mind as he shaped and reshaped the Shire. In a battered notebook dated 1899, Tolkien's younger brother Hilary wrote stories and reminiscences of the period in which the Tolkien family spent in Sarehole. Recently published as *Black and White Ogre Country*, they make interesting reading, for they confirm that J.R.R. Tolkien expanded his conception of the Shire in *LOTR* by drawing further on the childhood memories of Sarehole that he had used only fleet-ingly for the original setting of *The Hobbit*. Further information on Sarehole has usefully been gathered by Scull and Hammond, who cite interviews with journalists from the 1960s.[7] Tolkien had intensely positive memories of

Fig. 5b   Sarehole Mill courtyard

Sarehole as a lost paradise, with its millpond and swans, the dell covered in flowers and a scattering of old-fashioned houses.

The old mill with its tall chimney is still standing today, little changed since Tolkien's time. A recent view of the mill may be compared with a photograph in Blackham's collection showing the mill-house and yard in the year 1890; the miller George Andrew stands at the top of an external stone stairway leading to a doorway set high up in the outer wall of the grain-store; his son stands below in the courtyard on a horse-drawn cart, apparently taking a rest from the loading of the cart with sacks.[8]

From remarks in the Foreword to *LOTR* and in a letter of 6 May 1968,[9] it is clear that the miller and his son were formidable and memorable characters. In Hilary Tolkien's story they are transformed into ogres, and Black Ogre may well be the miller Sandyman, the rather unpleasant character who appears in the opening chapter of *LOTR*. White Ogre, on the other hand, sounds like a farmer:

> White Ogre wasn't so bad, but you had to go through his fields of wheat and barley with only a very narrow path, but if white Ogre saw you going into the corn after corncockles, poppies etc, he would swoop on you and tell you what dreadful things would happen to you if he ever caught you again, straying off his footpath. His cornland path led to the most delightful dell where the most enormous blackberries grew. We called them 'bumbles,' and the dell 'Bumble Dell.'[10]

Here in the dell are the blackberries, the orchids and the fresh mushrooms, like the mushrooms that figure so largely in the recollections of Frodo's childhood visits to the property of Farmer Maggot, as told in *FR*.

Farmer Maggot, of course, is the hero of 'A Short Cut to Mushrooms' (*LOTR*, book I, chapter 4), a positive 'helper' figure for the hobbits on the run from sinister Black Riders as they attempt to leave the Shire and reach the ferry across the river Brandywine to Bucklebury. But there is another side to Maggot. When the friends first arrive in this quiet and peaceful corner of the Shire, which Pippin identifies as Bamfurlong, old Farmer Maggot's land, Frodo is seriously alarmed at the prospect.

'What's wrong with old farmer Maggot?' we might ask with Pippin, and with good reason. But different versions of the Farmer Maggot episode are now available in Tolkien's *The Return of the Shadow*, and here it can be seen that even though the originally positive character is the one Tolkien finally stuck with, Maggot went through several permutations before he was returned to his original guise. In the 'First Phase' of *The Return of the Shadow*, Maggot is a benevolent figure and none of the travellers worry at their arrival on his land. His function is to serve beer to the travellers, to warn them of the Black Riders' visit to his farm, and to provide an opportunity for a minor practical joke, in which the invisible Bingo (the main hero of the narrative at this point in its conception) picks up Maggot's tankard of beer and drains it dry. This, of course, is very much to Maggot's consternation, but it is a harmless piece of tomfoolery.

By contrast, in the intermediate 'Second Phase', Maggot becomes decidedly ogre-like, and the trespassing incident rather ugly. Bungo recalls how once he and Bilbo were walking cross-country and became lost as it was growing dark, with a white river mist rising, and as they stumbled through a hedge into Maggot's garden, he set a large dog upon them. More like a wolf than a dog, it leapt on Bungo and Bilbo was forced to break its head with a great stick. Maggot's reaction was violent: he threw Bilbo back over the hedge shouting dire threats if he ever saw them again.[11] Maggot's strength here is almost that of a larger creature such as a man, or indeed ogre, rather than the helpful round-faced hobbit he is in *FR*. He has become a terror to people trespassing on his land, and perhaps Ronald Tolkien had his childhood in mind when he added this element to the story. In this version of the story the practical joke played on Maggot with the ring of invisibility is further elaborated: Bingo Baggins while invisible cajoles Maggot for his aggressive behaviour, and the scare he gives the farmer is his well-deserved comeuppance. This scene was received with great amusement by Tolkien's children when he first told them the tale in an early stage of its composition, but it did not survive the revisions.[12]

In the final version of *FR*, Frodo is terrified of the dogs and it is clear that Maggot has dealt severely with Frodo in the past for 'trespassing after mushrooms', but bygones are bygones and all is now past and forgotten.[13] Briefly Maggot's farmhouse now becomes an instance of homely 'guest-kindliness'. Indeed, in *FR* Maggot sees off the Black Rider, and he and his wife then give the hobbits good ale and a welcome break 'by the wide fireplace', before taking them by horse-and-cart safely to the Ferry. Though apparently as suspicious of foreigners as any other denizen of the Shire, the farmer turns out to be more broad-minded than he first appears.

As they later learn in the home of Tom Bombadil, Maggot is a friend of Bombadil's; in *The Adventures of Tom Bombadil* the two drink ale together, and in *The Return of the Shadow* it is even suggested that Bombadil and

Maggot are two of a kind, related in some way, which means that Maggot is not a hobbit but another kind of being altogether. Things were changing as Tolkien wrote the sequel. Not only were the inhabitants of the Shire becoming more interesting as characters, the Shire itself was expanding in scope, with its borders extending now right up to the marches of the Old Forest.

'The Adventures of Tom Bombadil'

In December 1937 in the face of his novel's rapid publishing success, Tolkien wrote to his publisher Unwin suggesting that the story of Tom Bombadil might make a suitable sequel to *The Hobbit*.[14] Although this plan was never implemented, as the new *Hobbit*-sequel progressed, Tolkien included Bombadil as the major character in the Old Forest and Barrow Downs episode. Rather like Beorn in *The Hobbit*, Bombadil is a provider of refuge and *guestkindliness*, but he is in some ways even more mysterious than the terrible shape-changer, as well as being more friendly and humorous, with his bright blue eyes and red countryman's face, 'creased into a hundred wrinkles of laughter'.[15] The magic of this 'old man' is less obvious than that of Beorn, based as it is on the authority of his spoken word, yet he seems to be Master of the whole region of the winding river Withywindle.

The 'merry fellow' Bombadil in fact already existed as a character in the poem 'The Adventures of Tom Bombadil' that Tolkien published in 1934, shortly after he finished working on *The Hobbit*.[16] According to Carpenter, however, Bombadil began his literary existence even earlier than this, as the hero of stories that Tolkien told to his children in the late 1920s, in the manner of *Roverandom*.[17] Possibly they were set in the woodland and the meadowland of the winding river Cherwell, which can be reached only about half a mile from the house where Tolkien used to lived in north Oxford.

As Christopher Tolkien has shown, an early extract of a Bombadil poem, a kind of humorous boating song, is extant among his father's papers. It begins as a dialogue:

> Ho! Tom Bombadil
> Whither are you going?
> With John Pompador
> Down the River rowing?[18]

The river journey takes this Bombadil to rural places with names like Little Congleby, Stoke Canonicorum and Bumby Cocalorum (names chosen more for their rhythmical and metrical attraction rather than for their geographical precision); his goal is to visit two characters with the comically rhyming names of Bill Willoughby and Harry Larraby. In fact, Harry is brewing ale, presumably in anticipation of the visit. In the refrain of this boating song, the willows and reeds are bending in the wind (with an obvious allusion to Kenneth Grahame's *The Wind in the Willows*) and the ripples of the flowing water gleam and shimmer, while the fair sun runs through the sky and there is laughter in the shady glades.

The poem 'The Adventures of Tom Bombadil' captures this playful mood very well, and Bombadil at times is the companion of badgers and otters, at times lover and then husband of Goldberry, the River's daughter (who is presumably a kind of river sprite), while in the later poem 'Bombadil Goes Boating' he drinks ale with his old friend farmer Maggot at Bamfurlong.[19] In the earlier of the two poems Tom sits by the waterside for hours upon hours until the trickster River-daughter Goldberry pulls him in by his beard that is trailing enticingly in the water. Later Tom has his chance for recompense, when he catches the River-daughter and holds her fast, though the water rats scutter, the reeds hiss and the herons cry – presumably in

Fig. 5c   Narrowboat on river

natural harmony with the River-daughter's fluttering heart.[20] On the whole, the mood is frivolous, and the lightness of touch is reflected in the many playful feminine rhymes on the unstressed syllable *-ing*: in words like *going* and *rowing* and *scuttering* and *fluttering*. But there is strong rhythm in these lines, and at its best the poem has moments of a deeper kind of joy. What Bombadil has in common with the singers of the Rivendell woodland is his playfulness.

The intimate connection between the setting and spirit of place deserves pondering further. In a provocative essay on 'Landscape and Character' (mentioned earlier in chapter 1), Lawrence Durrell once attempted to elucidate the sense of place in creative writing by suggesting that 'characters' in fiction could almost be regarded as 'functions' of a landscape. And Durrell goes on to suggest that good writers know how to tune in to 'the feeling, that mysterious sense of *rapport*, of identity with the ground'.[21] In fantasy fiction, with its added element of symbolism, this approach seems doubly appropriate. The earliest explanation of Tom Bombadil's identity is contained in some notes probably written in 1937–8; now published in *The Return of the Shadow* (p. 117), they suggest that Bombadil is an 'aborigine', older than any other denizen of the land, since he was there before men and hobbits, before barrow-wights and the necromancer, before even elves. Tolkien is still thinking here very much in the terms of *The Hobbit* that he had just published, hence the name *necromancer* for Sauron. He puts the term 'aborigine' in inverted commas to draw attention to its meaning and etymology *ab origine*, 'from the beginning'. And when he writes the story down (the original draft is very close to the final published version) it becomes clear that Bombadil belongs almost with the demi-gods of mythology. Tom Bombadil has been a part of the countryside since time began: he is, as Goldberry says, 'the Master of wood, water, and hill' just as she is daughter of the River.[22] As Tolkien wrote in his letter to Unwin in December 1937, Bombadil is the 'spirit of the (vanishing) Oxford and Berkshire countryside' – Berkshire of course being a rich area of ancient pathways, such as the Ridgeway, and ancient landmarks and burial mounds.

As a spirit of the countryside, Bombadil has affinities with the figure of Lob in the poem of that name by Edward Thomas, a writer who – as was suggested above – may be compared with Tolkien, for various reasons. Thomas and Tolkien are similarly preoccupied with the connections of language and landscape; they are also contemporaries, shaped by the same cultural forces, though they knew next to nothing of each other's work.

Edward Thomas was writing his poems in the years 1914 to 1917 and harking back to his earlier travel and nature writings, such as *The Icknield Way* and *The South Country*, which explore the southern English countryside much as Tolkien was to do when he moved to Oxford in the 1920s. The following comment may be seen as typical of Thomas's interests:

> You will find 'Welsh Ways' all over England. Walkers of Workaway Hill, where the Ridgeway descends southward from Wansdyke to the Pewsey Valley, is said to be a corruption of Weala-wege, and to have been called Walcway (or Welshway) by a shepherd not long ago.[23]

As Tolkien or any other contemporary philologist could have explained, the Old English *Weala-wege* means literally 'the way of the foreigners'; its first element was *wealh*, which according to Tolkien survives in the English word *walnut*, the 'foreign nut', as opposed to the native English *hazelnut*.[24]

In Thomas's poem 'Lob' the protagonist is a countryman with a weather-beaten face and sea-blue eyes; the poet-narrator meets him at hawthorn-time walking a footpath in Wiltshire near some ancient burial-mounds which (so says the old man) the archaeologists dug up sixty years before thinking there was something to find there – something which in the end they couldn't find by digging.[25] When years later the narrator returns in search of this man, he receives conflicting reports as to who he might be. According to one report the old man is Walker of Walker's Hill, a man linked closely to places on the maps; he is 'Old Adam Walker', a type of first man who keeps the pathways open; he is 'English as this gate'; he has been here 'as long as dove and daw/ calling the wild cherry tree the merry tree' (a line worthy of Tom Bombadil). A further informant, a 'squire's son' called Jack, another kind of traditional countryman, fills in the details that make up the second half of the poem. This young Jack then disappears rather mysteriously, as though he is a younger version of Lob himself. Before he makes his exit he gives the reader more to ponder, describing the old man as the one-time redoubtable hero of many trickster folk-tales, and calling him Lob-lie-by-the-fire, a kind of brownie or house-elf (as discussed in chapter 1 above), with many other traditional, almost hobbit-like names (Hob, Lob, Rob, Robbin and Jack).

Another early twentieth-century writer, contemporary with both Tolkien and Edward Thomas, was also interested in such folklore figures. In Kipling's *Puck of Pook's Hill* (1906) the protagonist of this story, based partly on Shakespeare's character Puck in *A Midsummer Night's Dream*, has a long-standing folkloric history behind him, evident in the place-name Pook's Hill:

> He pointed to the bare, fern-covered slope of Pook's Hill that runs from the far side of the mill-stream to a dark wood. Beyond the wood the ground rises and rises for five hundred feet, till at last you climb out on the bare top of Beacon Hill, to look over Pevensey Levels and the Channel and half the naked South Downs.[26]

Pook's Hill preserves the older pronunciation of the vowel in the name Puck, and goes back to the Old English *puca*, a word meaning 'goblin' or 'fairy' according to the *OED*, though that would be an appellation that the lively Puck of Kipling's tale would reject, or even refuse to mention. The idea of the People of the Hills had been hijacked for too long by the whimsy of 'little buzzflies with butterfly wings and gauze petticoats' glorified by the machinery of Victorian and Edwardian theatre productions and volumes of Fairy Poetry. Kipling, like Tolkien, was anxious to restore natural dignity and strength to the idea of a People of a parallel otherworld. Like the elves of Rivendell – as presented in *The Hobbit* rather than *LOTR* – Kipling's Puck also appears to dwell in the vicinity of a great house, as a spirit of the place, 'the oldest Old Thing in England', and like Bombadil he is intimately connected to the landscape and the region.

Why the Shire?

Why does Tolkien begin both his Middle-earth novels in the Shire? Why not start as, say, Peter Jackson does in his film version of *FR*, with the great battle when Isildur took the ring from the evil Sauron and then lost it again? Or why not start *The Hobbit* with the attack of the dragon on the Lonely Mountain, and the escape of the young Thorin Oakenshield from the terrible devastion of the halls of his grandfather, the last King under the Mountain? Another possibility would be to start with Gandalf finding Thorin's father in the dungeons of the Necromancer and being given the map of the Mountain, which is the invaluable guide that the dwarves need to find the side-entrance into the Mountain. There are at least two likely reasons why Tolkien did not begin his novels with sensational action-filled episodes. First, there is a need for a perspective: the reader who is going to be attracted to read a novel set in a mythical world needs to begin on solid familiar ground. Novels on the whole deal with realistic characters in realistic social settings, and this is what Tolkien provides with the Shire. By beginning in a relatively modern cultural world, the sceptical 'non-heroic' reader, with a modern perspective on events, can be wooed and drawn in; slowly but surely the reader loses his or her preconceptions; seen from an outsider's perspective (and in this respect a hobbit is just as much an uncomprehending outsider as the modern reader) the things of the legendary world are presented in a realistic manner and their existence becomes acceptable and authentic, or even plausible.

The Shire, then, has a literary function: it provides authentic grounding and a familiar perspective on the action. But there is another reason why Tolkien chose to base the start and finish of his two novels in the Shire. Like William Morris, as is discussed in chapter 7 below, Tolkien had what is nowadays termed an *eco-critical* turn-of-mind, and although he strongly disliked allegory, he felt his works should have *applicability* (*LOTR*, Foreword). Like many writers in the first three decades of the twentieth century, he felt that the real England was to be found in the rural regions.[27] And he might well have agreed with the village Poet as presented in *Akenfield*, the classic study of life in the English countryside:

> One has to have a leaning towards village life. It is often a life of poverty in contrast with that of the towns. Poverty is something believed to be a great stimulant of art, but I don't believe this. Except I am willing to forgo a lot of the things other people now take for granted in order to keep Akenfield, by which I mean the deep country. The power of wonder is here. In spite of machines and sprays, I still find Nature with a capital N in this valley. It is man's rightful place to live in Nature and to be a part of it. He has to recognize the evidence of his relationship to the great natural pattern in such things as flowers, crops, water, stones, wild creatures.[28]

PART TWO

Making the mythology

The Book of Lost Tales

A WHOLE MYTHICAL world lies behind the short novel *The Hobbit*, and it is alluded to in a scene during Bilbo's second visit to Rivendell on his way *back again*:

> When the tale of their journeyings was told, there were other tales, and yet more tales, tales of long ago, and tales of new things, and tales of no time at all, till Bilbo's head fell forward on his chest and he snored comfortably in a corner.

Bilbo falls asleep, and we do not hear any of these tales at Elrond's great house in *The Hobbit*. But here in one short passage is a playful allusion to Tolkien's creative activity up to and including the publication of *The Hobbit* in 1937. It is time to turn to these 'tales of no time at all' – the mythology – and examine the ways in which they developed in Tolkien's early writings. We will consider *The Silmarillion* in the early version that Tolkien wrote, known as *The Book of Lost Tales*, with its frame tale *The Cottage of Lost Play* that anticipates in conception the house of Elrond at Rivendell. This collection of tales, unfortunately never finished, is linked closely to Tolkien's plan to create a mythology dedicated to England.

The model is almost certainly medieval. Collections of tales were immensely popular in the Middle Ages, and the ones unified by a frame narrative are the best known, such as Geoffrey Chaucer's *Canterbury Tales*, for the frame adds dramatic interest and gives a further perspective on the stories being told. The famous *Decameron*, by the Italian author Giovanni

Boccaccio (1313–75), deserves mention in this respect, for in the frame story a number of noblemen and ladies take refuge from an outbreak of plague in Florence by fleeing to a country mansion, where they pass the time in song, music and tale-telling on the shaded lawns in the grounds of the house; the rest of the book contains all the tales, and after each tale is told the characters discuss and comment on its meaning. Whether consciously or not, Tolkien seems to have followed this model for his *The Book of Lost Tales*, not in terms of theme or type of story but certainly with regard to the structure: the visit of Eriol to a great house where he hears many stories. Each night a diversity of story-tellers and narrators gather in Lindo's house; they feature prominently in the 'frame', the link passages that occur between each tale.

As to content, the closest analogue is found in the *Prose Edda* by the thirteenth-century Icelandic writer Snorri Sturluson. *Gylfaginning* is the story of King Gylfi of Sweden, who visits a mysterious house known as the Hall of the High One. Here he asks many questions of his three hosts High, Just-as-high and Third, who then regale him with the creation myths and legends of the Æsir, the gods of Norse mythology. Since Tolkien as a student studied *Gylfaginning* as part of his special subject of Scandinavian Philology and must have known this set text well, it is very likely that the myths and stories told in *Gylfaginning* influenced his mythological writing project. A relevant example is the making of the light-ships of the Sun and the Moon, the latter myth resembling the one told by Lindo in part I, chapter 8 of *The Book of Lost Tales*. Another is the fantastical notion of a floating island physically moved by the gods, which has a parallel here too. Rather like Gylfi, Eriol hears stories that whet his appetite for more information on such matters as the making of the earth, the identity of the Valar and the departure of the Eldar from Valinor. Unlike the Eriol story, the structure of *Gylfaginning* is more clearly catechetical, in the sense of a short question-and-answer session, rather than a free dialogue, and it becomes in the end a contest of wisdom, as in some medieval didactic poems.

Many tales are told in Lindo's great hall, but the fullest narrative, and the one with many connections to *The Hobbit*, is *The Fall of Gondolin*, not the first legend in the sequence of the mythology itself, but certainly one of the first to be composed, probably in the period 1916–17. Aside from Tolkien's wife Edith, who probably read it at the time, its earliest audience consisted of members of the Essay Club at his old *alma mater*, Exeter College, Oxford. In 1920, while he was employed at the Oxford Dictionary, Tolkien was guest speaker at the Essay Club and chose to read an edited version of his story to the assembled meeting. Although, in his preamble, Tolkien modestly claimed that *The Fall of Gondolin* was not his best story to date, the reading was in fact very well received.[1] And with good reason. It is I think an interesting and powerful tale, with narrative tension, mysterious seascapes and landscapes, and vivid dramatic dialogue; it deserves more attention than it has so far received. It is also clearly the prototype of a common theme in Tolkien's fiction: the journey there-and-back-again, and there are a number of parallels to be drawn with the themes and plot of *The Hobbit*.

Chapter Six

The English country house and its myths

Rivendell and the house of Elrond in *The Hobbit*

ELROND'S HOUSEHOLD AT Rivendell, in the chapter 'A Short Rest' in *The Hobbit*, constitutes only a very brief interlude. The reader will have to await the sequel for further details on the quality of life there, and those who have read *LOTR* already will be able to imagine the scene rather differently from first-time readers of *The Hobbit*. From the story as given, it is clear that Elrond is a person of great knowledge and authority, with mysterious kindred and hints of a special character. And although Tolkien originally imported the name Elrond into the story haphazardly, that name nevertheless came along trailing its mythical significances. For Elrond was an important personage in the mythology that Tolkien had created before he ever wrote a single word of his two novels *The Hobbit* and *LOTR*.

One brief paragraph outlines the personal qualities of Elrond, and one scene is given in detail: we see Elrond identify the swords that the travellers have found in the trolls' lair, blades from the ancient kingdom of Gondolin, made during the old wars when King Turgon's hidden city was attacked and besieged by the forces of Melko. But no account of the 'Fall of Gondolin' is provided here; it is a mere name, offering the uninitiated reader perhaps a sense of hidden depth, of a greater background behind the story. But Gondolin is in fact a key location in Tolkien's cycle of legends *The Silmarillion*, and through his father Eärendel and his father's father Tuor, Elrond can trace his lineage right back to that fabled city. Moreover, Elrond's great house in Rivendell strongly recalls the house of Lindo in Kortirion in Tolkien's *Book of Lost Tales*, for Lindo also provides a symbolically charged 'short rest' and hospitality for guests.

The Cottage of Lost Play

Tolkien wrote his first mature piece of narrative fiction, *The Cottage of Lost Play*, at Great Haywood in Staffordshire in the winter of 1916–17. The Great War was at its height, and he was on convalescent leave from the trenches, visiting his wife Edith. As the introductory story in his unfinished (and, in his lifetime, unpublished) *Book of Lost Tales*, the *Cottage* makes an intriguing start to his fictional work. In the first paragraph it is revealed that the protagonist has been 'brought in a ship' out into the west to Tol Erresëa, the Lonely Island, otherwise known, says the narrator, as 'the Land of Release, and a great tale hangs thereto'.[2]

The theme is clearly one of travel and the desire for knowledge, and the mention of a 'great tale' serves as anticipation for what is to follow: it is the first of several hints that this is also a story about story-telling, a frame narrative. We are told that the traveller has wandered for a while until, in this opening scene, he reaches the heart of the island, a citadel or town where he decides to remain, seeking hospitality for the night and an opportunity to tell his own tale and hear a number of stories from his hosts, notably the myths of origin and the legends of the so-called Valar and Eldar; these then follow in the subsequent chapters, the actual 'lost tales' of the title of the book.

Both the setting and the traveller are mysterious at the start of the story, and they remain for some time unexplained as the reader continues reading. Tolkien uses the device found in some novels of only slowly introducing a traveller and the place where he is travelling, and of withholding facts in order to reveal them gradually as the opening narrative progresses. The initial scene of Hardy's *Under the Greenwood Tree* springs to mind:

> To dwellers in a wood almost every species of tree has its voice as well as its feature. [...] On a starry Christmas eve within living memory a man was passing up a lane towards Mellstock Cross in the darkness of a plantation that whispered thus distinctively in his intelligence. All the evidence of his nature were those afforded by the spirit of his footsteps, which succeeded each other

lightly and quickly [...] The lonely lane he was following connected one of the hamlets of Mellstock parish with Upper Mellstock and Lewgate, and to his eyes, casually glancing upward, the silver and black-stemmed birches, with their characteristic tufts, the pale grey boughs of beech, the dark-creviced elm, all appeared now as black and flat outlines upon the sky, wherein the white stars twinkled so vehemently [...][3]

This is the advantage for the novelist of choosing 'arrival' as the opening motif of a novel rather than, say, beginning with the two characters in conversation. The theme of the arrival of an unknown wayfarer allows the reader to identify with him and to become as it were also a traveller, and so to 'arrive' in the fictional world that the writer is seeking to present.

In *The Cottage of Lost Play* a similar technique is used. The time of the day is evening, the sun has set 'beyond the boughs of the elms that stood as far as eye could look about the plain'. Candles are being lit, and the traveller's thoughts turn to rest and stories to pass the long evening, and he is strangely attracted to this 'fair-seeming town' upon the hill, for it appears to hold 'many secrets of old and wonderful and beautiful things' both in its treasuries and in the memories of those who live there. A gentle breeze blows and there is a flight of rooks above his head making their way home to the tops of some elm-trees at the summit of the hill. As he climbs up he sees the stars appear through the great yew-trees that line one side of the road. Eriol now continues his way among the houses till 'stepping as if by chance' he turns down a winding lane that leads him to the house known as *The Cottage of Lost Play*, which rather fantastically and magically turns out to be much larger within than it appears without. Rather than a cottage as such, he enters a manor-house, with halls and turrets and an extensive garden. Here he enjoys the hospitality, the *guestkindliness*, of the lord Lindo and his wife Vairë.

As the opening passage of *The Cottage of Lost Play* shows, it is remarkable how the story picks up ideas and strands of plot that will appear in a number of different guises in the course of Tolkien's writing career. A major theme is travel, hospitality and tale-telling, and we will have occasion to explore this matter in detail below. But the following are also touched on: dreams and anticipation; the hints of far distant vistas; the beauty of a great city still at home in its natural surroundings; the love of trees and the interconnectedness or even communion between Man and Nature – the sense that the rooks are returning home just as the traveller reaches his place of

Fig. 6a   Building with turret (central Oxford)

rest. Above all the passage presents a moment of intuition, an epiphany in the mind of Eriol on seeing the city, where he senses a promise of wealth and secrets to be unveiled.

Coincidentally, the openings of the Hardy novel and the Tolkien story have features in common: the country setting, a lonely lane, the starlit sky glimpsed through the boughs of the trees. And the viewpoint or perspective soon settles on the traveller, through whom the new or even fantastical world is mediated to the reader. In the case of Eriol in *The Cottage of Lost Play* we as readers become involved with his perceptions and feelings, we sympathise with his predicament, his puzzlement, his delight. The traveller's arrival, his reception, his questioning of the hosts is a form of mediation that allows the reader to begin on familiar ground, before the main purpose of the book, the telling of the legends of a new mythology, takes the reader further, into decidedly unfamiliar territory.

The immediate context of *The Book of Lost Tales*

There is an autobiographical side to *The Cottage of Lost Play*, written in a Staffordshire village in the autumn and winter of 1916–17. In fact, the depiction of the 'fair-seeming town upon a little hill' with its golden elms matches closely to Tolkien's descriptions of the tree-lined, medieval city of Warwick, with its old castle and winding lanes. Here too he had heard a 'voice of home-coming', since his fiancée Edith had lived in Warwick from 1913 until their marriage in March 1916, and Tolkien had made frequent trips there, which he recorded in poems, letters and paintings. On a visit in 1913 or 1914, for instance, he went on a boating trip on the river Avon and made the drawing *Warwick Castle Seen from under the Bridge*, and in June 1913 he drew *Pageant House Gardens, Warwick*, a memoir of the Georgian house on Jury Street, which the couple had no doubt visited. In November 1915, while seeing Edith, he wrote the poem 'Kortirion among the Trees', dedicated to Warwick, the 'tower and citadel of the world'. It includes various evocative lines praising the 'gathered sound' of the breeze in the leaves of the elm trees, more overwhelming and musical than that of the other trees, the oaks, maple and poplars that once lined the streets of the city.[4]

It is clear that Tolkien envisages a close parallel between the town of the Eldar and the town of the English, which he later sought to explain in terms of the mythology that he was constructing. According to one legend (which he later put aside, though it has a parallel in a Norse myth) the whole island of Tol Eressëa was set adrift and drawn across the Ocean to the Great Lands, where it eventually became England.

In a poem of farewell called 'The Lonely Isle' (which opens with an address 'O glimmering island set sea-girdled and alone'), written in June 1916 as Tolkien embarked for service in war-beleaguered France, the theme of the elms of England again appears, and in a 'high inland tower' (perhaps Warwick again) the pealing of a bell is to be heard.[5] Tolkien's Lonely Isle is a kind of mythical, alternative, otherworldly England, as Christopher Tolkien suggests in his notes on the unfinished 'History of Eriol or Ælfwine', in his *The Book of Lost Tales*.[6] In this form of the legend, present-day Warwick really is the old, old city of Kortirion, with the root *Kor* or otherwise *Gwar* in the author's invented languages indicating an etymological connection with *War-*. In every sense Tolkien was relating his mythology to England.

The poem 'Kortirion among the Trees' has been dated quite closely to November 1915, when Tolkien took leave from training camp in order to meet his wife Edith in Warwick. The autumnal scene in the medieval town no doubt gave rise to lines 77–85 in which the elm foliage begins to fail, and turn pale amber at the onset of winter, and as the leaves fall from the

Fig. 6b   Warwick Castle

trees they appear to fly 'like birds across the misty meres'. His preface to the poem, also perhaps written in November 1915, serves as a kind of explanation of the imagery used:

> And it seems to the fairies and it seems to me who know that town and have often trodden its disfigured ways that autumn and the falling of the leaf is the season of the year when maybe here or there a heart among men may be open, and an eye perceive how is the world's estate fallen from the laughter and loveliness of old. Think on Kortirion and be sad – yet is there not hope?[7]

The hope was justified on a personal level, for Tolkien survived the war to return to his Land of Release and begin what he saw as his work of recording its stories and legends. The origin of this narrative, then, is biographical and historical: *The Book of Lost Tales* represents the life of a young soldier responding symbolically through literature to the times in which he lived.

The significance of elm trees was not only personal to Tolkien, since elm trees really were widespread in England at the time, and they took on symbolic weight for many authors. In the very same month and year as Tolkien was writing his poem in Warwick (i.e. in November 1915), a writer of a very different tenor, the novelist D.H. Lawrence, was staying as a guest of Lady Ottoline Morrell in the old country house of Garsington Manor, near Oxford. Lawrence felt a similar sense of loss and regret. And he was also about to depart from England. Under the pressure of the threatened censorship of his novel *The Rainbow* and with the obvious political difficulty of being married to a German woman, he felt he was being forced to leave England for America. In this context, at Garsington, he responds to the same clement autumn weather as does Tolkien at Warwick:

> When I drive across this country, with the autumn falling and rustling to pieces, I am so sad, for my country, for this great wave of civilisation, 2000 years, which is now collapsing, that it is hard to live. So much beauty and pathos of old things passing away and no new things coming: this house of the Ottolines – it is England – my God, it breaks my soul – this England, these shafted windows, the elm-trees, the blue distance – the past, the great past, crumbling down, breaking down, not under the force of the coming buds, but under the weight of many exhausted, lovely yellow leaves, that drift over the lawn and over the pond, like the soldiers, passing away, into winter and the darkness of winter – no, I can't bear it. For the winter stretches ahead, where all vision is lost and all memory dies out.[8]

The situation of the two men was utterly different, but the image of an ancient house in 'this England', with its elm trees and falling leaves, is strikingly similar.

From the 1880s and 1890s up to the First World War, there was widespread preoccupation with the symbolic significance of English houses and their gardens. Consider for instance the country houses idealised by the writers of the time, such as Rudyard Kipling, author of *Kim* and *The Jungle Book*, who bought his house, Bateman's, at Burwash in Sussex in 1902: 'a well-built Jacobean house of stone in a lonely valley, at the foot of a steep lane running down from an unfrequented village ... a gray stone lichened house, AD 1634 over the door – beamed, panelled, with old oak staircase, and all untouched and unfaked ... It is a good and peaceable place standing in terraced lawns nigh to a walled garden of old red brick'.[9] Here Kipling wrote his fictions celebrating a traditional view of England as a hierarchical society rooted in its countryside, perhaps the most famous of these being his children's novels *Puck of Pook's Hill* and its sequel *Rewards and Fairies* in which, by means of the magic of Puck, the two main characters meet figures from the historical and legendary past who tell their stories of England.

Another famous Edwardian celebration of a country house is E.M. Forster's novel *Howard's End*, published in 1910. Here the house Howard's End becomes a symbol of the reconciliation of English society, the return to connectedness that is the main theme of the novel. In one scene in chapter 33, Margaret Schlegel makes a visit to the house, which has not been lived in for some time. As she walks from the station, across the village green and up the avenue of chestnut trees towards the church, she begins to ponder the question of mythology:

> Up the avenue Margaret strolled slowly, stopping to watch the sky that gleamed through the upper branches of the chestnuts, or to finger the little horseshoes on the lower branches. Why has not England a great mythology? Our folklore has never advanced beyond daintiness, and the greater melodies about our countryside have all issued through the pipes of Greece. Deep and true as the native imagination can be, it seems to have failed here. It has stopped with the witches and the fairies. It cannot vivify one fraction of a summer field, or give names to half a dozen stars.

Interestingly, Forster in this novel shared with Tolkien the conviction that unlike other European cultures, England lacked a true native tradition of mythology, needed to restore its sense of rooted identity. Tolkien may or may not have read Forster, for such ideas were in the air at the time, part of the general literary culture, but certainly it was Tolkien who set himself the actual task of reconstructing or reinventing such a *legendarium*, a mythology for his time.[10]

Chapter Seven

William Guest

William Morris and the theme of hospitality

O NE OF THE strongest modern influences on Tolkien's writing is to be found in the work of the poet and designer William Morris (1834–96), author of a number of romances (*romances* here in the sense of novels or fantasies with legendary or exotic settings), which many scholars consider to be important precursors of *The Hobbit* and *LOTR*.

A number of parallels may be drawn. Both Morris and Tolkien were well read in Old English and Old Norse, in what Tolkien and his friend C.S. Lewis called northern literature, and its themes are everywhere apparent in their fictional writings. Both Morris and Tolkien were educated at Exeter College, Oxford, and Tolkien must have seen the tapestry *The Adoration of the Magi* in the college chapel, designed by Morris's long-term collaborator, the artist Edward Burne-Jones, and made at Morris's tapestry works at Merton Abbey. Morris and Burne-Jones were members of the Pre-Raphaelite Brotherhood, a movement in art that sought to revive medieval themes and styles in Victorian art and design; the notion of a brotherhood of like-minded writers is one that appealed to Tolkien and his school friends in their writers' circle the TCBS. Undoubtedly, Tolkien was influenced also by Morris's designs – the patterns of tiles and internal decorations – and he made his own designs in a similar manner.[1] Morris's medievalism extended into production and manufacture following the trail laid by John Ruskin: it was felt that all household goods should be valued equally for their beauty as well as for their function – such ideals of the Arts and Crafts movement surely influenced Tolkien, for instance, in his descriptions of the artistry and craftsmanship of the inhabitants of Rivendell or Lothlorien in *LOTR* or Nargothrond and Gondolin in *The Silmarillion*. Not that Tolkien drew all his inspiration directly from Morris, for, as a university teacher of Old and Middle English, Tolkien had direct knowledge of the same medieval texts that had influenced Morris.

As well as a writer, Tolkien was a moderately gifted cartographer, illustrator, painter and calligrapher, and this was also an ability he shared with William Morris. Tolkien sometimes began with an image, map or picture and worked out his story and characters on that basis: the most obvious example is *The Hobbit*, and there is a clear parallel in the cartographic plots of many of Morris's romances, from *The Roots of the Mountain* to *The Sundering Flood* or *The Water of the Wondrous Isles*. Tolkien never achieved great success as a painter of human figures, as he was the first to admit, and here again there is a similarity to Morris, who – though more gifted in this respect – was nevertheless also reluctant to paint human subjects. In both artists we can admire landscapes – impressive views of trees, mountains and

Fig. 7a   Exeter College, Oxford, rear quad and garden

water – and fine illustrations of buildings and interiors. And not content to be only passive admirers of medieval manuscripts and scripts both Morris and Tolkien developed skills in calligraphy (in Tolkien's case there was influence from his mother, and perhaps his grandfather), and they adapted and invented new scripts to suit the nature of their writing. In an ideal world, we ought to read their work in facsimiles of the original manuscripts, as can be done in some editions of the work of William Blake, in order fully to appreciate the artistry of both visual form and narrative content.

Tolkien seems to have known all of Morris's fiction and poetry,[2] and back in 1914 while a student he had even composed a story based on the Finnish legend of Kullervo, written in the same archaic prose-and-verse style that Morris had employed in *The House of the Wolfings* (1888), the first of two stories set in northern Europe in the so-called Dark Ages. For an example of that style, the following is a passage from the sequel *The Roots of the Mountains* (1889) dealing with the arrival of the man Goldmane, a stranger from Burgdale, at a mysterious house in the pine-forest, and his reception in the hall of the Wolfings or mountain-people (which may be compared to the reception of strangers in the Beorn chapter of *The Hobbit* or the chapter 'King of the Golden Hall' in *The Two Towers*):

> Therewith she led him gently over the threshold into the hall, and it seemed to him as if she were the fairest and the noblest of all the Queens of ancient story.
>
> When he was in the house he looked and saw that, rough as it was without it lacked not fairness within.[3]

Morris's *News from Nowhere* (1891) is another variation on the theme of *guestkindliness*, a utopian vision of a London of the future to which the main protagonist finds himself transported one morning. The rest of the novel narrates the journey he undertakes from a house in London to a house on the Upper Thames, and it bears some similarity with *The Book of Lost Tales*, in which, had he completed his task, Tolkien would have moved his guest from the house in Warwick–Kortirion to a country house at Tavrobel, a place corresponding to Great Haywood in Staffordshire (again significant to Tolkien for family reasons).

Both Morris and Tolkien open their narratives in a similar manner: a traveller responds favourably to the hospitality he receives in a wonderful house that he arrives at by chance. In *News from Nowhere* the traveller, who calls himself William Guest in this allegorical and partly autobiographical dream, begins with an account of 'a brisk conversational discussion' on the subject of the 'future of the fully-developed new society'.[4] Returning home, he retires to sleep, and wakes up – or more precisely seems to wake up – in his own bed, like Chaucer's dreamer in *The Book of the Duchess*, only to find his house and garden and city all changed for the better, with the air and water cleaner, the people brighter and freer. His reactions are partly those of a stranger (as the people he meets in the new world imagine him to be) and partly those of the time traveller who is shocked, though in this case pleasantly shocked, by the changes that have taken place in the world and the society with which he is familiar.

The buildings of this fictional world partly mirror Morris's inspirational work in architecture and design, for the story begins at a newly designed guesthouse in London and ends at an old country house on the upper Thames. In the fine illustrated edition of *News from Nowhere*, published by the Kelmscott Press in 1892, the frontispiece illustration reveals the second house to be Morris's property Kelmscott Manor itself, an old house that Morris saw as embodying pre-industrial architectural principles, while the guesthouse where Guest begins his river journey is reminiscent of Morris's own architectural creation Red House, designed to his own specifications. As Marcus Waithe has reminded us, Red House was made to embody, within a modern, newly designed building, something of the old values of hospitality as found at Kelmscott, or indeed in any other manorial hall of the medieval centuries. Pictures of Red House can be viewed for instance in Fiona MacCarthy's *William Morris* (1994): the large front door with its big strap hinges 'set in a deep porch, giving a sense of monumental welcome'; then the interior hall with its high ceilings, arched corridors and spaces that seem 'to flow from room to room'; finally the first floor drawing room below the roof that Morris wished to be 'the most beautiful room in the world', with its rugs and two carved oak chairs before the huge hearth and red-tiled fireplace and a huge celebratory wedding scene derived from a scene in the medieval writer Froissart's Chronicle, painted by Edward Burne-Jones to cover the whole of the far wall of the room.[5]

Morris's architecture and its influence on Tolkien

With the design of these rooms in mind, let us return to Tolkien's *The Cottage of Lost Play*. Like Goldmane in Morris's *Roots of the Mountains*, Eriol

Fig. 7b · Door to Exeter College Chapel

is invited to seek of the lord and lady a night's 'guest-kindliness' and pass across the threshold. He enters the building, which turns out to offer more attractions than the initial impression would give, since the house is delightfully spacious, and lord Lindo and his wife Vairë come forth to greet him. The *guestkindliness* or hospitality follows a time-honoured ritual pattern of word of welcome, naming, and stating of purpose. Eriol declares his name to be the Stranger, from the Great Lands (i.e. from Middle-earth), and that he was 'seeking whither so his desire for travel led him'. After this ritual has been fulfilled he is invited to join his hosts at dinner.

In a sequence anticipating the chapter 'The Last Stage' in *The Hobbit* and 'Many Meetings' in *FR*,[6] both set in the Last Homely House of Elrond at Rivendell, the company now repair to the great hall, a place of warmth generated by a fire burning in a hearth set in three out of the four walls of its internal space. A gong sounds and a throng of people of all ages and types gather to dine (compare this with the statement that 'the hall of Elrond's house was filled with folk' in *FR*). Again the ritual pattern is rehearsed, here one of song and blessing, followed by talk – the first word being given to the Stranger, allowing him to tell his story and then in return to ask his questions about the city he is visiting. At the end of the meal the cups are filled for a final ritual drink, then the big oaken doors at the far end of the hall are flung open, and the Stranger is conveyed even further into the interior of the house. Again one might compare Morris's *Roots of the Mountains*; there the rough but fair interior of the hall is similar to the hall of Beorn in *The Hobbit*, though more sociable and hospitable and more elaborately decorated:

> The hangings on the walls, though they left some places bare which were hung with fresh boughs, were fairer than he had ever seen, so that he deemed that they must come from far countries and the City of Cities: therein were images wrought of warriors and fair women of old time and their dealings with the Gods and the Giants, and Wondrous wights; and he deemed that this was the story of some great kindred, and that their token and the sign of their banner must needs be the Wood-wolf, for everywhere it was wrought in these pictured webs. Perforce he looked long and earnestly at these fair things, for the hall was not dark yet, because the brands on the hearth were flaming their last [...][7]

The hall of the mountain forest people is decorated with the tapestries depicting their myths and legends – the 'fair things' that catch and hold the attention of the newcomer. Similarly, in *The Cottage of Lost Play*, the assembled company passes through a short broad corridor whose walls are decorated with tapestries telling stories which Eriol cannot make out in the dark because the candle-bearers are behind him. Like the frame tale itself, the narrative art on the walls of the dark building further serves the function of mediation, attracting both the traveller and also the reader with the promise of stories to come.

At this point in the narrative, however, the pictured stories are still hard to make out in the darkness, and as Eriol walks the short broad corridor the only light comes from the room ahead, the Tale-fire burning in the Room of Logs. In some respects the Room of Logs is similar to the hall of the Wolfings in Morris's *Roots of the Mountains*. More to the point, it is not unlike the drawing room of Morris's Red House, since it is an attractive room lit by firelight dancing on the walls and the low ceiling, with many rugs and soft cushions placed around the hearth, and one 'deep chair with carven arms and feet'.[8] Lord Lindo the host will take the chair, and the listeners will take their places on the cushions or comfortably stretch by the great hearth fire. The scene is now set for the telling of the tales. This is a 'fair room' and, as already intimated, it will have a close analogue in the tale-telling at Rivendell in *LOTR* (a scene anticipated, albeit very briefly, on Bilbo's second visit to Rivendell in *The Hobbit*). In *LOTR* it is Elrond and Arwen his daughter who are the hosts, and in a similar manner they rise together at the end of the meal and lead the company down the hall. The doors are thrown open and they proceed down a passageway to another hall in which there are no tables, but a fire is burning brightly in the hearth between carved pillars.[9] Lindo's Room of Logs of course correspond to Elrond's 'Hall of Fire', the room where Frodo discovers Bilbo after the feast at Rivendell. This room is the place and occasion for 'many songs and tales'.

Tolkien's concept of *guestkindliness*

On the theme of hospitality Marcus Waithe makes the following salient point that 'the manner in which a household receives its guests – the unexpected as well as the expected – can tell us a great deal', notably about a society's ideals of cooperation and isolationism.[10] He goes on to consider the political ideal of openness to the outside that a hospitable society tends to proclaim and to contrast it with the suspicion and stasis, the unwillingness to change, of a closed society. As he demonstrates, there is – in the thinking of Karl Popper and others – a theory that western utopias have had an emphasis 'on perfectionism, on order, on social unity and on splendid isolation' that can verge on totalitarianism. In Waithe's view, it was Morris's medievalism that made the difference: the model of the medieval manorial hall open to travellers. In Morris this ideal of 'old English hospitality' cele-brated by William Cobbett and John Ruskin is commingled with a Marxist view of history in order to present a liberal, open-handed Socialist alter-native. And, in literary terms, Morris's project in the 1890s offered a way of dealing with such themes through the symbolism, the 'applicability' as Tolkien would call it, of imaginative fiction. In Morris's romances, different peoples at different stages of societal development are brought into contact in imaginary worlds set at different periods in the idealised past.

Tolkien shared Morris's views on ethnology, on the environment, home and work, arts and crafts, but all this without the Socialism that makes Morris the man so distinctive. This means that Tolkien is closer to, say, Ruskin than to Morris in his political attitude, which is hierarchic and traditionalist, if also environmentally aware. But Ruskin provided no liter-ary models for Tolkien to follow. Morris's influence on Tolkien on the other hand is literary rather than political. Through a writer such as Morris, Tolkien saw the possibilities open up for the use of medieval themes and styles in modern literature. And although Tolkien is not an overtly political writer, his work nevertheless shares in the context of debate on the appli-cability of the English past that is widespread in early twentieth-century fiction and poetry.

A good deal hinges on the nonce word *guestkindliness*. This is a partic-ularly apt example of a *hapax legomenon* (the philological term is used to identify a word appearing in a text such as *Beowulf* and then nowhere else in the surviving corpus of Anglo-Saxon literature). In fact, Tolkien employs his new coinage on three occasions in *The Book of Lost Tales*: in volume I, chapter 1 (with a hyphen, 'guest-kindliness') to describe the welcome at the Cottage of Lost Play and then again, this time naturalised without the hyphen as 'guestkindliness', in chapter 8, where the talk is of Eriol moving on to enjoy the hospitality of Gilfanon at the ancient 'House of the Hundred Chimneys' near the bridge of Tavrobel. (A third example occurs in volume II in *The Nauglafring*.) As a place-name Tavrobel was associated biographi-cally in Tolkien's writing with the village of Great Haywood in Staffordshire, where his wife Edith lived for a time while he served in the war.

Tolkien seems to have enjoyed coining words that, in his considered opinion, could or should have existed in Old English. His first published book was *A Middle English Vocabulary* (1922), to be discussed further in chapter 14, which was basically a glossary or dictionary to accompany the textbook of Middle English compiled by Kenneth Sisam (1887–1971), a young specialist in early English from New Zealand who had taught Tolkien at Oxford. The two books were soon amalgamated into one volume.[11] The *Vocabulary* contains a number of examples of words unrecorded in the surviving texts; each of these hypothetical words is marked with an asterisk to show that it is 'theoretically reconstructed'. One is the entry for Middle English *pypynge*, which is glossed as 'piping, playing on pipes' and given an Old English etymology: since the noun *pipe* existed in Old English, Tolkien feels justified in reconstructing a verb **pipian*, 'to play on pipes'. Similarly, *guestkindliness* is a reconstruction, a hypothetical Old English compound word apparently made up of the elements *giest* (guest), *cynde* (kind), *lic* (ly), *nes* (ness). Tolkien nowhere discusses the word. However, he does enter *kynd(e)ly* in his *Middle English Vocabulary*, as it appears twice in the selected texts in the accompanying textbook by Sisam, and Tolkien gives its Old English origin as *gecyndelic*, explaining its meaning 'having natural feeling' as a semantic development from the original idea expressed by *kynde* of 'inborn, naturally belonging to one'. In this way, then, *guestkindliness* is more suited to his theme, promising more 'natural feeling' than the Latin- and French-derived term *hospitality*, which more simply connotes the receiving of guests.

Frodo's sojourn at Rivendell is in fact the second instance of Elvish *guest-kindliness* in *LOTR*. The first occurs in *FR* in the Shire, the encounter with Gildor Inglorion in the chapter 'Three is Company', where Frodo is hailed as elf-friend because of his knowledge of their language. On this occasion Gildor and his men fashion a temporary guest-hall out of a suitable tree-lined location in the forest above Woodhall. In this encounter, there are two important factors: the closeness and connectedness of the elves to the land in which they move, and the notion of elf-friend, the special guest (for both Frodo and Eriol are granted this status). Eriol's story is one made round the notion of a wish: it is a reworking of the old legend of the elf-friend, the man who becomes a guest at Elvenhome and in the end develops a strong desire to join in kinship with his hosts. That this notion had an ancient pedigree is suggested by the existence of the Anglo-Saxon name Ælfwine, a compound name meaning 'Elf-friend' in Old English, with a related form in the cognate name of the early medieval Lombard King Alboin (where Lombardic *Alb-* corresponds to Anglo-Saxon *Ælf-* and *-oin* to *-wine*). In the later draft notes for the continuation of *The Book of Lost Tales*, Eriol's name is changed to Ælfwine, and Tolkien's later time-travel story *The Lost Road* again features a protagonist by the related name of Alboin Errol. In

The Hobbit, Bilbo himself formally receives the title 'elf-friend and blessed' from the Elvenking in exchange for his gift of a dwarvish necklace of silver and pearl at the end of the novel. This theme of the 'elf-friend', and the otherworldly hospitality that he enjoys, is remarkably persistent in Tolkien's writings.

Tolkien perhaps thought of himself as a latter-day Ælfwine. A driving force in his work is his rejection of the mechanical and the soulless, a hatred of bureaucracy and mechanisation as found for instance in modern factory production and experienced at its worst in modern trench warfare. By contrast he had a strong feeling for the world of nature: a love of trees, rivers, mountains and the tillage and husbandry of the land and the fruits of the earth, all embodied in the notion of the Eldar or elves. The earlier model for all this, the kindred spirit, was – as we have seen – the Victorian writer and designer William Morris. Ellen, a character in Morris's *News from Nowhere*, captures the feeling very well:

> She led me up close to the house, and laid her shapely sun browned hand and arm on the lichened wall as if to embrace it, and cried out, 'O me! O me! How I love the earth, and the seasons, and weather, and all things that deal with it, and all that grows out of it, – as this has done!' (chapter 31)

In Tolkien's writing the love of the earth can be equally intense, but because of his staunch Catholic faith he adds a theological twist to its expression that is absent from Morris's mostly Socialist perspective. In this he resembles the Catholic writer and poet Francis Thompson, who shares similar interests in the beings of other worlds.[12] Tolkien's concern is the immortality of the elves – those unfallen, near-human beings who seem to have their source on the margins of classical and above all medieval literature – and their relationship with the earth. As a passage in *The Silmarillion* makes clear, one of Tolkien's themes is the transience of human beings and the immortality of elves, whose love of the Earth is all the more poignant because of it, and who see human beings as transient guests or strangers among them.[13] Often in Tolkien's fictions, the children of men – mortal human beings – are literally the guests enjoying the hospitality or, as he calls it in *The Cottage of Lost Play*, the 'guest-kindliness' of the people of the Otherworld, whether this is Eriol visiting Lindo's hall at Kortirion on the Lonely Isle, or Tuor arriving at the city of Gondolin in *The Lost Tales*, or Bilbo reaching the Last Homely House at Rivendell in *The Hobbit*.

Fig. 7c   Exeter College inside passageway behind the chapel

Chapter Eight

'The lonely sea and the sky'

The hobbit and the sea

THE SEA IS a major archetypal image in Tolkien's mythology. He was fascinated by its changing aspects, its rolling breakers and wailing gulls, rocky coastline and far-off islands. In *LOTR*, the last we see of the character Legolas, son of the elvenking of the Forest of Mirkwood, is his departure downhill singing of the future time when his people will leave Ithilien and follow the course of the Anduin down to the sea, where a grey ship is waiting to take them across the sea to the undying lands beyond:

> To the Sea, to the Sea! The white gulls are crying,
> The wind is blowing, and the white foam is flying.[1]

There are echoes here of 'I must down to the seas again, to the lonely sea and the sky', the opening line of the popular poem 'Sea-Fever' by John Masefield (1878–1967), the Herefordshire boy who became a naval apprentice on the White Star Line, then a journalist and critic living in the countryside near Oxford, a writer of sea yarns and other stories, and eventually, in 1930, Poet Laureate. Tolkien met Masefield in Oxford in the 1930s, when Masefield recruited him to take part in the live recitations of Chaucer's *Canterbury Tales* in the original Middle English. Given that Masefield also wrote an account of the Battle of the Somme and was the author of children's stories and fantasies such as *The Midnight Folk* (1927), it seems likely that Tolkien knew his poems; here for comparison is the second stanza of Masefield's 'Sea-Fever':

I must down to the seas again, for the call of the running tide
Is a wild call and a clear call that may not be denied;
And all I ask is a windy day with the white clouds flying,
And the flung spray and the blown spume, and the sea-gulls crying.

The poem had been in the public consciousness for some time since it first appeared in the *Salt-Water Ballads* of 1902, and it is regarded as one of Masefield's best-known pieces. Tolkien's choice of phrase in 'white gulls are crying' and 'white foam is flying' sets up further verbal echoes of Masefield's 'white clouds flying' and 'sea-gulls crying', as well as expressing a similar theme of sea fever.[2]

At one stage early in his writing of the sequel to *The Hobbit*, before it took shape in his mind as the 'Lord of the Rings', Tolkien considered that Bilbo also might catch something of the sea-longing. Tolkien at this stage (early 1938) had written only one chapter, the essence of which is that Bilbo leaves the Shire. Scratching around to find the new direction for the sequel, Tolkien wrote various plot summaries in note form and fragments of narrative. In these it appears that Bilbo is short of money: this is one possible motivation for his journey. Another more serious urge to travel is also mooted: that Bilbo seems also to have caught the dragon-sickness, in the

Fig. 8a   Sea-mew

manner of Thorin in the early stages of *The Hobbit* as discussed above. He travels to Rivendell to consult Elrond and ask for his advice on how to heal his unsettlement and desire for money. The note is brief, but it appears that Elrond advises him to travel to an island (that may be Britain) called the Perilous Isle, far in the west where the elves still reign supreme. A snatch of their conversation is recorded in the fragment, and it appears that Bilbo tells Elrond that he has a great wish to look again on a live dragon.[3]

Bilbo of course does not make this journey to the Perilous Isle in any of Tolkien's extant writings. But the possibility is intriguing: the story would have sent Bilbo off on voyages in the wake of Eriol, the traveller who hears all the lore and wisdom of his hosts in *The Book of Lost Tales*. There is also a hint that perhaps Bilbo's adventures might have mirrored those of the great mariner of Tolkien's mythology, Eärendel.

Early experiences of the sea

Tolkien's appreciation of the sea was deep-rooted, going back to his childhood. In 1891, his father Arthur, a descendant of German émigrés, married Mabel Suffield: her respectable mercantile family from Worcestershire in the Midlands seem to have agreed to the match only with reluctance. The Tolkien family firm had gone bankrupt, and Arthur Tolkien's solution was to take up a post in a South African bank and set up house in Bloemfontein with his wife and the young family that appeared soon afterwards (Ronald was born in 1892, his brother Hilary in 1894). From a European perspective, the town of Bloemfontein was a distant inland outpost: a 'horrid waste' is how Mabel described it. A photograph of the Tolkien house reproduced in Carpenter's biography shows a long dusty street lined with houses and shops with wooden frontages not unlike a (Hollywood) Dodge City.[4] The open veldt was not far away. In this rough township, several incidents in the life of the boy are of arguable effect on the later life of the man, or at least of the writer; they include a brief (and only playful) abduction by the house boy, a painful encounter with a tarantula spider and bouts of ill-health – attributed to the climate and followed by convalescence at the coast, and then the return back permanently to England with his mother and brother Hilary.

In England, Ronald was to live for settled periods in various villages, towns and cities: in Sarehole, in Birmingham, in Warwick, in Leeds and in Oxford, all locations in the Midlands or north of England, all inland places roughly equidistant in any direction from the various coasts of the island of Britain. But the coast had been a place of refuge in Tolkien's very early years in South Africa: he remembered 'a wide flat sandy shore';[5] and of the long voyage home to England he recalled in later life 'the clear waters of the Indian Ocean' and also the harbour of Lisbon at sunrise, with the 'great city set on the hillside above'.[6] During his childhood in England the sea continued to be a place of escape for Ronald and his brother Hilary. With their mother Mabel there were visits to the English Channel, recorded in an image of the two boys on a beach in Dorset, painted by Ronald at the age of ten. Later, after their mother's untimely death, there were visits with their guardian to the east coast, to Yorkshire and the North Sea, seen in sketches of Whitby harbour and the ruins of the Abbey on the hill overlooking the town to the north and the open sea to the east.

These summer visits to the relatively gentle English seaside resorts did not prepare him for what was to be the essentially overwhelming experience of the 'Great Sea' as a young man. In the period 1910–12, he made two visits to St Andrews in Scotland, probably to see his aunt Jane Neave, née Suffield, his mother's sister, a school-teacher who (as was pointed out in chapter 1) turned out be a great encourager and patron of his poetry. Contemplating the coastline at St Andrews, he wrote his unpublished twelve-line poem 'The Grimness of the Sea'.[7] The title reflects well the direction of his thoughts at the time, although this was not to be the final version. According to Christopher Tolkien, a new poem was eventually written, and it passed through three distinct versions: 'The Tides' dated 1914; 'Sea Chant of an Elder Day' of 1915; and 'The Horns of Ulmo' of 1917. The titles are significant, indicating the line of development. From what was purely a nature poem set in the present day of 1914, Tolkien moved to a legendary setting in the 'elder day' in the text of 1915, and thence to a specifically mythological incident in *The Fall of Gondolin*, one of the stories from *The Book of Lost Tales*, which he wrote in 1917.

In the mythology of Tolkien's *The Book of Lost Tales*, men had appeared in the world from great lands to the east and thus had no knowledge of the ocean. And in *The Fall of Gondolin*, Tolkien narrates the first moment of human contact with the sea. The hero Tuor, who at the start of the tale is living alone on the shores of Lake Mithrim, has been singled out as a man of destiny by Ulmo the Lord of the Waters. One day, by the banks of a secret river, Tuor takes up his quest, the challenge of his life, and sets off downstream following the river through strange caverns and dark passages.

Fig. 8b   The lonely sea and the sky

He emerges near the coast and for the first time in his life hears the mournful calling of the gulls and feels against his face the wine-fresh wind from the Great Sea. As will be seen below, the story originates in the imagery of the poem 'The Horns of Ulmo', which is extant in three versions of 1914, 1915 and 1917. The way the poem changed is important. The textual history of Tolkien's poem 'The Horns of Ulmo' in fact mirrors the germination of Tolkien's mythology over a period of four significant years in his life.

An artist at work: the three revisions of 'The Horns of Ulmo'

During this eventful period Tolkien finished his university studies in English philology at Exeter College, Oxford, married Edith Bratt, and went to fight in the Great War. He attained the rank of lieutenant in the Royal Lancashire Fusiliers, serving as a signals officer in the Battle of the Somme; then, after contracting trench fever, he spent a period of recovery and creative convalescence in the north of England. Here he completed the third and final version of the poem.

The poem can be read in Christoper Tolkien's edition of *The Shaping of Middle-earth*; the 1914 version, 'The Tides', begins as follows:

I sat on the ruined margin of the deep-voiced echoing sea.[8]

The occasion was a walking holiday on the Lizard Peninsula in Cornwall in the far south west of England in August 1914. Led by Father Vincent Reade of the Birmingham Oratory (the well-known Catholic church of Cardinal Newman that Tolkien as a child had attended with his mother), there were hikes along the cliffs with views of the Atlantic; and there were inland walks across fields and steep valleys with streams, with the ever-present sound of the ocean in the background. As he recorded in a letter of 8 August to his fiancée Edith, the walk passed over moorland above the cliffs as far as Kynance Cove. The summer sun was hot but there was a huge swell out on the green Atlantic Ocean sending breakers against the rocky coast. The cliffs had wind-holes which made trumpet noises and there were holes right down to the sea which sprayed water like the spout of a whale.[9]

Out of this experience came the new, forty-line poem, along with several new paintings, as Tolkien the artist sat on the 'ruined margin' and drew and painted what he saw. He made a sketch of the Lion Rock, a huge cliff jutting out into the sea from Pentreath Beach on the west coast of the Lizard; here the sea is in gentle mood. Sitting at some elevation with a stretch of coastal water below him the artist/observer looks across to the Lion Rock in the

Fig. 8c   Rough sea

mid-distance, to the dark rocks of a sheer cliff that falls abruptly into the water and against which the Atlantic swell is breaking in large white waves. Above and behind the summit of the Rock is a warm balmy sky, stirred by the lines of a breeze. The ocean in another mood is seen in the painting *Cove near the Lizard*.[10] Again the artist–viewer sits near the water's edge, but now he depicts a cauldron of white foam and breakers washing the dark rocks, and he looks up towards tall cliffs that curve around the coastline to his right. The breakers smash against the sea-walls in the distance while above the grassy cliff-tops there is a dark line of fierce cloud.

The two moods – fierce and calm – are captured also in the words of the poem 'The Tides', written in 1914.[11] First there is the 'embattled tempest' conceived in imagery of siege warfare in which the armies of the grey sea rise to war like 'billowed cavalry advancing at the shore' (lines 23–4). Initially the attack is flung back by the defenders but finally the full force of the waves strikes the land in explosive anger. In the vivid expression 'and their war song burst to flame' (line 32) the sense of something heard (war song) is transformed into something seen and felt (the flames). In an abundance of adjectives Tolkien seeks to convey the force of the collision: the 'shouting water' (line 43), 'catastrophic fountains' (44), 'deafening cascades' (44). But then the mood changes, the imagery of loud music and voices changes to 'an immeasurable hymn of Ocean' played by an organ 'whose stops were the piping of gulls and the thunderous swell' (line 46). But the sound stills to an 'endless fugue of echoes' (49), and 'a music of uttermost deepness' (51), until eventually a 'murmurous slumber' (60) overtakes the listener when he hears the music cease, and he eventually awakes 'to silent cavern and empty sands and peace' (66) at the end of the poem.

In January 1915, during the Oxford Christmas vacation, Tolkien revised this poem, giving it the new title 'Sea-Chant of an Elder Day', and an Old English title of the same meaning, 'Fyrndaga Sǽléoth'; two extra lines of verse at the beginning and end now framed the main text and emphasised the setting in ancient times, 'in those eldest of the days' (compare this with lines 14 and 62). Back in Oxford for the Hilary Term from January, Tolkien read out 'Sea-Chant' at a meeting of the Exeter College Essay Club, a regular gathering of undergraduates. Evidently encouraged, Tolkien sent the poem to his school friend and fellow TCBS member G.B. Smith, who showed it to others.[12]

At this stage Tolkien also painted a watercolour based on the text. This painting, entitled *Water, Wind & Sand*, appears alongside some lines from the poem in the notebook *The Book of Ishness*, along with an added comment 'Illustration to Sea-Song of an Elder Day'.[13] The composition here is far from what you would expect given the discussion so far: instead of a realistic sketch of a recognisable sea-view, abstract symbolist shapes and splashes of colour dominate the imagery, done in pencil and watercolour. On the left are iconic brown cliffs with high round arches over yellow sand, presumably representing line 19 of the text:

> And its arches shook with thunder and its feet were piled with shapes.

In the centre of the illustration is an explosion of jagged, pointed flames in red, white and grey; these must represent the waves of the sea at that key moment in the narrative of the poem when 'their war song burst to flame' (line 32). In contrast then to the two more conventionally realist seascapes of the previous year, this picture has been conditioned by the words of the poem; it is a verbally inspired symbolic picture, reflecting the images and metaphors of the written text.

Significantly, and again unlike the two other sea paintings, a single diminutive human figure stands in the foreground of the picture, highlighted in a small white circle that stands out against lines of black rock. This seems to be the 'I' persona of the poem, reduced as it were to insignificance by the elemental drama that surrounds him in his vision. Indeed, the observer figure in the white circle may not be part of the main picture: as in Tolkien's later painting of Bilbo with the dragon Smaug, he may be in a different 'plane' to the rest of the picture. Scull and Hammond suggest that the observer figure may also be the seed of a new idea: that this poem will come to illustrate a scene from *The Silmarillion*.[14]

In the third version of the poem, then, done in 1917 at Roos, not far from Hull in Yorkshire, during a highly creative period in which Tolkien wrote a good deal of his *The Book of Lost Tales*, the new idea burgeoned and came to fruition. The title now is 'The Horns of Ylmir' (Ylmir being an alternative spelling of the name Ulmo), and it is stated that the song derives from events in the story *The Fall of Gondolin*, when Tuor sings a song to his son Eärendel about the visions he once experienced on hearing the horns of Ylmir when sitting by the river at dusk in the Land of Willows.

The figure in the painting *Water, Wind & Sand* is now clearly to be identified as that of Tuor, lulled into inaction and tarrying in the Land of Willows, where for a time he forgets his quest. The Vala, or god, Ulmo now intervenes directly, hurrying to the river where he plays 'deep melodies' (compare the poem's 'music of uttermost deepness' in line 51) 'of a magic greater than any other among musicians hath ever compassed'. Seeing in a vision the strife and music of the sea, Tuor listens and is 'stricken dumb'.[15]

In accordance with the new idea, Tolkien revised the text of the poem once again in order to bring it in line with his mythology, adding a new, more mythical introduction and conclusion.[16] In the final version of the main text there are now specific mythogical references: thus the 'anger' is attributed to the trumpets of the mythological figure of Ossë, a fierce and unpredictable spirit of the sea, whereas the 'music of uttermost deepness' and the calming of the sea are attributed to Ulmo himself, the Lord of the Waters, a figure akin to the Greek god Neptune. As for the narrator, Tuor, the sea-longing has clearly come over him by the end of the poem, and never to the end of his days will he forget the dream music he has heard.

By 1917, then, Tolkien had become a *myth-maker* – what his later Inkling friend and collaborator C.S. Lewis would call a *mythopoeic* writer. In the process of painting a view of land and ocean, and writing and rewriting a poem on this theme, Tolkien invented a character, Tuor, who goes on to act significantly in a wider and more complex story. In terms of *The Fall of Gondolin*, the prose tale that now accompanies the newly revised poem, it is this experience of the horns of Ulmo which incites Tuor to leave the Land of Willows and resume his quest to find Gondolin, where he has a greater purpose to fulfil. For Tuor will marry the Gondolin princess Idris; he will play a major role in the defence of the city; and he will become the father of the half-elven Eärendil, the great mariner who was to assume an even more significant place in the developing text of Tolkien's *The Silmarillion*.

Theories of myth-making

The process by which Tolkien turned a nature poem into a mythological poem is an interesting one, for it mirrors in some ways the reflections on poetry and myth-making to be found in Victorian and Edwardian anthropology, particularly in the work of Friedrich Max Müller (1823–1900), professor of comparative philology at Oxford, and Sir Edward Burnett Tylor (1832–1917), who became the first person to hold a chair in the new academic discipline of anthropology. In chapter 8 of his *Primitive Culture*, Tylor had presented his famous theory of *animism*, which he also called 'the doctrine of universal vitality' and defined as 'that primitive mental state where man recognises in every detail of his world the operation of personal life and will [...] sun and stars, trees and rivers, winds and clouds, become personal animate creatures, leading lives conformed to human or animal analogies'.[17] For Tylor, it is modern poets who recreate this old worldview through the imagery and metaphors they employ:

> The best poetry of our own day is full of quaint fancy and delicate melody, the setting of lovely thought in harmonious language, at once pictures for the imagination and music for the ear. But besides this it has a curious interest to the student of history, as keeping alive in our midst the ways of thought of the most ancient world.[18]

In particular, Tylor had the Romantics in mind, who had the ability, he thought, to 'throw their minds back into the world's older life':

> Wordsworth, that 'modern ancient,' as Max Müller has so well called him, could write of Storm and Winter, or of the naked Sun climbing the sky as though he were some Vedic poet at the head-spring of his race, 'seeing' with his mind's eye a mythic hymn to Agni or Varuna. Fully to understand an old-world myth needs not evidence and argument alone, but deep poetic feeling.

Andrew Lang, the folklore collector and literary critic, in whose memory Tolkien was to give his well-known lecture *On Fairy-stories* in 1939, lent his support to the Tylorian view:

> Homo, in the earliest stage at which we make his acquaintance, is already the philosopher, artist and man ... We cannot escape from him in any field of activity; we repeat his theories without knowing; or knowingly, as when Mr. F.W.H. Myers boldly proclaimed his reversion to 'Palaeolithic psychology'. Without the ideas of the savage (as Keats averred) we should have no poetry worthy of the name, and these fruitful rudiments, not to be styled 'superstitions', Mr. Tylor named 'survivals'; a term which implies no reproach.[19]

The etymological pursuit of the 'old poetic thoughts' involved tracing back words to their roots in the postulated Germanic parent language. Thus we find Max Müller, one of the great philologists of the Victorian period, speculating on why the word 'soul' (Gothic *saivala*) should be related to Gothic *saius* (sea) and Greek *seio* (to shake): 'we see that it was originally conceived by the Germanic nations as a sea within, heaving up and down with every breath, and reflecting heaven and earth on the mirror of the deep'.[20] There was a long tradition of using the comparative method in this way, and it was Max Müller among others who had sought to apply this methodology to the reconstruction of early European myths out of the 'survivals' of these ideas in the various early literatures of the Indo-European family of languages.

It is clear that Tolkien in his imaginative writings also sought to recreate the old-world myths, 'the ways of thought of the most ancient world' that so fascinated the Oxford anthropologists and comparative philologists of the previous generation. But where in the end Tylor or Müller were sceptical about their value, Tolkien sought through his literary work to create a world in which the old myths could ring true. In short, then, although *The Cove near the Lizard* is an accomplished picture, the painting *Water, Wind & Sand* is far more striking because of its symbolic importance. Similarly, 'The Tides' is a readable poem, but 'The Horns of Ulmo' is more arresting, since it takes the conventional imagery as literally true and reinterprets it in terms of the developing *Silmarillion* mythology. The poem now deals with the elf-friend Tuor, his quest for the sea, and his momentous encounter with the Lord of the Waters on the banks of the river Sirion. Thus Tolkien's holiday in the Lizard peninsula was enlightening in many and various ways. Over the years, as his imagination worked on his first literary endeavour, he transformed it into an image that came to be part of his wider and far more original project of myth-making.

Chapter Nine

'Far over the Misty Mountains cold'

I N *THE FALL of Gondolin*, Tolkien combines two elements that were to recur again and again in his work. The first is the theme of 'sea-longing', in this case a journey to the coast that leads to the momentous encounter with the god (or Vala) Ulmo, Lord of the Waters, the genesis of which was discussed in the previous chapter. The second is the motif of the mountain quest, the journey 'far over the Misty Mountains cold' which was to become the basis of the there-and-back-again plot structure of *The Hobbit*. For the actual details of walking in the mountains Tolkien drew on his own life-changing experience: a journey to Switzerland at the age of nineteen.

Mountain journey (Switzerland 1911)

He had left school at the end of July 1911 with the customary Speech Day and prize-giving and, typically for him, his participation in a school theatrical production of Aristophanes's *The Peace*, performed in the original Greek. The summer was a particularly fine one, with hardly a drop of rain from April until the day of George V's coronation in October. Tolkien, now at the end of 'a poor boy's childhood', as he called it, was ready for adventures.[1] In August he travelled by boat to the Continent and by train to Innsbruck in southern Austria with a party of twelve people; at Interlaken they began their walking tour. As will be seen from the following account, many of the places Tolkien saw on the trip became models for the mountains and

mountainous landscapes of the fictional world that he began to create in
the years leading up to his service in the army in the First World War. He
would go on many walking trips in the future, but this was the only Alpine
mountain expedition that he ever experienced.

Participants in the tour included the Brookes-Smith family, the organis-
ers of the trip (i.e. James the father, his wife Ellen, their daughters Phyllis
and Doris, and their young son Colin); with them was their friend Jane
Neave (who was Tolkien's aunt), and Tolkien's brother Hilary. The *Tolkien
Family Album* has preserved a photograph of eight members of the party,
all wearing hats to shade them from the bright sunshine: there are two
males in the picture: Tolkien appears to be sitting on the grass at the front
next to a woman, perhaps one of the Brookes-Smiths? A boy, either Hilary
Tolkien or Colin Brookes-Smith, is seated on a rock at the back behind a
row of six women, apparently of different ages (because of the effect of the
bright sunshine it is difficult to make out the details). In his memoir of
the trip to his son Michael, written in 1967–8 when apparently Michael
had also visited Switzerland, Tolkien mentioned an 'uneducated French-
speaking member of the party', perhaps one of the Swiss guides, and 'one
of the hobbits of the party (he is still alive)', who was involved in the fun of
damming a stream at Belalp near the Aletsch glacier and then breaking the
dam with his alpenstock and allowing the accumulated waters to descend in
a rush down the slope at the back of the inn, just as an old lady was going
to the rill to fetch water: 'she dropped the bucket and fled calling upon the
saints'.[2] As Tolkien occasionally referred to himself as a hobbit, it is tempting to see this as his coded reference to himself; certainly he was soon to be
involved in practical jokes while at university, so that such behaviour would
not have been out of character.

The walking route took them 'mainly by mountain paths' to
Lauterbrunnen, and they then ascended via Mürren to the head of the
Lauterbrunnen valley. They then appear to have walked eastwards to
Meiringen by crossing the Scheidegge to Grindelwald, with views of the
two mountains the Eiger and the Mönch on their right. As the journey
went on, it left an indelible impression of the eternal snows of the Jungfrau
on his mind, so Tolkien writes; and he remembers the sharp outline
of the Silberhorn against the dark blue background of the sky, calling it
'the *Silvertine* (*Celebdil*) of my dreams'. The name Silvertine (Celebdil in
Elvish) refers to one of the three mountains of Moria in *LOTR*; it is here
that Gandalf fights and overcomes the monstrous balrog, but is pulled with

it into the abyss. The fictional name derives clearly from the Silberhorn (which in English would be 'Silverhorn') that Tolkien saw on his Alpine tour in 1911.

From Meiringen the walking tour went on over the Grimsell Pass and down to the Rhone; they stayed in the city of Brig where they spent a wakeful night disturbed by the noise of the trams. Spending some time at Aletsch, they took a long march one day onto the glacier, another eventful day on the journey, and in the end the most dangerous of their experiences. They were walking in single file along a narrow path with a ravine on their left and a steeply rising snow-covered slope to their right. Since the summer of 1911 had been so hot the upper layer of snow had melted, leaving exposed rocks and boulders which in the heat of the day started to break loose and roll down onto the hapless walkers below. Tolkien remembers it as a 'hard pounding', by implication like an artillery attack in the war. By luck and careful dodging, no one was hit, but Tolkien remembered that one 'elderly schoolmistress' let out a stifled scream and lurched forward as a small boulder passed between them on its way down to the ravine below.[3] The mention of an 'elderly schoolmistress' in this account is a bit of a surprise on a tour of this nature, unless again this is a coded reference in the letter to his

Fig. 9a   Snow on the Misty Mountains

Aunt Jane, who was of course by 1967 an elderly and retired schoolmistress. In another letter (to Joyce Reeves, written in November 1961) he recalls the trip of 1911 and admires his 'shrewd sound-hearted' aunt, who had just been to Switzerland again on a 'botanising' tour.[4]

Mountain scenery in *The Hobbit*

The mountain crossing in *The Hobbit* draws directly on the details of the above episode, with boulders coming loose and galloping down the mountainside and passing between them, 'which was lucky', or over their heads, 'which was alarming'. The passage is from 'Over Hill and Under Hill' (chapter 4), and it conveys the same sense of a danger that never became serious; the accident that never happened is one that people can afford to write about in light, almost humorous terms.

Eventually in the same chapter the party meet a great storm, which again is described in authentic and convincing detail based on experience,[5] and there is an accompanying illustration by Tolkien in the standard editions of *The Hobbit* which shows the fork lightning spreading across the sky with the snow-peaks beyond it; the path winds up to the right and there is a precipitous drop into the deep and narrow valley to the left. The picture works well with the text at this point in the story. The narrator still loves his wordplay but uses it for rhetorical emphasis – the travellers do not meet a *thunderstorm* but a *thunderbattle*, when two storms from east and west wage war on each other. Tolkien evokes the sound effects of such a storm, the clashes that split the air, and roll and tumble around the mountainside.

The account of the Swiss mountain expedition back in 1911 is not yet complete. After the episode on the glacier, the party went on into Valais and then later continued to Zermatt, where they stayed in a high mountain hut of the Alpine Club; here Tolkien remembered seeing the bright white snow-desert between them and the black horn of the Matterhorn a few miles away from them.[6] The mention of this famous Alpine peak recalls Tolkien's Caradhras, or Redhorn, the most northerly of the three mountains of Moria, with its sheer red sides and snow-covered peak, and its difficult mountain pass which the travellers in *FR* fail to cross because of the falls of heavy snow. They flee a blinding blizzard and the apparent animosity of the mountain itself, with its eerie cries and laughter sounding in the crevasses and gullies of the rocky mountain wall; again boulders are described as coming down between or flying over their heads.[7] The humorous account of the falling stones in *The Hobbit* is here given a rather more serious treatment, and the game played by the stone-giants has disappeared, only to be replaced now with vaguer but more menacing howls on the air, as though the mountain itself is alive and malevolent and deliberately hindering their progress. Mountains are not to be taken lightly.

One of the immediate consequences of the mountain tour of 1911 was its effect on Tolkien's art. On his return, he inserted into his notebook a large pencil-and-watercolour entitled *The Misty Mountains*. In many ways it is an impressive picture, rightly given pride of place at the very end of *Artist and Illustrator*.[8] Basically its title is fitting: in the mid-foreground an old stone road-bridge straddles a river flowing from left to right; over the bridge there passes a yellow road which – proceeding through areas of green foliage – disappears into a remote distance dominated by a skyline of tall, sharp grey mountain peaks outlined against a yellow sky. This is the very picture of alpine mountains in summer, and it was to be followed by many other illustrations of a similar nature. In a scene from the story of Tuor, another of Tolkien's illustrations shows a ring of similar high mountains surrounding a plateau in the middle of which is the great city of Gondolin.[9] A further classic example is the painting of the dragon Glorund emerging from the entrance of Nargothrond against a backdrop of snow-covered peaks not unlike Japanese prints (which Tolkien is recorded as owning at the time in his rooms at Exeter College).[10]

The picture *The Misty Mountains* provided, one may suspect, a possible model for at least two passages in *The Hobbit*. So, for example, in the 'Roast Mutton' chapter, the road is described as 'fortunately' passing over 'an ancient stone bridge, for the river, swollen with the rains, came rushing down from the hills and mountains in the north'. As with the painting in the notebook, there is no further explanation given as to who built the stone bridge and when; it is simply there, a concrete image of the journey and the road ahead. Another passage of description in *The Hobbit* captures a similar scene at the beginning of chapter 3, 'A Short Rest'. The hobbits ford a river and ascend the far bank; at the top they see that the mountains have marched down to meet them; the nearest one looks 'dark and drear', though behind it can be seen the gleam of snow on the taller mountains beyond. The snow-covered peaks would come to figure in various ways in Tolkien's fiction. In fact, they are ever present, for mountains of many kinds remain the backdrop, the given setting in many of his stories. In his two most famous works, the Misty Mountains are a major hindrance to be overcome, and the crossing of that mountain range, or in the event the passing under this obstacle, is a necessary part of the plot.

'Of Tuor and his Coming to Gondolin'[11]

The legendary story of Tuor, as we have seen, begins as a quest narrative that takes him from the shores of Lake Mithrim to his vision of the Sea at Falasquil, then further to his momentous experience of divine favour and his vision of 'the piper at the gates of dawn' on the banks of the river Sirion. This in fact is only the first stage of the quest, for the story then divides into further stages of there-and-back-again as a theme. Unlike Bilbo and Thorin, who want to recover a treasure and regain a kingdom, Tuor must undertake a long and dangerous journey to find the hidden mountain city of Gondolin and to deliver Ulmo's message to its king, Turgon.

As in many such narratives, Tuor meets helpers who become his guides on the journey. In *Tuor and the Exiles of Gondolin*, the helpers are various: the three seabirds and the three swans are instances of helper-figures from the natural world; then there are the Noldoli, or elves. Eventually, with the help of Bronweg-Voronwë, the father of Littleheart, the narrator who is recounting the story to Eriol in the frame narrative to *The Book of Lost Tales*, Tuor discovers in a gully in the upper reaches of the river Sirion the hidden entrance, a magically protected passage to the City of Stone. The two travellers find 'a way dark rough-going, and circuitous', and full of echoes, which the fearful Voronwë wrongly interprets as the footsteps of 'Melko's goblins, the Orcs of the hills'.

Again there is the passage underground, with all its implicit symbolic import. The theme of a fearful passage through tunnels is one that Tolkien knew from the Victorian novelist George MacDonald, and one which he reintroduced in both the *Hobbit* and *LOTR*, for in both the later novels the travellers are forced to journey under the mountains, where the goblins live, rather than passing over them, through the high passes. Eventually, in *Tuor*, the two protagonists find their way by fearful groping and falling over stones, out of the blackness and into the light, into the brightness of the open air, where a great sight awaits them. The hills encircle a wide plain in the middle of which stands the great citadel of Gondolin 'in the new light of the morning'.[12] The scene depicted here verbally is the same in essence to that shown visually in Tolkien's pencil drawing of 1928, *Gondolin and the Vale of Tumladen from Cristhorn*.[13]

Here a formal spoken dialogue of challenge and identification finally takes place, a statement of identity, kindred and allegiance. The newcomer declares himself to be Tuor son of Peleg, son of Indor, of the house of the Swan of the sons of the men of the North, and he announces that he has come to Gondolin on a much higher authority, the will of Ulmo, the god or Vala of the Outer Oceans.[14] The amazed reaction of the citizens is one shared by the reader of the story, who as it were for the first time hears Tuor's 'deep and rolling voice' and measures its startling effect on the citizens, 'for their own voices were as the plash [sic] of fountains'. This is the first time Tuor speaks in any lengthy dialogue in the narration, and the fact that the reader has had to wait so long to hear it simply adds to the dramatic effect. There is a similar scene in *The Hobbit* in the chapter 'A Warm Welcome', when Thorin the bedraggled wayfarer arrives at Laketown and the guards snatch up their weapons and spring to their feet, demanding to know who he is. But Thorin declares in a loud voice that he is Thorin the son of Thrain, the son of Thror, and despite outer appearances the guards believe him, for his inner worth is there to be heard, and to be seen in the look in his eyes and the gleam of gold on his neck and his waist. Naturally, in both cases the citizens accept the impressive newcomer and lead him to the city hall to be welcomed by the head of the city.

After the inevitable fall of Gondolin, the theme of there-and-back-again recurs, and the mountain quest takes place in reverse as the beleaguered survivors make their escape from the devastated city over the encircling mountains to eventual safety. Long before the writing of *The Hobbit*, Tolkien's Alpine journey to the Silberhorn now finds its first literary expression in his description of the severe climb and the harsh weather. The fugitives come to the Cristhorn, a dangerous place, so high that the snow lies all year round. As they try to cross along a narrow path with a sheer wall to their right, the wind howls and the snow blizzards swirl round them.[15] In this first version of the theme of the mountain crossing, the falling stones, which in *The Hobbit* are to be attributed to melting snow or in *FR* to a hostile mountain spirit, are hurled down by an ambush of orcs, to the grievous harm of the refugees. Other motifs that anticipate people and events in *LOTR* are the names of the Gondothlim heroes such as Legolas Greenleaf, 'whose eyes were like cats' for the dark, yet could they see further',[16] and Glorfindel the great lord, who like Gandalf in *FR* defeats the balrog but is pulled down into the abyss in the moment of his triumph. Eventually the company win through, much depleted, and Tuor with his wife Idril and their son Earendel tarry for many years at the Land of Willows, where the whispering winds bring peace, healing and respite.

There is a discrepancy between the high style of *Tuor and the Exiles of Gondolin* and the context in which it was composed: written in two battered exercise books as Tolkien sat surrounded by the accoutrements of war and military life in a crowded army hut with the gramophone playing loud ragtime music (which he detested), and written up later as he was recovering in a military hospital. One detail from the story – the seven names of the city of Gondolin – was apparently composed on the back of an army-issue leaflet detailing 'the chain of responsibility in a batallion';[17] in *The Book of Lost Tales* these names are: Gondobar the City of Stone, Gondothlimbar the City of the Dwellers in Stone, Gondolin the Stone of Song, Gwarestrin the Tower of Guard, Gar Thurion the Secret Place, Loth the flower, and Lothengriol the flower that blooms on the plain.[18] The contrast between the bureaucratic list and the poetic enumeration could not be more blatant. This was a world away from what had been his first adventurous expedition to the European continent, back in 1911, and it is tempting to see Tolkien as a lonely soul lost in the world of the modern military machine. Something of this attitude seeps through into *The Hobbit*, as will be seen shortly.

Chapter Ten

Goblin wars

Mentions of Gondolin in *The Hobbit*

I T IS WORTH remembering that Gondolin is one of the more obvious of a number of allusions to *The Silmarillion* that Tolkien allowed to slip, mostly unnoticed, into his novel *The Hobbit*. During their 'Short Rest', in the chapter of that name, Elrond one day examines the swords the dwarves had taken from the troll-hoard, and he identifies them immediately, and with good reason, as it turns out. They are swords made in Gondolin for the Goblin wars many ages before. Thorin's new sword is called Orcrist, or Goblin-cleaver, while Gandalf's is the sword Glamdring, meaning 'Foe-hammer', which was once worn by Turgon the king of Gondolin. Turgon, who fell with the city, was Elrond's great-grandfather, and Elrond is in fact Elrond Half-Elven, one of the wielders of a ring of power. His father is Eärendel, son of Tuor, who married Idril of Gondolin, the daughter of Turgon. A key figure in the mythology, Elrond reveals his long life and ancestry in *LOTR* to the great amazement of the hobbits. But here in *The Hobbit* his identity is played down, although he does admit that the High Elves of Gondolin are his kin.

In the original draft of *The Hobbit*, Tolkien had not fully decided that this Elrond was in fact the same as the Elrond of the mythology. He is described as an elf-friend, 'kind as Christmas', an attractive alliterating phrase that was later changed to 'kind as summer' to remove the overt Christian reference. And the passage where Elrond identifies the swords is considerably shorter; he knows them to be old swords, made in Gondolin

Fig. 10a   Short sword or seax

Fig. 10b   Long sword

for the Goblin wars, and he wonders whether they came to the trolls from a dragon's hoard, perhaps from one of the dragons that plundered the city at its fall.[1] At this point in the writing of *The Hobbit* the High Elves are still referred to as gnomes, and the two swords do not as yet have special names that can be identified with their previous owners (Tolkien actually names the swords in a later passage in this draft version). And at this stage in the conception of the character of Elrond, there is no assertion at all that he might be related to these people from ages past.

In the published version, there is a much longer discussion of the origin of the swords. Thorin looks at his sword with a new interest and he asks Elrond how the swords came into possession of the trolls. Elrond is uncertain, but he hazards a guess that the trolls plundered from earlier plunderers or perhaps came upon forgotten treasure abandoned in the caverns of the mines of Moria since the dwarf and goblin war. Elrond's words cause Thorin to ponder and he vows to keep the sword in honour until a time when he may use it, a wish that Elrond feels will soon be granted when the expedition proceeds onward to the mountains. The mention of Moria is a reference forward to *LOTR*, when Gandalf and his company are again compelled to give up an ascent of the mountains and try their luck passing through the tunnels under the mountain. In all this discussion goblins figure chiefly as the collective enemy, and the passage neatly anticipates the events of the coming chapter.

The nature of goblins

As we discussed above, *The Hobbit* gives a vivid account of the 'over hill' journey of the hobbit and the dwarves, of the rock-falls and storms and wind and rain, as well as the grandeur – if not overwhelming grandeur – of the mountain country through which they must pass. Similarities were also noted with the story of Tuor's 'under hill' journey to Gondolin, when he travels with his companion Voronwë through the rocky underground passages which, despite their fear of 'Melko's goblins, the Orcs of the hills', lead them safely to the gateway of Gondolin itself (see p. 136 above). In chapter 4 of *The Hobbit* this pattern of 'Over Hill and Under Hill' is repeated when the harsh weather forces the company of travellers to take refuge in a cave which Fili and Kili find round the next corner of the winding mountain path. Here the fear of the orcs would be justified, but none seems to feel it save perhaps Gandalf and Bilbo. It is Gandalf who asks whether they have *thoroughly* explored this cave, and it is Bilbo who has trouble sleeping and when he does finally sleep has dreams filled with nightmarish fears. Certainly the ever-present narrator shares their fears, for he comments to his young readers on the dangerous nature of caves, the fact that 'you don't know how far they go back, sometimes, or where a passage behind may lead to, or what is waiting for you inside'.

The narrator's hint is enough for most to guess what sort of thing will happen next. The cave becomes a deceptive refuge, a place to talk and forget the storm, to send smoke-rings dancing up by the roof, a place to make plans, a place to sleep. The narrator's hint now becomes a warning, for this (so he says) is the last time they will use their ponies and all their other gear on the journey. Bilbo wakes up just in time to shout a warning to Gandalf as all their ponies and baggage disappear through a sudden gap at the end of the cave. The narrator's hints and warnings have all led up to this moment, which he relishes in a sentence with a characteristic phrasal verb '*Out jumped* the goblins', several repetitions of the subject, and a whole set of suitable qualifiers of size, manner and quantity:

> Out jumped the goblins, big goblins, great ugly-looking goblins, lots of goblins, before you could say *rocks and blocks*.

The 'out jumped' construction might be compared with the phrase 'up jumped Bilbo' used twice of the protagonist when he oversleeps and hurries out of bed for a late breakfast (it is the opening phrase of chapter 2, repeated again when Bilbo sleeps long and deep in Beorn's great hall in chapter 7). There is a kind of robust jolliness to this account (despite the potential seriousness of the theme) which suits Tolkien's purpose – at least in this part of the novel – to imitate the oral style of a narrator telling a comic tale to a listening audience of children. Echoing the 'rocks and blocks' tag, the narrator then says that the goblins immediately snatched and grabbed all the sleeping travellers and carried them through the crack 'before you could say *tinder and flint*'. The rhyming proverbs only add to the humorous effect, and of course when the goblins pinch Bilbo roughly as they carry him away he once again wishes he was back home safely in his nice bright bachelor den. The humour continues as the goblins whisk him down underground passages deep and dark; for though their dark depths compare well for their fearfulness to those through which Tuor and Voronwe pass in The *Fall of Gondolin*, here the goblins run through them precipitously since they know the way 'as well as you do to the nearest post-office'.

Two opposing traditions about goblins as creatures of folklore and folk-belief collide here: on the one hand goblins are mischievous; on the other hand they are evil. However, the first time Tolkien ever used the word *goblin* back in 1915 in his published poem 'Goblin Feet', it referred probably to small sprites or brownies and had no evil connotations whatsoever; nor did the creatures observed in the poem appear even mischievous. But this was soon to change, and Tolkien came to regret ever having published that particular poem. In *The Book of Lost Tales* the word *orc* is the preferred designation for the same kind of creature, but in 1932 he went back to the word *goblin* for his children's stories in *The Father Christmas Letters*,[2] and retained the word when he wrote *The Hobbit*. The *OED* provides a working definition for *goblin* as 'a mischievous ugly demon' and traces the word itself back to Middle English *gobelin*, also spelt *gobolyn*, *gobelyn*, a loan from Anglo-French *gobelin*, which derives it in turn from medieval Latin *gobelinus*. The word is related to the rare English word *kobold* (derived from German), 'a familiar spirit, brownie, or underground spirit in mines etc.'; the name of the metal *cobalt* derives from the same source. The notion of

Fig. 10c   Goblin with sword

'mischievous' seems relevant here, as is the German connection, for one of the sources of the idea must be German folk-tales of the kind collected by the brothers Grimm in their *Household Tales*. A well-known example would be the mischievous ugly little man in the story *Rumpelstiltskin*.[3] Another would be the story *The Prince Afraid of Nothing* about a king's son who has to free a castle and a princess from enchantment by spending three nights in the great hall, enduring the torments of little devils but without being afraid or making a sound. In the German text the little devils are called *Teufel* or *Teufelspuk* (i.e. 'devils'), but at one point in Margaret Hunt's 1884 translation of the *Household Tales* they are *hobgoblins*:

> The hob-goblins came again: 'Art thou there still?' cried they, 'thou shalt be tormented till thy breath stops.' They pricked him and beat him, and threw him here and there, and pulled him by the arms and legs as if they wanted to tear him to pieces, but he bore everything, and never uttered a cry. At last the devils vanished, but he lay fainting there, and did not stir, nor could he raise his eyes to look at the maiden who came in, and sprinkled and bathed him with the water of life. But suddenly he was freed from all pain, and felt fresh and healthy as if he had awakened from sleep, and when he opened his eyes he saw the maiden standing by him, snow-white, and fair as day.[4]

Are these really *devils*, or are they in fact *goblins* under another name, creatures of German folklore rather than the fallen angels of Christian theology? Certainly the pricking and beating are reminiscent of how the goblins behave in *The Hobbit*.

A Victorian novelist well acquainted with the German folklore tradition was George MacDonald, a favourite writer of Tolkien's Oxford friend and colleague C.S. Lewis. MacDonald's *The Princess and the Goblin* was an overt influence on both Lewis's Narnia and Tolkien's Misty Mountains. This children's novel tells of an eight-year-old princess living somewhere in mountainous central Europe, whose father has confined her indoors in their castle, under the constant supervision of a nurse, because of the threat of kidnapping by the goblins – otherwise known as gnomes or kobolds – who haunt the mineworkings in the surrounding countryside. MacDonald's goblins are small, misshapen creatures apparently descended from a race of people banished for their misdemeanours, who then retreated into the underground caves and tunnels of the mountain, where they plot their mischief and revenge on the people 'upstairs'. Rather like Gollum in *The Hobbit* they hate the sunlight, though they do use torches, and like hobbits they walk barefoot – this is what the miner's son Curdie discovers is their weakness, for though their heads are hard, their feet are soft. They are ruled by a king, like the Great Goblin in *The Hobbit*; this king also holds court in a large cavernous hall beneath the mountain. And although they plot to destroy the miners, the goblins are nevertheless figures of fun, easily outwitted by stamping on their feet or chanting verses at them, which is painful to their ears. The mischievous snatch-and-grab goblins of the early chapters of *The Hobbit* are clearly of a similar kind to those of MacDonald,[5] and they do not, at least at first, seem quite as dangerous and malicious as they perhaps should.

In English in particular, as well as meaning mischievous sprite, *goblin* and the related *hobgoblin* refer also to the demons of Christian theology, as in the line from Bunyan's hymn 'Hobgoblin nor foul fiend shall daunt his spirit'. One of the earliest citations offered by the *OED* for *goblin* is from the late fourteenth-century Wyclif Bible translation: 'Of an arowe fliynge in the dai, of a gobelyn goynge in derknessis' (Psalm 90:6). The idea of a goblin walking in the darkness is of course highly relevant to the present context, but what is noteworthy of course is that the mischievous element of the German mountain sprite is lacking here. This demonic, wholly evil sense of *goblin* is in the end the one most relevant to Tolkien's purpose: the goblins are Melko's orcs, the perversions of nature brought into being by this Satanic figure of the mythology. As three present-day editors of the *OED* point out in their study of Tolkien's vocabulary, it is likely that the mischievous folktale associations of the word *goblin* caused Tolkien to replace it with *orc* as the usual term for such creatures in *LOTR*.[6] Similarly, he tended to remove such words as *gnome* and *fairy* in his later writings, and replace *dwarfs* and *elfin* with *dwarves* and *elvish* for the simple reason that the earlier words had the wrong feel: they were too frivolous and had the wrong associations in the minds of most readers. Incidentally, it has been shown that the word *orc* most likely derives from *orcneas*, a word for 'demons' that occurs appropriately in *Beowulf*. Again Tolkien took care in a prefatory note in *The Hobbit* to point out that *orc* means goblin or hobgoblin and is not the English word applied to 'sea-animals of dolphin-kind'.

In the period between *The Hobbit* (1937) and *LOTR* (1954–5), not only did the word for this evil creature change but also its presentation in Tolkien's fiction. It is appropriate to consider, for a contrast with the cave episode from *The Hobbit*, other scenes involving goblins or orcs, this time from *LOTR*. The chapter 'The Bridge of Khazad-dûm' in *FR* sees the first fighting against orcs in the novel, and these orcs are of sterner stuff than the goblins of *The Hobbit*. Where one might even be tempted to feel sorry for the goblins blasted by the wizard's wand in the episode in the cave in *The Hobbit*, one feels no such pity for the orc-chieftain in black armour, with red tongue and eyes like coals, who charges into the room and attempts to butcher Frodo on the end of his great spear. Similarly, the orcs who kidnap Merry and Pippin in *The Two Towers* (*TT*) demonstrate real cruelty, and the more realist style of writing only serves to highlight the genuine hardships: the whipping, the sore wrists, the hunger and thirst that they suffer.

There is one thematic difference between the two novels which is worth stressing. The goblins of *The Hobbit* seem to be acting independently, at least from the point of view of Thorin and Bilbo and their friends. There is never any sense that the Necromancer of Mirkwood (i.e. Sauron) is controlling them or guiding their actions; though he may well be involved, we are never told this, even when the goblins team up with the wolf-like wargs. Similarly, the dragon is a very independent self-seeking operator, and does not appear to be a creature of Melko, though that may be his origin. By contrast, *LOTR* is very similar to *The Silmarillion* in presenting orcs and other such beings as wholly dependent on their masters – that is, either Sauron or Saruman – who have bred them or even in a sense created them. This last point throws up a whole host of problems, theological and philosophical, that have exercised the commentators about whether any creatures can be created wholly evil and irredeemable.[7]

In 'Over Hill, and Under Hill' in *The Hobbit* the true nature of the goblin captors only becomes clear when the action pauses after the goblins with their prisoners reach the great cavern in the heart of the mountain. Here the narrator stops to evaluate the nature of goblins, emphasising their cruelty and wickedness, their filth and untidiness, and their skill in mining and engineering: 'they make no beautiful things, but they make many clever ones'. It is perhaps here that the 'mischievous' connotations of the word *goblin* begin to fade and the reader begins to worry. Speculating further in his colloquial style, the narrator suggests that it is 'not unlikely' that goblins and orcs eventually invented all the machinery of modern warfare, 'especially the ingenious devices for killing large numbers of people at once'. Goblins, the narrator asserts, take delight in 'wheels and engines and explosions'. Clearly this is Tolkien's personal view of modern warfare, and it is found little changed in many of the asides and comments in his published letters, for instance in his comments on air raids that he makes during the Second World War. Orcs, he declares, are to be found on both sides of a conflict, even in wars that are morally justified.[8]

Attitudes to war

As Diane Purkiss has rightly pointed out, *The Fall of Gondolin* is Tolkien's war story, a distillation of his Great War experience into the form of 'his own epic romance version of the Somme'.[9] And although, as we have just seen, the story of Tuor's sea epiphany and mountain quest was based on earlier pre-war experiences, these two plot elements nevertheless form a necessary prequel to the main part of the narrative: the battle in which the great impregnable city of Gondolin falls to the forces of Melko. The immediate context for the composition of that narrative was Tolkien's participation as a soldier in the Great War, a shattering experience, for it was a war which killed two of his close friends and effectively put an end to the TCBS, the first literary circle to which the youthful writer had belonged. Tolkien himself saw active service as a signals officer at the Battle of the Somme before contracting the trench fever which brought about his return to England, where his convalescence outlasted the duration of the war.

Tolkien had been ready to enlist as soon as he had finished his degree at Oxford in 1915. This was not unusual; there was huge social pressure on young men to fight (from families, girl-friends, local communities) whether they wanted to or not. And most young men decided to fight. A dialogue in *The Book of Lost Tales*, probably written during Tolkien's time in France or shortly afterwards, gives literary expression to the reasons for those decisions. In *Tuor and the Exiles of Gondolin* the protagonist Tuor delivers his message from Ulmo of the Valar gods, bidding the people of Gondolin prepare for war, but his plea is firmly rejected by King Turgon in his pride and indignation, for he simply will not risk his people in a battle against the Orcs, nor, so he says, will he endanger his city.

Gondolin is a hidden kingdom analogous to Switzerland, a city on a plain surrounded by a ring of apparently impenetrable mountains, and Turgon is reliant on the landscape and the city's defences and a policy of neutrality based an unwillingness to risk his resources in all-out war against the encroaching forces of Melko that have overrun most of the Great Lands. And he is indignant that the paths across the perils of the sea to Valinor and the home of the Valar are closed, and none of his messengers have ever come through or returned from their voyages successfully. Tuor's point by contrast is that there is no choice: the encroaching enemy has to be stopped or they will take over the world, but if Gondolin will fight, despite the hardship that will ensue, Melko's power will be diminished.

Tolkien was admittedly not a British jingoist, but he was at the very least an English patriot, and he felt that right and justice was on the side of the Allies, and that war had to be fought. He had heard lectures on the poet Rupert Brooke, and friends such as G.B. Smith had encouraged him to read this poet's verse. No doubt he knew Brooke's lines:

> If I should die, think only this of me:
> That there's some corner of a foreign field
> That is for ever England.

And perhaps he knew and recognised something of Thomas Hardy's cyclical view of history in his poem 'In Time of the "Breaking of Nations"':

> Only a man harrowing clods
>   In a slow silent walk
> With an old horse that stumbles and nods
>   Half asleep as they stalk.
>
> Only thin smoke without flame
>   From the heaps of couch-grass;
> Yet this will go onward the same
>   Though Dynasties pass.
>
> Yonder a maid and her wight
>   Come whispering by:
> War's annals will cloud into night
>   Ere their story die.

But for Tolkien in his literary work it is also the passing of dynasties and war's annals that interest him; for these are seen to be as equally important as the lives of ploughmen, farm labourers and rural lovers. The subject matter of his stories deals with both.

Depictions of modern warfare

Tolkien is often presented as an admirer of courage in the face of the enemy, and there is much truth in this, though not everyone, he concedes, is made of such stern stuff. For Bilbo in *The Hobbit*, the final terrible battle is the most dreadful of all his experiences, with good reason – since the slaughter is immense, though not reported in detail. The narrator adds ironically that it is the experience Bilbo was 'most fond of recalling long afterwards' (*The Hobbit*, chapter 17).

There is ambivalence in Tolkien's attitude to war; it is certainly peace-loving, though not pacifist. As his letters reveal, he hated learning the business of killing; he disliked the vulgarity of life in barracks and training camps; he hated the mechanisation and casual brutality of modern warfare. For an example, consider the following passage:

> Time passed. At length watchers on the walls could see the retreat of the out-companies. Small bands of weary and often wounded men came first with little order; some were running wildly as if pursued. Away to the outward the distant fires flickered; and now it seemed that here and there they crept across the plain. Houses and barns were burning. Then from many points little rivers of red flame came hurrying on, winding through the gloom, converging towards the line of the broad road that led from the City-gate to O...

The extract reads like a typical account of a retreat back to a defended town during the early stages of the Great War of 1914–18: perhaps a diary entry by Siegfried Sassoon, or a passage from *Goodbye to All That* by Robert Graves.

As I expect many readers will have realised, however, the final place-name should in fact read 'Osgiliath', revealing that the passage occurs in the chapter 'The Seige of Gondor' in *The Return of the King* (*RK*), where Tolkien returned to his theme of the siege of a great city. Apart from the similar names of Gondolin and Gondor (based on a root *gond* meaning 'stone' in Tolkien's invented language) there are further parallels to be drawn between the two besieged cities. Possible real historical resonances include the siege of Troy by the Greeks (Tolkien was steeped in the Classics at school), and the siege of Byzantium by the Turks. The two cities of Gondolin and Gondor both represent the height of urban civilisation at the time when the story is set – the word civilisation of course deriving from Latin *civitas*, city. Both cities have great magical trees at their heart, the two trees in Gondolin recalling the splendour of the Trees of the Moon and Sun in Valinor, the land of paradise in the West, as depicted in *The Silmarillion*. The dry tree in Gondor is symbolic of the dead royal line in that city, which is ruled now by stewards awaiting the return of the king.

The sieges, though written in very different styles, are vivid and convincing pieces, and the same may be said of the dragon Smaug's attack and siege of Laketown in *The Hobbit*. Tolkien is a writer who has seen the details of war at first hand. There is the sense of preparation, the arrival of reinforcements and preparation for bombardment; the individual at odds with the world, trying desperately to find out what is happening, frustratedly questioning orders given from high command that contradict other orders given earlier on the same day. As these and many other passages show, and as many commentators have remarked, Tolkien's experiences on active service in the Great War fed in a number of ways into his writing, lending it authenticity. One need only read these episodes in conjunction with the account of the war in John Garth's biographical study *Tolkien and the Great War* to realise the truth of the assertion.[10]

Even the fantastical and terrifying weapons of iron, bronze and copper, and burning fire that Melko designs for the assault on the city of Gondolin[11] are plausible in terms of the disgust that Tolkien felt for weapons of mass destruction and products of the modern technology of war, such as tanks and poison gas and bomber-planes. The description in *The Book of Lost Tales* of Melko's cunningly contrived technical weaponry almost sounds like the ethnological perspective of a writer or narrator (the tale is indeed being told by Littleheart, son of Voronwë) towards a technology that he perceives closely but does not fully comprehend.

Similar are the battle scenes, which again are given through Littleheart's perspective, and expressed in the archaic literary language that Tolkien used at this time. But the scene where the fire-drake is forced into the deep waters of the great fountain of the royal square is nevertheless vividly done, and from a modern perspective it is reminiscent of technological warfare, or even a gas attack. The pools of the great fountain on the square are instantly transformed into steam and a cloud of vapour rises and hangs over the city. The square is filled with blinding fogs and scalding heat and the people fight each other in their blind panic until a rally of men gather around the king.[12] With this episode might be compared the moment when the stricken Smaug falls onto the town of Esgaroth, splintering it to sparks and embers; the lake roars in and a vast white fog leaps up, lit by the moonlight (*The Hobbit*, chapter 14).

As was argued in chapter 3, Smaug is a real dragon, not an allegory, but nevertheless symbolic or allegorical readings of the story suggest themselves: at one point he is a kind of Leviathan, with biblical overtones. Similarly, an aspect of the battle for Gondolin that invites symbolic reading is the description of the two forces arrayed against each other. Where the men of Gondolin are pictured as belonging to great chivalric battalions, with

heraldic devices and splendid accoutrements (not unlike the various group-
ings in Morris's novel *House of the Wolfings*), the forces of Melko are, as we
have just seen, the epitome of ugly, perverted technology, and such detailed
imagery may be one of the essential themes that give this story its rather
grim, relentless fascination. By contrast the grim parts of *The Hobbit* –
Smaug's attack on Esgaroth and the final 'terrible battle' – are shorter and
more contained.

Chapter Eleven

Literary myth and the Great War

Robert Graves's *Fairies and Fusiliers*

IN 1917 THE young poet Robert Graves, who – like Tolkien – had been hospitalised at the Battle of the Somme in 1916, published his early volume of verse *Fairies and Fusiliers*. The title is revealing, for it shows clearly that the 'fairy theme' was alive and well in the later stages of the war in the writings of one of the most talented of the poets of that generation. Though many of the poems are direct realist pieces, the following touch on folklore or myth in various ways: 'Babylon', 'The Cruel Moon', 'Finland', 'Faun', 'I'd love to be a Fairy's child', 'Love and Black Magic', and 'Cherry-Time' with its repeated refrain 'And you'll be fairies soon'.[1] Not all of these poems have survived into later editions of Graves's *Collected Poems*, and copies of some are difficult to locate, but the evidence of the 1917 volume is clear: this was a literary fashion in which Graves participated, and the alliterating title shows a startling juxtaposition of the imagery of the fairy with that of modern warfare.

As the previous chapter sought to show, a similar juxtaposition is to be seen in Tolkien's *The Book of Lost Tales*. His Andrew Lang lecture *On Fairy-stories*, given at St Andrews in 1939, sought to praise his great predecessor where praise was due, but Tolkien disagreed strongly with Lang's assertion that fairy-tales belong only to childhood, and that in the same way mythology and folklore belong to the childhood of the human race. Myth, Tolkien felt, was much more universal, much more important and significant than this. In an autobiographical passage in the same lecture, Tolkien claimed that a liking for fairy-stories was not at all characteristic of his own 'nursery days'; some interest in fairy-stories certainly developed as he learned to read for himself in the years before he attended school (when he was taught at home by his mother) but he also liked and even preferred other things: history, astronomy, botany, grammar and etymology. As for poetry, this was something he usually skipped if it came in tales (as do, ironically, some present-day readers of Tolkien's *LOTR*) but he acquired a liking for poems at school when he came to study them in other languages such as Latin and Greek. He goes on to assert that he developed a liking for this kind of story only after he grew up, and that it was kindled into flame by his experiences in the war.[2] The claim needs to be tested further: how was Tolkien's taste for fairy-stories 'quickened to full life by war'?

'Goodbye to all that'?

Tolkien's own planned book in the period of the Great War, a collection of poems with the title *The Trumpets of Faerie*, had been submitted for publication, but it was fairly quickly rejected by the publishers Sidgwick & Jackson. Tolkien and his fellow TCBS-ite Geoffrey Bache Smith had however achieved the moderate success of having poems published in *Oxford Poetry*, their names appearing in the list of contents alongside modernist poets destined for greater poetic fame in the future. Tolkien's poem was 'Goblin Feet', a poem about the open road, and little sprite-like creatures disappearing beyond the poet speaker's reach; it is very much in the same mode as a poem about Tinfang Warble that he also wrote in this period. Less folkloristic is Smith's contribution, a short piece of historical reflection on the old roads built by the Romans. But since the TCBS claimed to be antithetical to the subject matter of modernism, Tolkien and Smith were not happy with the reviews of the volume, which tended to favour the more experimental or modernist poets in the anthology, such as the editor T.W. Earp. Tragically the young writer H.R. Freston, one of the poets in the anthology whom they did admire, was killed in action, and Smith himself was to succumb to shrapnel wounds later in 1916. Events seemed to be weighted against their project.

The value of the fantastical was under threat. It is the contention of some literary critics that the Great War said 'goodbye to all that', and indeed

Robert Graves, the originator of the phrase, produced the following couplet in one of his poems of the period:

> Wisdom made him old and wary
> Banishing the Lords of Faery

It is easy to see why he would write this, for it certainly seemed as if the modern world was driving out the old. One of Rudyard Kipling's stories in *Rewards and Fairies* pictures the departure of the fairies overseas as taking place at the time of the Reformation, the time when the old beliefs were done away with; since the story was published in 1910, it was perhaps symptomatic of what was to come. Graves's collection *Fairies and Fusiliers* marks the onset of the new realism, though as we have seen a number of the poems (such as 'I'd love to be a Fairy's child', 'Love and Black Magic', 'Cherry-Time') still hark back to the Edwardian and Victorian fairy themes that were in danger of dying, like Tinker Bell on the Edwardian stage, through lack of belief.

But there may be reasons to rethink this rather commonplace conclusion. Both the readers (i.e. the young men who fought in the war) and the writers (i.e. the intellectuals who wrote about their wartime experiences) were intensely interested in myth, of various kinds. Among the writings that Fussell in his *The Great War and Modern Memory* emphasises is allegory, especially John Bunyan's *Pilgrims' Progress*.[3] But there was also the romance quest, exactly the kind of story that Tolkien was writing in his hospital bed in the winter of 1916–17. The example Fussell cites is William Morris's *Well at the World's End* (1896), now regarded as a classic of its kind, the story of a young man's trial and testing, his first love and loss, and his second love, and his quest to find the fabled well on the farthest eastern shore of an unknown country, all of this nevertheless taking place in a partly familiar English medieval world. According to Fussell, who rather surprisingly claims not to particularly appreciate *The Well at the World's End* himself, 'there was hardly a literate man who fought between 1914 and 1918 who hadn't read it and been powerfully excited by it in his youth … for a generation to whom the terms like heroism and decency and nobility conveyed meanings that were entirely secure, it was a heady read and an unforgettable source of images'.[4] Fussell cites a number of writers such as C.S. Lewis, Hugh Quigley and Siegfried Sassoon; all these allude to it or couch their wartime experience in terms of images and episodes drawn from Morris's great work. One such moment is the valley of the Dry Tree at the centre of a kind of dismal valley or amphitheatre, with its poison pool and dead and mummified pilgrims scattered around it.[5] One writer cited by Fussell, for instance, compares the war-torn landscape and dead soldiers to the strange image of the Dry Tree in Morris's novel.[6] Tolkien himself perhaps recalled this kind of imagery in the dry tree of Gondor, and especially in the Dead Marshes through which Frodo Baggins and Sam Gamgee pass on their journey to Mordor in *RK*.

A Spring Harvest: the mythological poems of Geoffrey Bache Smith

Not long after Tolkien himself was hospitalised, his close friend and fellow TCBS member Geoffrey Bache Smith died at Warlencourt in France in December 1916 from shell wounds he had sustained a few days before. At the end of the war, and after his own recovery, Tolkien determinedly set about arranging, editing and publishing his friend's oeuvre with the help of fellow TCBS member Christopher Wiseman. The result was *A Spring Harvest*, which appeared in June 1918.[7] Tolkien's arrangement of the poems is instructive: it tells us much not only about the common literary project on which the TCBS was engaged but also about Tolkien's own poetic and creative concerns in this period.

Smith shares with Tolkien a similar preoccupation with ancient kingdoms and legendary history in 'Rime' (p. 24), 'A Sonnet' (p. 30) and 'O There be Kings whose Treasuries' (p. 38). Smith has his own preoccupation (a recurrent metaphor is one of the wind blowing constantly over the sea, the hills, the cities), but there is also some classic Tolkien-style diction and vocabulary: the dialogue in 'Rime' between the man of action and the *scholar of gramarye* is suggestive of Tolkien's later projects. All three of these poems are worthy of further study, and are printed in Appendix 1 at the end of this book. 'O, One Came Down from Seven Hills' is another poem rich in mythic themes; its mysterious opening scene recalls Tolkien's Gondolin with its seven names, and the insistent numerology hints at symbolic meanings to be uncovered. The poem then becomes a dialogue between the mysterious visitor and the old men that stand at the market-place, in which the theme is war and peace and the easement of the city's ills, and the need to love honour more than life: a debate which was of contemporary relevance to the war years, and which echoes (it might be argued) Tuor's arrival in Gondolin and his debate on the city square with King Turgon in Tolkien's

The Fall of Gondolin. The idea of a stricken city appears elsewhere in Smith's poems, either as a literal or metaphoric image: there are 'windy citadels' and 'fast-walled cities' in 'A Preface for a Tale I have Never Told' (p. 29). Another short piece 'Over the Hills and Hollows Green' (p. 66) speaks of the spring-tide air which 'Over the desert towns doth blow/ About whose torn and shattered streets/ No more shall children's footsteps go'.

There are however signs of hope. In the short poem 'It Was All in the Black Countree' (p. 31, see Appendix 1 for the text), the Middle English or dialectal spelling suggests a traditional song of local patriotism, which reso-nates with Tolkien's similar love for the West Midland shires. It also centres on the symbol of a tree, and though it is 'all gaunt and grey' a message is there to be heard.

If there exists a key to the line of thinking behind Smith's recurrent imagery it is to be found in the 'Two Legends' that form part I of *A Spring Harvest*; both deal with the theme of a springtime epiphany. The second – entitled simply 'Legend' – is a kind of supernatural time-travel story; it tells of a monk returning from centuries past to sing a new poem to the season. The first – the narrative poem 'Glastonbury' – has deeper, more complex themes. Though Smith is by no means a myth-maker in the sense that Tolkien was – and this makes Tolkien stand out from his TCBS fellows

Fig. 11a   Castle ruin

– there is a similarity of purpose: a revisiting and remaking of the old myths and stories of England in particular and Britain more generally. The two friends shared an interest in Welsh language, literature and mythology, and Tolkien inherited some of Smith's books, including a copy of a diplomatic edition of *The Four Branches of the Mabinogion*, and a study of the tale Peredur by Mary Williams.[8]

Glastonbury is an evocative name in its own right, the old Anglo-Saxon name Glæstingabyri suggesting (at least to place-name specialists in Tolkien's day) an early Anglo-Saxon settlement; later – from the tenth century – it became a famous monastery, the home of the celebrated St Dunstan in the 940s and a great centre of learning. Through the influence of Arthurian literature from Geoffrey of Monmouth's Latin history in the twelfth century to Thomas Malory's *Morte D'Arthur*, an English reworking of the myth of the fifteenth century, Glastonbury is associated with the legendary Avalon, 'a lake island mythically set' as Smith calls it, and with the final tragic events of King Arthur's reign in the fifth century. It is these events that Smith revisits in his poem (pp. 13–20).

The point of the poem is a miracle, a symbolic moment, a sudden flowering of a 'barren tree' (p. 19), apparently a retelling of the legend of the Glastonbury Thorn. Smith carefully lays the ground for the epiphany in the preceding stanzas. The poem begins with the aftermath of a battle, in this case the final battle between the forces of Arthur and the invaders under Mordred, his 'base son'. Like Tolkien's later poem *The Homecoming of Beorhtnoth*, which presupposes knowledge of the Anglo-Saxon heroic poem *The Battle of Maldon*, during which the East Anglian governor Beorhtnoth died in a final stand-off against the Vikings, so Smith's poem presupposes a knowledge of Arthur's last battle in the final elegiac section of Thomas Malory's heroic romance *Morte D'Arthur*.

Both poems present a dialogue between survivors, looking back at the events of the final battle and struggling desperately in their minds to find some hope for the future. There is an echo perhaps in *The Hobbit*, for after the final Battle of the Five Armies, Bilbo Baggins wakes up after a blow on the head to find himself alone on the battlefield, on a cold, cloudless day. Sorrow seems to hang in the air, 'a very gloomy business', and there is no one around (*The Hobbit*, chapter 18). In Smith's *Glastonbury* the king's right-hand man Bedivere arrives at a hermitage 'at the gloomy breaking of a winter's day'. The hermit helps him as he staggers in a faint through the doorway, watches over him and treats him till the crisis is passed and

Bedivere's wound starts to heal. In conversation it transpires that the hermit too is a fugitive, the former royal bishop who fled the court 'when at last the whole was overthrown' (p. 14).

As their talk unfolds, Bedivere recalls the summoning to war of the heralds, a summoning that seemed to bring the whole world into conflict: 'Come gather all unto the fronting hosts' (p. 15). The description of 'the last dim battle' has the same grim force as seen in Tolkien's *The Fall of Gondolin*, but here the battle takes place in a desolate wasteland:

> I saw the last dim battle in the mist
> There, where a dreary waste of barren sand
> Doth mark the ultimate leagues of this fair land

The fight itself is a nightmare, totally destructive (note the use of the later Tolkienian word *wraiths* in this passage); its outcome is apocalyptic:

> [...] like thin wraiths
> Fit to throng Lethe banks the warriors
> Struck and o'ercame, or fell, unseen, unwept;
> And alien hopes, lives, peoples, alien faiths
> Were all confounded on those desolate shores.
> And ever the mist seethed, and the waves kept
> A hollow chanting, as they mourned the end
> Of all mankind, and of created time. (p. 15)

Bedivere goes on to narrate the departure of the dying king in a bark across the mere, and the hermit reports a secret burial at the ancient chapel, where the golden letters 'once and future king' are engraved on the covering stone. Bedivere now recalls the prophecy that Arthur would 'escape mortality' and lie at rest in a cavern or on a shore 'where faery seas do break' (p. 16) until at the return of the old enemy he would waken, and 'his own victorious arm/ shall rid the stricken land of hate and foes' (p. 16).

A new dialogue now begins with the arrival of Lancelot. He tells the hermit of his last audience with the queen and predicts that someone in the future will sing 'the immortal loveliness of Guinevere'. But his dominant mood now is not hope but near-despair 'beneath the pitiless skies' (p. 17); he expresses his feeling in an invocation of the pagan gods of antiquity:

> Gods of the burnt-out hearth, the wandered wind,
> Gods of pale dawns that vanished long ago,

Gods of the barren tree, the withered leaf,
The faded flower, and the ungarnered sheaf,
Gods half-forgot in the wild ages' flow
Yours am I, that all for nought have sinned. (p. 18)

The litany evokes images that recur frequently in Smith's verse: the ruin, the wind, the dawn, forgetfulness and war – the old Gods represent war in Smith's thought (e.g. pp. 61, 68). In the above passage the barren tree recalls the 'tree all gaunt and grey' of the poem 'It Was All in the Black Countree'. As we have seen, the arid tree is a symbol found in Morris's *Well at the World's End* as also in Tolkien's mythology: the trees of Sun and Moon poisoned by Melko and the ruined trees of *The Fall of Gondolin*.

But this is not the end of the story. As the winter turns towards spring, the fields all white with snow remind Smith's Lancelot of the purity his soul once enjoyed. Yet he feels he can no longer regain it. At this point he touches a dead shrub, a 'barren tree', claiming that he will not see the gates divine until this tree 'shall bud and blossom':

But even as he spoke the hand of God
Worked on the sombre branches, and straightway
They were all green with sap, and bud, and leaf
As at the very bidding of the spring,
Burst forth [...] (p. 19)

Smith mentions the rod of Jesse, a biblical parallel, and the theme of the revived tree occurs in medieval writing, in the anonymous Latin *Life of Edward the Confessor*. But in this particular context it is hard not to think once more of Tolkien's later writing. In *LOTR*, notably, the dry tree of Gondor is replaced with a young sapling by the new King Aragorn after the fall of Mordor. The project of the TCBS – continued by Tolkien – was preoccupied with a myth of revival and rejuvenation.

Smith's poem 'The New Age and the Old' (p. 59) views such a revival as a new period in history:

Like the small source of a smooth-flowing river,
Like the pale dawn of a wonderful day,
Comes the New Age, from High God, the good giver,
Comes with the shouts of the children at play:
As an old leaf whirls faster and faster
From the sere branch that once gave it fair birth,

Into the arms of the devil, its master,
Be the old age swept away from the earth!

The *envoi* 'So we Lay Down the Pen' (p. 78) – the final piece in the book –
ends as follows:

When the New Age is verily begun,
God grant that we may do the things undone.

Its authorial first person plural suggests a communal project, and one which
is also divinely inspired. It confirms the sense that the reader, and more to
the point Tolkien as editor and literary successor, is called upon to continue
the 'things undone' and take them further.

The uses of myth

Though the Great War did hasten the departure from the medievalist
themes in poetry and in art that the Victorians had loved, it is important
not to overstate this tendency, for there are many qualifications to be made.
It should be noted that both before and after the war there were modernist writers who remained fascinated by myth as a literary mode. Many
employed the imagery of medieval poetry in their own writings; these
include poets such as Edward Thomas (who wrote versions of Celtic and
Norse tales), Ezra Pound (who was fascinated like Tolkien with the imagery
of the Old English poem 'The Seafarer') and T.S. Eliot (who was widely read
in medieval Arthurian literature and in Frazer's *Golden Bough*). As Thomas
Honegger has pointed out, Eliot praised 'mythical method' as a 'simple way
of controlling, ordering, of giving a shape and a significance to the immense
panorama of futility and anarchy which is contemporary history'.[9]

One telling example is the modernist writer David Jones, a Catholic poet
intensely interested in the recovery of myth, particularly images from older
Welsh as well as Anglo-Saxon heroic legend. His poetry may be seen as fusion
of that older myth with Christian theological symbolism. In 1937 Jones
published his *In Parenthesis*, a long poetic account of the men of 'B Company'
of an Anglo-Welsh battalion and their disastrous final attack on 'Acid Copse'
during the battle of the Somme.[10] As well as Arthurian material, Jones alludes
to the early Welsh poem the *Gododdin*, about the warriors who went to battle
at Catraeth and never returned. He was also very much under the influence of

the Anglo-Saxon poem *The Dream of the Rood*, which depicts Christ's passion in terms of a warrior willingly mounting a tree, and of a personalised tree or Rood, who becomes a hero wounded together with his Lord. In part III of *In Parenthesis*, Private John Ball dreams, while waiting in line, of Christ in the manger; he later invokes the 'silver hurrying' of the Moon and calls on her to transform into silver all the equipment of war, to turn into 'faery bright' the barbed wire, to turn the trees into 'silver scar with drenched tree-wound' (p. 35); it is almost but not quite a prayer to the Moon as a divine figure bidding her 'grace this mauled earth – transfigure our infirmity – shine on us' (p. 35). In part IV, Ball again contemplates a wounded tree:

> The hanged, the offerant:
> himself to himself
> on the tree.

This time the image recalls the figure of the god Odin in *Havamal*, one of the poems in the medieval Norse anthology of mythological verse known as *The Elder Edda*. Here is the text, in the translation entitled 'The Words of the High One', by Paul B. Taylor and W.H. Auden (a book dedicated to J.R.R. Tolkien):

> Wounded I hung on a wind-swept gallows
> For nine long nights,
> Pierced by a spear, pledged to Odin,
> Offered, myself to myself:
> The wisest know not from whence spring
> The roots of that ancient rood.[11]

The last two lines offer a comment on the role of myth in modern literature: for, apparently, even the wisest do not know where the 'roots of that ancient rood' spring from.

Despite what he wrote in his poem, Robert Graves cannot in all fairness really have believed that the Lords of Faery had departed; his strange and eccentric *White Goddess* (1948) is a testimony to his belief in the power of the otherworldly muse as an essential force in the writing of poetry.[12] In the light of all this concern with myth, critics such as Fussell interpret the trends of the literary world of the time rather differently:

> Such leanings towards ritual, such needs for significant journeys and divisions and returns and sacramental moments, must make us sceptical of Bernard

Beronzi's conclusion; 'The dominant movement in the literature of the Great War was ... from a myth-dominated to a demythologised world.' No: almost the opposite. In one sense the movement was towards myth, towards a revival of the cultic, the mystical, the sacrificial, the prophetic, the sacramental, and the universally significant.[13]

Fig. 11b   Tree trunk with foliage

Chapter Twelve

Visions of peace

'I'm back'

BOTH *THE HOBBIT* and *LOTR* have war as one of their major themes, and both in their own way deal with the aftermath, the last stage in the journey. In *The Hobbit* the first task of the narrator is to get the protagonist *back again*, and he tells this part of his story far more speedily than the journey *there*, in a matter of a few pages.

There are many precedents for this sort of accelerated narrative strategy. In one of Tolkien's favourite medieval English poems, *Sir Gawain and the Green Knight*, Sir Gawain heads back through the Wild after his fateful encounter with the Green Knight. His journey is recounted in a handful of lines of verse (2489–94); there is no time to give any details of 'mony aventure in vale', for the main purpose of the story has been achieved. The parallel in *The Hobbit*, probably intentional, is not hard to see. At the end of chapter 18, Bilbo Baggins 'turned his back on adventure' and begins his return journey. He and Gandalf visit Beorn again, but very little is told of their stay, though like Gawain at Bertilak's house, they spend an agreeable Yuletide feast. The narrator now looks ahead, speaking of how Beorn became a great chief whose descendants would rule the wide region between the mountains and the wood. In their time the last goblins disappear from the Misty Mountains, 'and a new peace came over the edge of the Wild'.

Peace has been declared. But in the last stage, chapter 19 of *The Hobbit*, we see that the protagonist is not yet at peace in his heart. The travellers are returning to Rivendell, and they reprise their original visit. They come to the brink of the valley, ride down the steep path and hear the elves singing in the trees, just as before, 'as if they had not stopped since he left'. At first even the song seems just the same, with its fair nonsense of a 'tra-la-la-lally' refrain. But things have changed; there is loss and grief to bear; and the singers know it. Their song reflects the news they have heard, the death of the dragon and the loss of Thorin, and the burial of his great treasure the Arkenstone. But the song goes further and proposes alternatives: the stars for jewels, the moon for silver, the fire for gold – these are the compensations that the guest-hall can provide for sad and weary travellers. And through all this, though it is not stated in so many words, the river is flowing. Consolation is at hand: tale-telling in Elrond's house; the story of their experiences; the hearing of myths from time out of mind. (Here more than anywhere else there is a strong hint of the story of Eriol of *Lost Tales I* and the comfortable hall where stories are told by the burning hearth fire.) After this comes drowsiness and the cure of sleep. The elves' second song, which Bilbo hears at dead of night, though it is called jokingly a lullaby, is a kind of hymn to the blossoming stars, the flowering moon and the silver river, and it brings rest and peace to the wanderer's spirit.

Recovery from the war

As soon as he was discharged from the army in 1918, Tolkien returned with his wife and young son to Oxford. The town and university were recovering from the war. Looking for permanent work he started teaching part-time for various colleges in the university, while retaining membership of Exeter College (where he had been an undergraduate) for its dining rights and academic connections.

An impression of change in the air can be felt on the pages of issue no. 25 of the biannual *Stapeldon Magazine*, the newsletter of Exeter College, Oxford.[1] Almost in every article, on whatever subject, there are instances of recovery from the war. The college rowing club, for instance, had forty members in December 1919, of whom twenty-eight were first-years or Freshers; for obvious reasons to do with wartime service, there was a 'shortage of senior oarsmen' (p. 33). Even more explicit is the editorial that opens the magazine: 'the work of gathering together the threads of pre-war life was successfully accomplished' and it was now clear that student numbers

Fig. 12a   Cloister shadows

had reached a record high; and despite the normal practice of allowing all students to 'live in' during their first year, the College was unable to accommodate all the newcomers (p. 1). The debating club, known as the Stapeldon Society, even complained that the JCR (student common room) was too cramped for their meetings (p. 37). A sign of the times in this issue of the magazine is a travelogue entitled 'Constantinople 1919', in which the writer called on his fellow Exonians to send in their own travel experiences of peasant life or foreign cities that they had had while on active service abroad. Even more pertinently, the same issue records a speech by the Rector (i.e. Principal) of Exeter College:

> A university should be a rallying point in the conflict with those disintegrating forces, commonly summed up in the word 'Bolshevism', which threaten the very existence of our civilisation.[2]

In the following Hilary Term, as we know, Tolkien read his *The Fall of Gondolin* – his own story of a threat to civilisation – to the Essay Club, and the *Stapeldon Magazine* reported that Mr Tolkien 'entertained the Club with an unpublished work of his, an imaginative mythological fairy story after the manner of Lord Dunsany, entitled "The Fall of Gondolin"'.[3] In fact, Tolkien's name appears a number of times in *Stapeldon Magazine* in this period. An entry in the magazine for the Michaelmas (i.e. autumn) Term of 1919, for example, lists Tolkien as 'Critic', one of the officers of the Essay Club, the college literary society. Papers read to the society that term included:

> October 29: H.D. Hancock, 'The Comic Spirit in Molière'
> November 12: C.H.B. Kitchin, 'World Progress and English Literature'
> November 26: E.C. Dickinson, 'The Place of the Ballad in English Literature'.

Tolkien possibly influenced the choice of topic for the third of these papers, by the poet Eric C. Dickinson, while the second is surely a mirror of the times. The literary contributions to the magazine make for some revealing comparisons.

'The Happy Mariners'

Tolkien had originally written his mythological poem 'The Happy Mariners' back in July 1915, while staying with his Incledon relatives at the village of

Barnt Green in Worcestershire. (It often happened that Tolkien worked on his poems and stories while on vacation.) He revised it at training camp in Bedford on 9 September 1915.[4] During the war years it was put to one side. He now returned to the poem, and it was published for the first time in issue 26 of *Stapeldon Magazine* (June 1920). Tolkien's poem is one of a number of discrete items, linked apparently by their theme. A short, bleak sonnet 'Ypres, 1917', by F.A. Greenhill, describes 'the tortured city [...] deep plunged in the abyss of agony' and pictures the 'shrine of Beauty' that has been 'blasted into ruins' (p. 64). Another sonnet, 'The Radcliffe Camera' by M.A. Cardew, printed immediately after Tolkien's 'Happy Mariners' on p. 70, pictures the 'magnificent dome' of the Radcliffe Camera of Oxford University, one of the most prominent landmarks in the city, a stone's throw away from the walled garden at the rear of Exeter College.

The author of the poem 'The Radcliffe Camera' imagines a time in the distant future when the dome, now ruined, still stands majestic – in sad contrast, it must be said to be the blasted ruins of the museum at Ypres, described only five pages before. On the same page as 'Ypres, 1917' a moralistic piece 'So Strange it Is' by J.H. divides young people into two bands: the pleasure seekers and the adherents of 'Truth and Beauty' (p. 64). There follows a short story 'The Vision of Ludovico Neroni' set in medieval Italy by the poet Eric C. Dickinson (the same who had spoken to the Essay Club on the subject of the Ballad), recounting a dream vision in the style of the great medieval Italian writer Dante's *La Vita Nuova* (pp. 65–8). Whether by chance or design, word or ideas in the poem 'Ypres, 1917' on the facing page are taken up in the first and second sentences of the story. Here is the opening (written, it should be noted, in a deliberately archaic medievalising English):

> And the days were ill of my suffering till I longed for the cool of that garden and the splash of the fountain which had once been vouchsafed to me in a vision as the goal of my grievous wandering. For one day when I was an hungered and athirst for peace, I rose and went out upon the high hill above my city, and slept a little while. There while I did sleep I dreamed a dream. (p. 65)

The dream is set in a garden, where the dreamer meets a guide who tells him of his life and asks him:

> My son, tell me. Have you left your love without my garden?

Fig. 12b   The Radcliffe Camera seen from Exeter College

Evidently all this has great symbolic import, though it is hard to fathom. The dreamer finally awakes to find the 'sun's last radiance all about the towers of the city' (p. 68). His troubles are not over, but now he has had a vision, a goal towards which he can work. Here are the closing lines of the story:

Again I am longing for the touch of his sweet garden, the wondrous rest of his mien, the murmur of his singing fountain. And lastly, I would learn the riddles he had left unanswered, some of which appeared within his garden, and some upon the faces of his pupils that have been so much with the pictures of Messer Sandro Botticelli. Messer Sandro, I would come to you, and lay the matter before you of this riddle which vexes me, and of these troubles about my heart. (p. 68)

In short, the narrator of the short story is inspired through his dream to attempt to restore his love, both in a personal and social sense but also apparently in a more spiritual direction.

Following the end of Dickinson's story, on the facing page (p. 69) is Tolkien's poem 'The Happy Mariners', and it is tempting to see a connection, a thematic link perhaps perceived by the editor in the arrangement of pieces for the magazine. Set in Tolkien's mythical landscape, 'The Happy Mariners' belongs to the Eärendel cycle of poems. Reprinted most recently in *Lost Tales II*, it opens as follows:

I know a window in a western tower
That opens on celestial seas.[5]

Fig. 12c   Celestial sea

Given the context in which it appears the poem seems an apposite choice in its theme. Rather than dreaming a vision as in Dickinson's story, the narrator of the poem sees it with his waking eyes: he looks through the window of his Tower of Pearl at the fairy boats making their way to the celestial seas, and he longs to travel with the happy mariners, as far as the star-dashed, dragon-headed portals of the Night where they 'follow Eärendel through the West'.[6] The mythical figure here named is of course Eärendel son of Tuor, the fabled seafarer of Tolkien's private mythology, and at the time only someone well versed in Old English could make any sense of the name, perhaps seeing it as a personification of the 'dayspring', which is the meaning of the word in Old English. Another of the mythical or even fantastical themes of the poem is the notion of starlight as a liquid dashed against the blue night like water out of a fountain, or of sunlight as a tangible substance collected by divers in the 'waters of the unknown Sun'. All these details must have been very mysterious and obscure, and even more difficult to interpret than the preceding piece by Dickinson.

Despite the obscurities, there are continuities of theme. The longing to return is very strong in the passage by Tolkien in which he addresses the mariners who continue on their journey 'chanting snatches of a mystic tune' (line 28), just as it is in Dickinson's story. The narrators in both the story and the poem are overcome with longing in a time of trouble, a time of trial in which the Great War clearly played a significant role as background to the act of writing, and in which the recounted visionary experience seems at one and the same time to be very personal and intensely spiritual.

A Northern Venture

In 1920 Tolkien took a teaching job at Leeds University and again he returned to his poem 'The Happy Mariners' in a university publication. *A Northern Venture*, an anthology of 'Verses by Members of the Leeds University Association', is a small green paperback pamphlet of a mere twenty-five pages, published in 1923 at Belle Vue Road in Leeds, by the Swan Press, the publisher of the periodical *Yorkshire Poetry*.[7] Its theme is signalled by a woodcut print on the front cover showing a dragon-ship on the tossing waves, presumably a Saxon or Viking longboat. The collection contains four poems by Tolkien: a reprint of his poem 'The Happy Mariners' (here provided with an additional Old English title 'Tha Eadigan

Saelidan'); the folklore piece 'Why the Man in the Moon Came Down too Soon'; and two riddle-poems written in an Anglo-Saxon style. Again the arrangement and juxtaposition of poems makes for interesting comparisons, and again the theme of vision and recovery seems to dominate the selection, four years after the war had finished. In the following discussion the themes of this anthology will be explored and Tolkien's 'The Happy Mariners' will be compared to the poems contributed by his colleagues and friends W.R. Childe, E.V. Gordon and A.H. Smith. These are printed in Appendix 2 of the present book.

The broad 'northern' theme of the anthology covers myth, medieval literature and Yorkshire country dialect, as well as more personal themes, and all this probably had a special significance to readers in the English department at Leeds, which was home to the Viking Club, a student society founded by Tolkien and his friend and colleague E.V. Gordon, probably in 1922. Its aims were both educational and recreational: to encourage the reading of Old Norse language and literature, especially the Icelandic sagas and the verse of the Norse *skalds* or court poets; to attract students to take English language options offered by the department; and to allow them to socialise over a glass of beer, for which purpose songs and poems were composed in Old Norse and Old English for singing to well-known tunes. Gordon is nowadays a well-known name among medievalists, chiefly through his *Introduction to Old Norse* (1927), a textbook still widely in use, and through his editions of Old English poems, in particular *The Battle of Maldon*, published in 1937, and *The Seafarer*, adapted and completed by his wife Ida Gordon in 1960. Just as Tolkien worked together with his former tutor Sisam, E.V. Gordon was a former student of Tolkien's who cooperated with him on various projects, in particular an edition of the Middle English poem *Sir Gawain and the Green Knight* published in 1925, the same year that Tolkien became Professor of Anglo-Saxon at Oxford. The two men got on well, and Tolkien jokingly referred to him as 'an industrious little devil'. In 1926 Gordon was appointed Tolkien's successor as Professor of English Language at Leeds, and eventually he finished his career as Smith Professor of English Language and Germanic Philology at Manchester University, where he went in 1931.

A prominent undergraduate member of the Viking Club was A.H. Smith, who contributes two poems to the anthology. Hugh Smith was to become a distinguished figure in English language studies, and professor at University College London, with various special interests. He maintained a life-long interest in the craft of printing with hand-presses, and taught it to students at London: he later printed, for private circulation, *Songs of the Philologists* (1936), many of which were based on songs penned for the Viking Club by Tolkien and Gordon. Like Gordon, Smith was a respected editor of Old English texts, such as *Three Northumbrian Poems* (1933), and he worked also in Old Norse and Middle English studies as well as in linguistics; while the related work that he carried out during the Second World War on the decipherment of documents for army intelligence earned him an OBE.[8]

Probably his chief academic glory is his work in place-name studies, covering in particular in many volumes the place-names of the three Ridings of Yorkshire, as well as of Gloucestershire and Westmorland. The earliest of these volumes is *The Place-names of the West Riding* (1928), in which he thanks Tolkien for his philological advice and encouragement. Linked to this work was his knowledge of northern English dialects. While still an undergraduate, Smith published *The Merry Shire* (1923), a short book of six dialect poems, in a similar green pamphlet format to that of *A Northern Venture*, with a picture of a horse-drawn Romany caravan moving towards a crossroads in the middle of the countryside.[9] The title could, or perhaps should, have been used by Tolkien for his late collection of poems and light verse *The Adventures of Tom Bombadil* (1962). A major theme of these poems is nature: the opening piece 'Gnats' is printed as 'Spring' in *A Northern Venture* (see Appendix 2 for the text). Other themes include the difference between countryside and town, folksong and dance, legends of hobs, and cities drowned by supernatural means.

The woodcut on the cover of *A Northern Venture* is likely to be Smith's work, since he is credited with a similar printed image of a galleon in full sail on the cover of the slightly later companion volume *Leeds University Verse 1914–1924*. In its artistic style, the image of the Viking longboat is almost a caricature, for its dragon figurehead appears to smile, and the flag at the top of the mast is flying in the wrong direction, towards the stern, whilst the decorated sail nevertheless bellows out towards the prow. The dragonship is of course an iconic symbol of the north, but the picture is an allusion possibly to Tolkien's poem 'The Happy Mariners' and also more obviously to Gordon's humorous poem 'A Skald's Impromptu', which appears on page 6 of the anthology (for which see also Appendix 2). This contribution by Gordon to *A Northern Venture* is an edition of a 'Norse verse composed by Skull, Earl of the Orkney (in the twelfth century), while launching his ship at Grimsby'. Gordon provides an edited text of the Old Norse poem and follows it with his own verse translation.

Fig. 12d   Viking longship in full sail

'Grumblingly at Grimsby' seems well placed in the anthology: the theme of tarrying in towns resonates with that of three preceding poems: the jaunty 'Tumbledown Town' by W.D. Chapman (p. 3), and the visionary 'Fairy Tales' and mystical 'The Summer Creek' by W.R. Childe, with its 'little and narrow and strange sea-shipman's-town' (pp. 4–5). Grimsby is appropriate not simply because it is a Yorkshire sea port but also because it is a Viking place-name dating back to the ninth- and tenth-century Norse settlement of the area. In his modern English version, which is arguably a new poem rather than a literal translation, Gordon the Old Norse expert seeks to imitate and follow closely the metre, internal rhymes and alliterative patterns of the medieval original. The dominant mood is a mixture of humorous complaint and serious theme: there is a strong sense of release in the poem, as the boat finally sets off on its return voyage to Bergen. Based loosely on the words of the original, Gordon begins with a marvellously apt wordplay 'Grumblingly at Grimsby', matching and contrasting with the sound effects on the vowel of the final line 'Merrily to Bergen'.

Wilfrid Rowland Childe (1890–1952), another friend and collaborator of Tolkien while he was at Leeds, joined the English department there as a lecturer in 1922, the same year as E.V. Gordon. His previous university education had been at Oxford, and he was one of the joint editors of *Oxford Poetry* in 1916 and 1917 (Tolkien and his school-friend Geoffrey Bache Smith had contributed poems to the 1915 volume). He remained at Leeds making his career there, and served as Dean of the Faculty of Arts from 1943 to 1945. Childe was a fellow Roman Catholic, and in 1924 became godfather to Tolkien's son Christopher. In a letter to his publishers in September 1937, Tolkien mentioned Childe as a possible promoter of *The Hobbit*, since he was 'specially interested in elves and related creatures'. This interest is reflected in 'Fairy Tales', the first of his two contributions to *A Northern Venture*. Set in the narrow streets of an ancient town, the poem speaks of a 'Child ... wiser than his heart was ware', who perceives 'a certain Presence' brooding everywhere, in the calm statues on a monument 'an aery steeple lone amid the blue', and in the 'gracious speech' of the doves that circle round it. The poem suggests that fairy-tales contain 'visions' of truths behind surface appearances to which privileged persons are granted access. It is hard not to think of the theological slant of Tolkien's later work *On Fairy-stories* when reading this poem.

A similarly suggestive vision of faery occurs in the dialect poem 'A Vision' by Smith, the other philologist contributor to the book; here it is combined with the same grouchy kind of good humour that is seen in Gordon's 'A Skald's Impromptu'. In the anthology, Smith's 'A Vision' (pp. 13–14) immediately precedes Tolkien's 'Tha Eadigan Saelidan' or 'The Happy Mariners' (pp. 15–16), and whether deliberately or not the theme of 'vision' also pervades both poems, though their style and tone differ considerably. Smith's northernness is his language, for he writes in Yorkshire dialect, and he begins with the classic adventure formula 'T'neet war dark an' stormy' ('the night was dark and stormy'). Everyone, as might be expected, is abed; everyone, that is, except the Yorkshire shepherd, the poet narrator, who is out and about on the mountain fell in search of a lost 'yowe-lamb', otherwise referred to by the more opaque dialect word of 'gimmer'. The stage is set for the vision in stanza 2, the poet's 'unkerd seet', his strange sight, of Roman soldiers, ghosts or reminiscences of the past, which then in the next stanza transform into dancing elves, rather like figures in the Middle English poem *Sir Orfeo* or in Tolkien's Mirkwood in *The Hobbit*. In a humorous scene in the fifth stanza the shepherd finds the lost 'yowe-lamb'. It seems to appear suddenly in the ditch in which he finds himself sheltering when he eventually awakens from his vision. Giving a stark physical reminder that he is back in everyday reality, the lost lamb licks his face:

> I'm swaimish in this place [my head swims]
> I waken up i' t' delf-hoil;
> T' lost gimmer licks my face.

Another moment of vision appears in the opening piece in the anthology, 'A Kiss of Peace' by H. Brearly, which tackles memories of the war and its consequences. In this short narrative, the I-narrator and a close companion are walking in the Yorkshire countryside of hill and valley when they encounter 'fair Peace, gray-clad, with gentle eyes':

> Where the long ridges stare across the dip,
> Changeless and still against the changing skies,
> We met fair Peace, gray-clad, with gentle eyes
> The daughter of our quiet companionship.

The personification of Peace perhaps recalls the closing lines of Shakepeare's *Richard III*, where 'smooth-faced Peace' is evoked at the moment when the new King Henry VII takes to the throne. The visionary experience, expressed in terms of 'presence', is one that recurs regularly in the anthology:

> Content, we watched her grave and shining way
> Across the austere line of moor and hill
> By windy tracks; yet felt her presence still,
> When moonlight faerily on the river lay
> And lit the valley.

The moon here is a sign of the peace that now bathes the landscape in light; to decribe its light Brearly uses the unusual adverb 'faerily', and sets up a faery theme to which other poets (in particular Childe and Tolkien) return later in the volume.

Brearly's poem continues in the following lines, which eulogise the personified figure of Peace in terms of affection and song:

> Her restrained caress
> Gave meaning to the sound, in quiet places,
> Of water welling through soft moss and grasses –
> Her benediction and voiced loveliness,

And all the undistinguished homely stir
Of daily life together, sang of her.

The benediction of water is suggestive also of a recurrent theological motif, one which becomes explicit in the themes of 'vision wonderful of joy' and 'God of the great infinite, thou / Quest of my heart' in two of the poems by G.M. Miller (pp. 8–9), and of 'radiant secret' and 'God's great love' in those by M.A. Northgrave and H.S. Pickering (pp. 10–11).

Following Tolkien's poems the final section of the anthology (pp. 21–5) is given over to six poems by Geoffrey Woledge (1901–88). A graduate of Leeds who became a well-known librarian, Woledge began his career in 1919 at Leeds University Library, where he remained until 1931; in 1938 he became University Librarian at Queen's Belfast, and from 1944 to his retirement in 1966 he served as Librarian at the British Library of Political and Economic Science. In the 1920s his poems appeared regularly in the periodical *Yorkshire Poetry*, which was also published (like *A Northern Venture*) by the Swan Press at Leeds. Though arranged alphabetically, Woledge's pieces nevertheless trace a path of ideas that move from earthly love to regret, penitence (p. 23), return and sunrise. The last poem 'The Sunrise' (p. 25) begins and ends with a refrain:

The sun-deserted clouds were pure as water
That wanders cold over the mountain pebbles.

The image of the flowing stream in this final poem resonates well with the first poem; the theme there is the benediction of water, welling through soft moss and grasses. In this way, flowing water and its healing powers become the opening and closing image of the anthology.

PART THREE
Finding the words

I~n~ J~anuary~ 1919 Tolkien started work in a temporary post at the *Oxford English Dictionary*, and in the same period he also began what was to be his first research publication, *A Middle English Vocabulary*, to be published eventually in 1922 after he had moved to Leeds. In every respect, Tolkien was well equipped to undertake these two tasks, for both involved tracing English words back to their origins. He had a first-class degree in English Language and Literature behind him, and despite the intervention or 'parenthesis', as David Jones was to put it, of the war years, Tolkien still had support from his *alma mater* Exeter College, who gave him college membership and the opportunity to supplement the etymological and lexicographical work with part-time tutoring in Old English (Anglo-Saxon) at the university. This work at Oxford was extremely beneficial to his career; in 1920 he was appointed a Reader in English at the University of Leeds, and then in 1924 he became Professor of English Language, in a department of two professors and several lecturers, his counterpart as Professor of English Literature being the poet and critic Lascelles Abercrombie. In 1925 he made a successful bid for the chair of Anglo-Saxon at the University of Oxford, and returned again to his home university, where he was to stay for the rest of his career.

In this period, Tolkien became committed to the language research that was to form the basis of his professional life: *A Middle English Vocabulary* was followed three years later with the text of the Middle English poem *Sir Gawain and the Green Knight* (1925), edited jointly by Tolkien and his Leeds colleague E.V. Gordon. Though not all his work ended up in print, Tolkien was editing texts, and reading widely in general philology. In 1928 there appeared Haigh's *A New Glossary of the Dialect of the Huddersfield Dialect* with a preface by Tolkien that reveals the importance he attached to the speaking and writing of dialect. Various important articles also appeared: in the mid-1920s he provided survey articles on 'Philology: General Works' for *The Year's Work in English Studies* for 1924 and 1925; in 1929 he published an article on the text *Ancrene Wisse* (i.e. on Early Middle English in the west of England and its continuities with the past), an article that has been described as 'the most perfect though not the best-known of his academic pieces'.[1] Then, as he began work on *The Hobbit*, he published articles in 1932 and 1934 for *Medium Aevum* in which he discussed the etymology of the Old English *Sigelwara Land*, and in 1934 in *The Transactions of the Philological Society* he discussed Chaucer's remarkably perceptive use of dialect in *The Reeve's Tale*.

In short, Tolkien was publishing a good deal of research on language in the period up to the writing of *The Hobbit*. Accordingly, the third part of this book explores aspects of Tolkien's philology, his work in language studies, the fundamental foundation for all of his writing. Tolkien's creative writing of poetry and prose depends on this groundwork: his knowledge of language history, his work on etymology and semantic change, his scholarly interest in the history of stories. The writing of *The Hobbit* comes out of all this groundwork in philology.

In traditional terms, philology is the scientific study of language, usually on a historical and comparative basis. In Tolkien's case it involves the history of the various stages in the development of the English language from Anglo-Saxon through Middle English to present-day English, and it includes knowledge of related languages such as Old Norse and German, both of which are 'cognate' or sister languages going back to the same distant parent. Philology as it had developed in the late nineteenth century was engaged language study, concerned with the sounds of living speech, the soul or spirit of a language rather than just the dead letter. As a discipline it had its drawbacks, since there was a tendency to accumulate too much detail and shrink away from theory. But philologists thought long and hard about how languages develop and they included the study of dialects and other varieties of English within their remit.

Philology also involves etymology, and takes a reconstructive approach, in which the history of a linguistic form, a sound, a syllable, a word or phrase, or even a motif in a story, is reconstructed out of the vestiges that have survived the passage of time, copied in manuscripts and documents. The drawback here, as we will see, is the reconstructive approach that tends to dominate proceedings, though many of its results are plausible and useful.

In addition, unlike its sister discipline linguistics, which is more interested in how 'language' in general operates, philology is usually connected more closely to literature; its purpose is the elucidation of the texts: the poems, stories and romances that survive. In short, philology is about the 'growing neighbourliness of linguistic and literary studies';[2] Tolkien felt strongly about this – it was the goal and purpose of his work. As an author or writer, then, he felt that the language literally forms and informs the writing of the text, whether that text is merely a set-phrase or formula, a rhyme or riddle, a poem or song, or a whole story or novel.

Chapter Thirteen

Early lessons in philology

In February 1973 Tolkien wrote a note on the pastedown of the well-thumbed and battered family copy of *Chambers' Etymological Dictionary* that he had owned since childhood. The note records for posterity the fact that this dictionary marked the start of his interest as a child in language and philology. In fact, it was so well used that the introduction to the dictionary, in which the user was initiated into the mysteries of *Lautverschiebung* and other technical terms, became so tattered that it fell out and was lost.[3] The German technical term *Lautverschiebung* (literally 'sound shift') is a key one in historical philology; it refers to the sound changes, or rather patterns of sound change, that have been observed by historical linguists in various languages. The classic example is 'Grimm's Law', formulated by Jacob Grimm (brother of Wilhelm Grimm and co-author of *Grimms' Fairy Tales*). Grimm showed that a word in a Romance language beginning with *p-* such as Latin *pisces* or Italian *pesce* (or even Spanish *pez* and *pescado*) is related by a regular consonant shift to the equivalent or cognate word in a Germanic language, where it begins with *f-*: thus Old English has *fisc* and Danish *fisk* and modern English *fish*. The interrelation of the European languages is one of the initial fascinations in the study of philology.

It was at King Edward's School Birmingham that Tolkien's predilection for language history took an intensively philological turn. His official education went through the traditional curriculum of an English public school, with its heavy emphasis on the Classics: the intense study of the Latin and Greek languages, and the reading of the literature and history of the Classical

Fig. 13a   Cloister and tower seen through arch

periods. Such a syllabus had existed for centuries, and in many nineteenth-century schools Classics had been literally the only academic subject studied, pupils being steeped – with good and bad results depending on the pupil – in the languages of ancient times.[4] Though by Tolkien's time the syllabus had been broadened and reformed, it still encouraged pupils to read and write Latin poetry and – perhaps with influence from the Cambridge school of Latin studies – even to speak and debate in the language. 'I was brought up in the Classics', Tolkien once said in a letter to Rob Murray, grandson of Sir James Murray, the first editor of the *OED*; Homer was his first introduction to the appreciation of poetry, and he discovered that he enjoyed the fresh association of the form of the word with its meaning – an experience he found when studying the poetry of a foreign language or poetry written in older forms of the English language, such as Anglo-Saxon.[5]

Anglo-Saxon and *The Making of English*

One lively introduction, Henry Bradley's *The Making of English*, which Tolkien confessed to having read with delight, resonates well with Tolkien's experience of languages as a boy, both at home and at school. Indeed, Bradley appeals to exactly that kind of schoolboy reader (the gender bias is unconscious), for he begins with the core vocabulary of English, presenting it by means of what he calls 'the likeness of German and English':

> An Englishman who begins to learn German cannot fail to be struck by the resemblance which that language presents to his native tongue. Of the words which occur in his first lessons because they are most commonly used in everyday conversation, a very large proportion are recognisably identical, in spite of considerable differences of pronunciation, with their English synonyms.[6]

Bradley gives an illustrative list of resemblances, beginning with the family relations of *Vater* (father), *Mutter* (mother), *Bruder* (brother), *Schwester* (sister); then moving to the theme of country life with *Haus* (house), *Feld* (field), *Gras* (grass), *Korn* (corn), *Land* (land), *Stein* (stone), *Kuh* (cow), *Kalb* (calf), *Ochse* (ox); he turns next to common verbs *singen* (to sing), *hören* (to hear), *haben* (to have), *gehen* (to go), *brechen* (to break), *bringen* (to bring); and continues to chart the connections in adjectives, pronouns and prepositions. The list of resemblances is now expanded as Bradley brings in some rudimentary comparative philology, pointing out the phonetic correspondences:

German	English
z, tz, ss	t
d	th
pf, ff	p
t	d
-b- (in the middle of a word)	-v-

Examples illustrate 'the fundamental identity of a vast number of English words with German words which are very different from them in sound and spelling, and often also in meaning':

> *Zaun*, a hedge, is our 'town' (which originally meant a place surrounded by a hedge, a farm enclosure); *Zeit*, time, is our 'tide'; *drehen*, to turn, is our 'throw', and the derivative *Draht*, wire, is our 'thread'; *tragen*, to carry, is our 'draw'; and so on.[7]

His exposition goes on to demonstrate the many similarities that exist in the grammars of the two languages, as well as the differences: the inflectional endings on verbs, adjectives and nouns. It is precisely these kinds of differences between German and English, he points out, that also distinguish present-day English from Anglo-Saxon (or Old English as it is also called).

Having begun with a series of facts familiar to his readers' experience, Bradley now continues by exposing one or two popular fallacies, often still believed today: that English is somehow derived from German. This is manifestly not the case. In fact, the two languages have 'descended, with gradual divergent changes, from a pre-historic language which scholars have called Primitive Germanic or Primitive Teutonic'. English and German are sister languages, with a parallel history. The rest of the *Making of English* goes on to show how Anglo-Saxon gradually evolved, in its grammar and vocabulary, into the modern language spoken today. Bradley traces the 'the making of English grammar' (chapter 2), and examines in detail 'what English owes to foreign tongues' (chapter 3), in particular the Norse influence on English, which came about through massive Viking migration and settlement in northern and eastern England in the Anglo-Saxon period, and then also the French influence, chiefly during the ascendancy of French as a prestige language in England in the Middle Ages, and finally the influx of Latin words into the language during the Renaissance.

In brief, Henry Bradley's book still constitutes a sound introduction to the way English developed and expanded over a millennium and a half, and provides a still valuable guide to the history and development of English words. It clearly helped to kindle Tolkien's interests. Coincidentally, Tolkien later met and worked with Bradley and the two struck up a good working relationship.[8] At the beginning of his career, from January 1919 to may 1920, Tolkien was employed on the staff of the *OED*, for which Bradley was senior editor from 1915 to 1923.

An Anglo-Saxon Primer

While still at school, then, Tolkien began studying extra-curricular languages, such as Anglo-Saxon (Old English). George Brewerton, a perceptive teacher of English and the Classics, placed a textbook of the language in Tolkien's hands. Likely as not this was *An Anglo-Saxon Primer* by the Oxford philologist Henry Sweet, the standard introductory textbook in England at the time, or just possibly the same author's *First Steps in Anglo-Saxon*.[9] Both of Sweet's primers give a summary of the language followed by texts for practice in reading the language; these reading sections would have provided Tolkien with interesting material, some with stimulating creative potential.[10] The texts in *An Anglo-Saxon Primer*, for one, are well chosen for their descriptive and/or literary-stylistic qualities: passages from the Bible such as the Tower of Babel, Solomon and Sheba, or the Parable of the Sower; extracts from the Anglo-Saxon Chronicle; an interesting saint's life set in ninth-century East Anglia, *The Life of Edmund King and Martyr*, by the writer Ælfric. There is not time or space to examine all these texts, but let us take two which stand out for their potential interest to Tolkien.

It is not hard to see why the philologist and linguist Henry Sweet chose the Tower of Babel as a passage for his *Primer*, nor why Ronald Tolkien, the schoolboy with a philological inclination, may have wished to study it. This narrative has symbolic potential for its moral content: a tale of hubris that harks back to an ancient time when the language of all people was one. In the Babel story, humankind is motivated by overweening ambition and has chosen to build a great tower. Depicted over many centuries in European art, the Tower of Babel in the biblical story is also the symbol of the perfect language, the Victorian philologist's ideal narrative, a *mythos* of how the one language became divided and scattered into many different tongues and vernaculars.

Though the Old English narrative is a close paraphrase of the Latin Bible, two words in the text are worthy of note: *boc-leden* and *steapol*. The term *boc-leden* or Book-Latin neatly reflects the general situation in early medieval Europe, where Latin was the one principal language of written record – Tolkien in 1938 was to coin his own word on a similar pattern, *elf-latin*, referring to his own invented language Qenya.[11] In medieval terms, book-latin was for the 'literate' while all other languages were for the 'illiterate'. A notable exception to this attitude, of course, was England in the years before the Norman Conquest, when (Old) English became the second language of government and record.

In the Old English text, *steapol* signifies the tower of Babel itself, clearly the modern English word 'steeple', here signifying a construction that is *steap* (exceedingly tall), perhaps a prelude to the many tall towers that feature in Tolkien's writing, from Tower of Pearl in 'The Happy Mariners' to the Necromancer's tower in *The Hobbit* to the *Two Towers* of *LOTR*.

Select passages from the Chronicle constitute the next chapter of Sweet's *Primer*, and these undoubtedly had an influence on Ronald Tolkien's developing sense of early literature. A chronicle is a set of brief records or annals – the years are listed and important events are briefly noted alongside the relevant date. The Anglo-Saxon Chronicle was one of the first sets of annals in Europe to be recorded in a vernacular language rather than in the Book-Latin. This is its attraction to philologists: the ancientness of its language, the suggestiveness of its linguistic forms. It can be shown that Henry Sweet felt strongly this enticement: his scholarly article on the vestiges of old poetry preserved in the language of the Chronicle is a paradigm of philological speculation, the process of reaching back into the past of a word or phrase in order to reconstruct the hidden concept, or the hidden poem that lies behind it.[12] In one instance, there is a record of a battle in 473 AD between Hengest and his son Ash, leaders of the *Engle*, the 'Angles' or 'English', and the *Wealas*, literally 'the foreigners', also referred to as the *Brettas* – in other words, the Britons (text here adapted from Sweet's *Primer*):

> Her Hengest and Æsc ge-fuhton with Wealas, and ge-namon un-arimedlicu here-reaf, and tha Wealas flugon tha Engle swa swa fyr.

> [Here Hengest and Ash fought with the foreigners, and took countless plunder, and the foreigners fled the English like fire.]

Here the crucial phrase depends on alliteration of f-sounds on *fought*, *fled*, *fire*, and translates quite literally into the present-day language as 'the foreigners fled the English like fire'. Sweet's speculation was that the Chronicle entry was a memory or an echo of an old poem long since lost, for Anglo-Saxon poetry used alliteration as the basis for its rhythm and metre. And Tolkien followed suit, at least in creatively re-imagining contexts for Old English poems in the legendary world he was inventing and discovering. He even imagined through his Ælfwine legend a situation in which a speaker of Old English would come to record the events of *The Silmarillion* in his own language. In such texts as the Annals of Beleriand, therefore, he records the legends in Old English, in its typically sparse, annalistic prose style.[13]

The appeal of philology

For Tolkien, above all, language study had an aesthetic appeal. In his view, the riches of a language were to be found in what linguists would term its phonology, in its system of *phonemes* or meaningful sounds, and their combinations, and in the rule-based patterning of those phonemes into words. This is Tolkien's celebrated language-aesthetic.[14] While still at school, he discovered it in Anglo-Saxon (i.e. Old English), as we have seen, but also in the related early medieval language Gothic, spoken by the Goths, a nation from Scandinavia and the Baltic that spread across Europe in the fifth century during the decline and fall of the Roman empire. Records in Gothic chiefly survive through a Bible translation made by bishop Ulfilas in the fourth century, a proponent of the teachings of Arius, which eventually lost favour in the western Church. The kind of speculation that followed from this, the *might-have-been* of history, was that, if Arius and Ulfilas had been more orthodox in their Christianity, Gothic could have become one of the great languages of the medieval church, alongside Greek and Latin.

Tolkien first came across this language in the *Gothic Primer* by Joseph Wright, the professor who was to become his tutor in comparative philology at Oxford. He later recalled 'the vastness of Joe Wright's dining-room table' where he sat 'alone at one end learning the elements of Greek philology from glinting glasses in the further gloom'. Wright, an autodidact from a Yorkshire working-class background, was a rigorous and demanding tutor, and must have conducted his university tutorials from the comfort of his own home, a common practice at that time, especially for professors.[15] The *Gothic Primer* gives a grammar and a few passages, all taken from the Gothic version of the Gospels, the only major text extant in this language. This fact is significant, for there is no surviving poetry in Gothic to provide any kind of more strictly literary or poetic enjoyment. Nevertheless, for Tolkien the encounter with Gothic was akin to poetic enjoyment, and it became a creative catalyst: he attempted on its basis to invent, or in a way to reconstruct and re-invent, a similar ancient Germanic language in which other more strictly literary texts could then be produced. His love of Gothic, then, was strictly philological – that is, stemmed from 'a love of the words'.

Likewise also was his attraction to Finnish, which he discovered as an Oxford undergraduate while supposedly working towards his intermediate examination (known at Oxford University as Honour Moderations); at the time he was studying the Classics, though he subsequently changed to medieval English studies for the second half of his degree. The attraction of Finnish was its mythological literature, especially the nineteenth-century collection of ballads known as the *Kalevala* or *Land of Heroes*. Its mythical themes, heroic stories and cold bright northern landscapes fascinated Tolkien, and inspired him to write an appreciative essay which he delivered as an undergraduate paper to the Sundial Society at Corpus Christi College, Oxford on 22 November 1914 and then again to the Essay Club at Exeter College, Oxford in February 1915. This paper, now published, demonstrates

Fig. 13b   Quad at Exeter College

at first-hand his love of the archaic literary style and above all of the texture of the Finnish language itself, which he sees as euphonious and musical, and 'anything but ugly'.[16] He later regarded his discovery of Finnish as a defining moment; in a letter to W.H. Auden in 1955 he compared his finding the Finnish grammar in Exeter College Library to discovering a wine-cellar filled with strange intoxicating vintages.[17]

Finnish thereafter became the basis of his Quenya and (to a lesser extent) Sindarin, the invented languages that were to provide the nomenclature, and hence generate the characters, personalities and even the whole narratives, of his fiction. As the two talks he gave to the Oxford college essay clubs show, all this creativity had started while he was still a student supposedly studying Latin and Greek. With so many extra-curricular linguistic interests, Tolkien did not perform outstandingly in his Honour Moderations in Classics, and his Exeter College tutors encouraged him to switch to the School of English for the second half of his undergraduate degree.

In these early encounters with Gothic and Finnish, it must be said that Tolkien was certainly not unique, nor was he the first to feel in this way the pull of philology as language-aesthetic. The following are a few examples from the late nineteenth-century world of language studies. A classic case is the German-trained philologist Friedrich Max Müller (1823–1900), Professor of Comparative Philology at Oxford, whom Tolkien was to mention in his later lecture on fairy-stories. Müller famously lectured on the 'Science of Language' in the 1860s; the published lectures sold widely, in many editions, and in them Müller expresses a similar feeling for language, in his case the experience of studying Turkish, a language related generically to Finnish. Though Müller is rather more focussed on the beauty of structure rather than the euphony of sound, his reaction is not unlike Tolkien's initial response to the discovery of the sounds and textures of Finnish:

> It is a real pleasure to read a Turkish grammar, even though one may have no wish to acquire it practically. The ingenious manner in which the numerous grammatical forms are brought out, the regularity which pervades the system of declension and conjugation, the transparency and intelligibility of the whole structure, must strike all who have a sense of that wonderful power of the human mind which has displayed itself in language.[18]

Like Tolkien with Finnish, Müller does not wish to acquire a practical ability to speak Turkish: rather, he is impressed by its pattern and structure.

Sound symbolism and onomatopoeia

A younger contemporary of Max Müller was the Oxford anthropologist Sir Edward Burnett Tylor (1832–1917), who became the first person to hold a chair in the new academic discipline of anthropology. Tylor was particularly fascinated with language and was well read in the scholarship of the German philologists; he particularly appreciated the aesthetic aspects of Jacob Grimm's work, for instance on the phenomenon of vowel gradation, by which a word can symbolically express fine 'colourings' or distinctions of meaning, simply by ringing the changes on its root vowel. Here, for example, is Tylor's discussion of the sound-symbolism inherent in the words *stand* and *stop*; the passage is characteristic of nineteenth-century philology at its most lively and enthusiastic:

> Thus, again, to stamp with the foot, which has been claimed as an imitation of sound, seems only a 'coloured' word. The root *sta*, 'to stand', Sanskrit *sthâ*, forms a causative *stap*; Sanskrit *sthâpay*, 'to make to stand', English to *stop*, and a foot-*step* is when the foot comes to a stand, a foot-*stop*. But we have Anglo-Saxon *stapan*, *stæpan*, *steppan*, English to *step*, varying to express its meaning by sound into staup, to stamp, to stump, and to stomp, contrasting in their violence or clumsy weight with the foot on the Dorset cottage-sill – in Barnes's poem:–
>
> > 'Where love do seek the maïdens's evenèn vloor,
> > Wi' *stip-step* light, and tip-tap slight
> > Ageän the door.'
>
> By expanding, modifying, or, so to speak, colouring, sound is able to produce effects closely like those of gesture-language, expressing length or shortness of time, strength or weakness of action, then passing into a further stage to describe greatness or smallness of size or of distance, and thence making its way into the widest fields of metaphor.[19]

By 'metaphor' is meant here the metaphorical use of certain vowel-sounds such as the effect of lightness in the vowel in *step*, contrasted with the heaviness expressed by the vowels in *stamp* and *stomp*. Tylor here combines historical inquiry with analysis of the structure of present-day English, and he cites the Dorset dialect poetry of William Barnes, a poet with whom Tolkien had affinities, both in his love of dialect and linguistic variation and in his preference for the Old English and Germanic roots and stems of the English language.

Another poet thinking along the same lines was Gerard Manley Hopkins, whose experiments with sprung rhythm and alliterative metre might well have appealed to Tolkien. Hopkins had the same love of etymological connections that we also find in Tolkien's work. In the following paasage he speculates on the origins and connections of the word *grind*:

> Original meaning to *strike*, *rub*, particularly *together*. That which is produced by such means is the *grit*, the *groats* or crumbs, like *fragmentum* from *frangere*, *bit* from *bite*. *Crumb*, *crumble* perhaps akin. To *greet* to strike the hands together (?) *Greet*, grief, wearing, tribulation. *Gruff*, with a sound as of two things rubbing together. I believe these words to be onomatopoetic. *Gr* common to them all representing a particular sound. In fact I think the onomatopoetic theory has not had a fair chance. Cf. *Crack, creak, croak, crake, graculus, crackle*. These must be onomatopoetic.[20]

This diary entry of September 1863 alludes to the work of F. W. Farrar, who had proposed the theory that human language had originated in cries imitative of the sounds of the external world.

One of the new turning points in science in the mid-1860s was the realisation of the great age of the earth. Rather than being a few thousand years old, as many scholars and scientists had previously assumed, the evidence of geological strata, fossils and biological variation pointed to the earth being millions of years old, and to modern humanity itself being tens of thousands of years old. No longer was it possible therefore to regard an ancient recorded language such as Sanskrit as fairly close to the original human language, the tongue spoken by humankind at a 'primitive' stage of development; for example, at the time of the Tower of Babel. The difficulty is that all languages for which we have records are relatively speaking 'modern', for two reasons: first, languages were not recorded in writing for many millennia in the unwritten story of humanity; and, second, it is impossible to find a 'primitive language' since (apart from socially constructed pidgins) all natural human languages in existence have complex systems of vocabulary and syntax. Despite the chronological problems involved, however, speculations on the origin of language, often linked to an aesthetic of sound symbolism, continued to enthral philologists and anthropologists at the end of the nineteenth century. Max Müller, rejecting Farrar's imitative–onomatopoeic theory, proposed his own, equally speculative, theory that phenomena of the external world ring and resonate and so give rise to the sounds of human speech that are consonant with them.

In the early twentieth century, when Tolkien was as it were a trainee in the field, historical philology remained traditional in its methods, even if the philologists had to make some allowance for the new sophistication of the exponents of 'linguistics', such as the great Swiss linguist Ferdinand de Saussure and his structuralist disciples, who further developed his work from the 1920s onwards. Tolkien described himself as old-fashioned in his philological work; the old theory and methodology suited him. Not surprisingly, continuations of nineteenth-century language reflection are found among the Inklings, the loosely associated group of Oxford scholars and writers headed by C.S. Lewis to which Tolkien belonged. As Verlyn Flieger has recently argued convincingly, the Inkling Owen Barfield's book *Poetic Diction* was a key formulation.[21] In Barfield's insistence that words preserve an ancient unitary meaning – this despite the ceaseless processes of semantic change – Barfield seems closer to the originary linguistic roots of William Barnes, Farrar and Max Müller (even though he disagreed with them) than he does to anything in contemporary twentieth-century structuralist linguistics or linguistic philosophy. Barfield's ideas do, however, chime well with some recent attempts to explore the notion of phono-semantics and the connection between sound, meaning and landscape.[22]

Reconstruction as a method

All this language background is highly relevant to Tolkien's epiphany, his discovery of the Anglo-Saxon word *éarendel* in the poem *Christ I*. It was a moment of aesthetic appreciation, and the effect was exhilarating, as though he was about to grasp something remote and unusual, just beyond his fingertips.[23]

Tolkien eventually used this word denoting the evening star as a name in his own mythology, in an elaborate process of reconstruction and re-invention that is famous in Tolkien studies.[24]

But, as we are about to see, *éarendel* was not the only word that he adopted creatively from earlier forms of English. He was now (from 1913) 'studying A-S professionally'.[25] The course was demanding, and the tutor, the well-respected Kenneth Sisam, was rigorous but also inspiring in his coverage of set texts. The main edition from which the set texts were drawn was Henry Sweet's *Anglo-Saxon Reader*, the standard textbook since its publication in 1876; by the time Tolkien was at university it was already in its eighth revised edition (1908).[26] Just as his *Primer* was aimed at beginners in the language, Sweet's *Reader* took them to the next stage; it consisted of a short grammar (aimed at advanced students) followed by a large anthology of reading texts in both prose and verse, selected by Sweet from all the periods and regions of Old English literature before the Norman Conquest. Notes and a glossary completed the book. Sweet's principle in presenting the texts was to keep the notes to a bare minimum and to refrain wherever possible from historical or cultural commentary, for he felt that it was the role of the teacher to comment on the texts when using the *Reader* with students.[27] The result of the policy is that the small number of cultural comments that are actually included in the textbook stand out prominently, and it is arguable that they influenced student users of the *Reader* considerably. Two examples are telling. Chapter 27, headed 'Selections from the Riddles', has the rubric:

> Many of these riddles are true poems, containing beautiful descriptions of nature.

While chapter 28, 'Gnomic Verses', has the following comment:

> The so-called gnomic verses show poetry in its earliest form, and are no doubt of great antiquity, although they may have been altered in later times. While abrupt and disconnected, they are yet full of picturesqueness and power; the conclusion of the present piece is particularly impressive.

The problem with a comment of this nature is that it goes back to the first edition of 1876, when Sweet, despite some pioneering linguistic work that was ahead of its time, was still under the spell of the older philology. At that time, as was pointed out above, the scientific demonstration of the great age of the earth had only recently been made and the new ways of thought were taking a while to filter through. Even a rigorous, forward-thinking scholar like Sweet still felt that the writings in the earliest Old English must be 'of great antiquity', when in point of fact thousands of years must actually separate the writers of Old English from 'poetry in its earliest form'. Clearly the attitude was entrenched and difficult to dislodge. The temptation was to date Old English poetry far earlier than it really was, or to see it as somehow a vestige or record of something far more ancient.

In fact, the *Gnomic Verses* appear in a manuscript of the eleventh-century version C of the Anglo-Saxon Chronicle, and though it is likely that these versified proverbs or maxims are traditional, the composition of the poem need not necessarily be very ancient: it is possible that the verses were put together to accompany the new manuscript of the Chronicle that was compiled in the 1040s. The title of course is not part of the original poem, for none of the manuscripts of Old English poetry contain titles. These have mostly been invented by nineteenth-century scholars, and their successors employ them as convenient labels. Sometimes a poem title is changed: nowadays this particular poem is referred to as *Maxims II*. Not a terribly inspiring title for a poem, it must be admitted, but the Roman numeral serves to remind scholars that there are two very similar poems of this genre in the surviving corpus of Old English poetry. Since the term 'gnomic' suggests 'wisdom', or even ancient wisdom, the nineteenth-century title of the poem has now been replaced. The antiquarian bias of Victorian Anglo-Saxon studies is the flaw, as it were, in the traditional philological method of reconstruction of lost earlier realities.

Nevertheless, there is something very attractive in the reconstructive approach, and Tolkien certainly must have found it so; for him the philological method of reconstruction was creative and stimulating. If we look for instance at the opening lines of the *Gnomic Verses* in the textbook that he studied, a rich variety of Tolkienesque terms and concepts simply leap out from the page. Here is the Old English text (I have modernised the spelling of the letter thorn as 'th' for the benefit of readers who do not know Old English); a translation follows:

> Cyning sceal rice healdan. Ceastra beoth feorran gesyne,
> orthanc enta geweorc, tha the on thysse eorthan syndon,
> wrætlic weallstana geweorc. Wind byth on lyfte swiftest,
> thunor byth thragum hludast. Thrymmas syndan Cristes myccle.
> Wyrd byth swithost.

> [The king must rule over a realm. Cities are conspicuous from afar, those which there are on this earth, the ingenious constructions of giants, ornate fortresses of dressed stones. The wind in the sky is the swiftest thing and thunder in its seasons is the loudest. The powers of Christ are great: Providence is the most compelling thing.[28]]

This is a poem about kingship, the marvels of old cities, the power of the elements, the strength of *wyrd*, an old word for 'fate'; even conceptually there are echoes of Tolkien's world here.

Line 2, with the words 'orthanc' and 'enta geweorc', is the clearest verbal resonance: the original meaning is 'cunning work of giants', and rather like the proverbial 'standing on the shoulders of giants' this maxim probably referred not to literal giants but to the skills of the Roman architects and masons who built what they called the *castra* – these are the towns that the Anglo-Saxons named *ceastra* (pronounced roughly as 'chastra'); in other words, the ancient fortified 'chesters' such as Chester or Winchester that were and still are to be seen across the length and breadth of Old England, among the oldest stone-walled cities in the country. When Tolkien presumably turned to the glossary in Sweet's *Reader* he would have found that *orthanc* is an adjective meaning 'cunning'; and with the help of grammar and glossary he would have found that *ent* means 'giant' and *enta* means 'of giants', while *geweorc* is in fact the perfective prefix *ge-* plus the noun *weorc* meaning 'work, fortification'. Here already are the first inklings of an idea that was to take many decades to crystallise in Tolkien's mind as he wrote *LOTR* in the 1940s. First came *Orthanc*, the tower of the wizard Saruman, a name which (as Shippey has pointed out) is *searo-mon* in standard Old English and signifies 'the cunning man, the artificer'. With this image in mind Tolkien hit upon the *ents*, the tree-giants of Fangorn Forest. The two images then were linked in *TT* as two symbolic figures in the War of the Ring: on the one hand Treebeard and the ents representing nature and the voice of defenceless trees; on the other hand Saruman the artificer, the industrialist and destroyer of the environment. The juxtaposition of the two images is the revenge of nature against artifice, the symbolic theme of the narrative. Intrigued by the implications of the Old English words, Tolkien adapted them to the narrative world of his own stories set in ancient times.

Old English words and concepts in *The Hobbit*

As with *orthanc* and *ent*, the same process took place with other Old English words; with regard to *The Hobbit* the following non-exhaustive list covers some of the more significant: *ælf, beorn, eorcanstan, orcneas, smugan, wearg*. All these words appear in *The Hobbit* in a modernised form, either as a type of being or creature in the case of *elf, orc* and *warg*, or as a proper noun in the case of Beorn, Arkenstone and Smaug (from the verb *smugan*: to investigate, worm one's way into something). For discussions of these particular words the reader can do no better than turn to the writings of Tom Shippey, in particular *The Road to Middle-earth*, in which he pioneered a philological approach to Tolkien's writings, and to *The Annotated Hobbit* by Douglas

Anderson.[29] An alphabetical treatment of these and other words is to be found in *The Ring of Words* by *OED* editor Peter Gilliver and his colleagues.[30] The following remarks highlight some of their findings and emphasise a few other points to be made about these once extinct Old English poetic words that had gone out of use in everyday English, until Tolkien revived them.

In its Norse cognate form, the word *alf* has already been encountered in the compound name Gandalf, one of the dwarves of Norse mythology, whose name Tolkien borrowed for his wizard with his staff (*gand* means literally 'staff'). The Old English cognate was *ælf*, spelt with the old letter known as 'ash', a ligature or blend of the two letters 'a' and 'e'. Ælf- is usually encountered as the first element in compound names such as Ælfræd and Ælfwine and Ælfgar, names common among the Anglo-Saxon nobility of tenth-century England. Alfred and Alwin and Elgar are their modern descendants, though the spelling complicates and partly disguises the etymology. The second element in the first instance is *ræd*, a noun which means 'advice' or 'counsel', hence Alfred means 'advice of supernatural beings' or 'counsel of the elves'. An archaic word in present-day English is *rede*; and the modern German cognate is *Rat* (advice), heard for instance in *Rathaus* (town-hall), where traditionally counsellors meet. The second elements respectively of Alwin and Elgar are *-wine* (friend) (pronounced as two syllables 'wi-nuh') and *-gar* (spear). These were productively used to generate other names such as Eadwine/Edwin the Blessed Friend, a name that Tolkien used in his unfinished novel *The Lost Road*, and Eadgar/Edgar the Blessed Spear.

A passage in the poem *The Dream of the Rood*, the well-known Old English religious poem celebrating the victory of Christ at the crucifixion, which David Jones used in his poem *In Parenthesis*, provides a context for two other Anglo-Saxon poetic words that Tolkien adopted and made his own: *beorn* and *wearg*, which appear in their plural form *beorn-as* and *wearg-as*. Generically, the poem is a dream vision in which the Cross itself is given a personalised voice, telling the story of the Passion from his own perspective, lamenting how strong enemies (*feondas*), criminals (*weargas*) and warriors (*beornas*) – all these words appear to be near-synonyms in the rhetoric of the verse – carried the Cross to a hilltop where they raised it up.[31] As was discussed above it is clear that Tolkien used his knowledge of the sister-languages and their cultures, especially Old Norse, when adopting words into Old English. The name Beorn is the case in point: its poetic meaning 'warrior' is coloured by its older meaning 'bear', which Tolkien then associated with the story of Bothvar Bjarki, the man-bear or shape-changer in Norse saga. As for *wearg*, this meant a criminal or outlaw in Old English; also spelt *wearh*, the word appears in the poem *Maxims II*, which declares that it is right and proper for a criminal to hang in order to atone for, or pay back for, crimes against humanity. The lupine nature of the word is found in the Old Norse cognate *vargr* meaning either 'outlaw' or 'wolf'. Tolkien combined these two ideas in order to invent an intelligent but malevolent wolf-like creature that fitted the polarities of good and evil which he had fashioned for his mythology. As Tolkien himself pointed out, the spelling *warg* is an older form that points to the prehistory of the word in the original Germanic language that eventually gave rise over time to its descendants Old Norse, Old English and Old German.[32] As with Eärendel from Old English *éarendel*, Tolkien used the method of reconstruction to create imaginatively a person or creature in the reconstructed 'real world' of prehistory who would fit the poetically rich term that he had come across in his study of the Old English language. This attention to finding the right word is part and parcel of Tolkien's philology, and the success of his fiction depends very much on the suitability of his choice of words and, as we saw in chapter 5, his nomenclature, his finding the right name.

Fig. 13c   Warg

Connected with this also is Tolkien's attention to the right sound of his words, since his thinking was as much phonetic as it was calligraphic or typographic. He loved scripts and alphabets, but he also thought in terms of sounds as well as spellings, and when using his Tengwar script, for example, he spelt English words phonetically.[33] (The Tengwar script can be seen, for example, in editions of *The Hobbit* on the large pot of gold in the picture of Smaug resting on his treasure.) The preference for phonetic writing was in keeping with the results of comparative philology, which showed to the satisfaction of most scholars (though there were sceptics) that on the whole Old English scribes wrote phonetically, using a consistent system of letter-to-sound correspondences. Their system for spelling vowels for instance followed very much the values of continental languages like Latin, Italian and German. Tolkien adhered to this traditional use of the roman alphabet in the names he used for people and places. The first syllable of Sauron, for instance, rhymes with 'now'; the 'au' spelling represents the diphthong, the phonetic term for two vowels combined into one syllable, pronounced as though it is one vowel, with a glide between the sound 'a' of *cat* and the 'u' of *full*. The spelling 'au' in Tolkien's nomenclature is one consistently used for that sound, as in modern German *Haus, Maus, laut*, which correspond roughly in their sound to their English cognates *house, mouse, loud*. The name Smaug should also be pronounced with the same vowel-sound. More difficult is the pronunciation of the diphthong in Eärendel. Learning to pronounce Old English can provide useful assistance here (as well as giving access to the riches of early English literature that Tolkien knew so well).[34] In *éarendel* there are three syllables *éa-ren-del*, the first syllable having the open 'æ' sound which then glides briskly down to a short 'a' vowel; the name 'Arundel' spoken quickly comes close to the same sound.

One final pronunciation point concerns the 'v' sound in Tolkien's plural noun *dwarves*, which he favoured over the traditional English proofreaders' preference for *dwarfs* when he published *The Hobbit*; likewise the adjective *elvish*, which famously he preferred to the diminutive *elfin*; he also on occasions favoured *roof–rooves* on analogy with *hoof–hooves*.[35] There was no letter 'v' in Old English: the final '-f' of *hrof* (meaning 'roof of a house') was pronounced 'f', but between vowels the medial letter '-f-' had the sound 'v' as in *lufu*, modern English 'love', or indeed the plural *hrofas* (rooves). The reader may be tempted to suspect that Tolkien's love of Old English as a language to be heard and enjoyed also influenced the way he pronounced and wrote modern English.

Tolkien's choice of words in *The Hobbit*

With respect then to the way Tolkien thought and felt about the living history of English words, it makes sense to cultivate an appropriate linguistic awareness when reading and thinking about his fiction. And occasionally, though of course not too often, it is worth taking a break from reading to linger over Tolkien's choice of word and phrase. A highly illuminating exercise is to take a short but significant passage and examine the history of a selection of its words, using etymological dictionaries and glossaries (such as Sweet's *Anglo-Saxon Reader*) as well as the *OED* as a guide and reference tool.

One key passage, already alluded to in chapter 9 above, concerns the 'thunderbattle' in 'Over Hill and Under Hill' (*The Hobbit*, chapter 4) which prevents the travellers from crossing the Misty Mountains:

> You know how terrific a really big thunderstorm can be down in the land and in a river-valley; especially at times when two great thunderstorms meet and clash. More terrible still are thunder and lightning in the mountains at night, when storms come up from East and West and make war. The lightning splinters on the peaks, and rocks shiver, and great crashes split the air and go rolling and tumbling into every cave and hollow; and the darkness is filled with overwhelming noise and sudden light.

The passage is of interest from a historical point of view in showing a word in the act of changing its meaning. In the adjective used to describe the emotional effects of the storm on the observer, this passage (published of course in 1937) demonstrates one of the last uses of the word *terrific* in its detrimental sense of 'causing terror, terrifying'. The *OED* states this use is 'now rare' and cites the poet Milton as a first user of the adjective with this meaning in 1679, and gives a war report of 1914 as its last citation. The *OED* sense 2a, 'of great size or intensity', is first attested in 1743, while sense 2b, 'an enthusiastic term of commendation: amazing, impressive; excellent, exceedingly good, splendid', is first observed in 1871 and is still current. It is unlikely given the related pairing *terrific/more terrible* that Tolkien meant the word in this latter, positive sense, though we may be fairly sure that as a philologist he was aware of it.

The compound *thunderstorm* is a relative newcomer to the language, despite the fact that its constituent words *thunder* and *storm* both go back to Old English. The *OED* finds no trace of it until the seventeenth century, from which time it gains in popularity. *Storms*, however, are a long-standing veteran of the English lexicon. The word occurs for example in the wind-swept seascape of the Old English poem *The Seafarer*, where storms 'beat' the cliffs: 'stormas þær stanclifu beotan'.[36] The use here verges on the metaphorical, and, as the *OED* reports, a similarly figurative take on the word occurs in *Beowulf* (line 3117), where the meaning is transferred to warfare: 'stræla storm' – that is, a storm of arrows shot over the shield-wall, rather like the 'hail of dark arrows' shot at the dragon in *The Hobbit* (chapter 14). *Thunder* is another veteran, attested in Old English as *thunor*. Old English *Thunor* as a proper noun was also the Anglo-Saxon equivalent of the Norse god Thor, after which Thursday or Thunres-dæg is named.

The main theme of the passage is *thunderbattle*, Tolkien's word to describe the situation when two separate storms 'meet and clash' – and 'come up from East and West and make war' – here the verb *meet* has the military sense of 'to come together as rivals in a battle' (*OED meet*, sense IVb). There is no *OED* entry at all for this compound *thunderbattle*. It is of course Tolkien's original comic invention to play on the military connotations and replace the element *-storm* in *thunderstorm* with a word of full military import. The noun *battle* is one of the first French words to be introduced into English after the Norman Conquest; William I named the abbey founded on the site of his victory near Hastings as Battle, a name which the nearby village retains to this day. As the *OED* shows, the word derives from Old French *bataille*, which in turn goes back to Late Latin *battualia* from *battu-ere* (to beat). Similarly, the noun *war* is also a Norman import into the language (the Central French equivalent being *guerre*).

The mythic and warlike connotations of the word *thunder* and the compound *thunderbattle* may lie behind Tolkien's introduction later in the same scene of the stone giants hurling their rocks at one another for a game and smashing them into the trees far below in the valley. Is this nature personification rather in the manner of the theories of animism propounded by Max Müller and E.B. Tylor that we discussed in chapter 9? The effect of the description is terrifying, though some critics have objected that such mythic personifications do not fit well into Tolkien's overall concept. Elsewhere, in particular in his treatise *On Fairy-stories*, Tolkien was sceptical of the reductive attempts by the late Victorian armchair anthropologists to explain away the gods solely as personifications of the weather; for instance. the highly personable and irascible character of the god Thor 'explained away' as a personification of thunder.[37]

Probably with deliberate intent, Tolkien plays on a number of etymological connections in the onomatopoeic words he uses in this passage. The verb *clash* and the noun *crash* are related in sound and echoic sense, as is *smash* which appears later on the same page; *splinter* and *split* are both derived from Middle Dutch. Sometimes he also matches synonyms from different language origins. The matching pairs 'rolling and tumbling' and 'cave and hollow' are words of related meaning but different derivations: *roll* and *cave* from French; *tumble* from Old Low German but related to Old English *tumbian* (to tumble, leap, dance); *hollow* from OE *holh* (hole). The latter word *holh* (hollow) is related to *hol* (hollow place, cave, hole, den). A hollow is exactly the place the travellers are about to retreat to as the storm worsens. It is also a reminder of the word *hobbit*, which in the language of Rohan in *LOTR* (Part III, chapter 8) is *holbytla* or 'hole-builder'; in this pseudo-etymology Tolkien actually invents an Old English word **holbytla* (the asterisk marking it as hypothetical or reconstructed), in order to provide a life-history for his invented modern English word *hobbit*.

Chapter Fourteen

Tolkien as word-collector

Dictionary work

TOLKIEN'S *MIDDLE ENGLISH Vocabulary* (1922), his first academic book, is a natural offshoot of his work for the *OED*. The *Vocabulary* was effectively a small paperback dictionary for use in conjunction with the textbook *Fourteenth-Century Verse and Prose* (1921) by his former tutor Kenneth Sisam, who later went on to pursue a career in publishing with Oxford University Press. The two books, small brown paperbacks aimed at the student market, were published by the Clarendon Press, part of Oxford University Press, and were intended to supersede the earlier textbook by Morris and Skeat, *Specimens of Early English*, which Tolkien had studied as an undergraduate.

It was a prestigious series, and although Tolkien was at the time still a young academic, his name was now appearing alongside those of the great experts in the field of English language studies. The list advertised on the back cover of the book as 'Oxford English Dictionaries and Glossaries for Students' included *A Glossary of Tudor and Stuart Words* by the Cambridge philologist and professor of English W.W. Skeat, and *A Shakespeare Glossary* by the *OED* sub-editor C.T. Onions (1873–1965). Onions was one of Tolkien's superiors at the *OED*, and since he was also a lecturer at the university they later became colleagues together at Oxford. Listed also was *The Concise Oxford Dictionary of Current English*, adapted from the *OED* by H.W. Fowler and his more famous brother F.G. Fowler, author of *Fowler's English Usage*.

Fig. 14a   The White Horse, Broad Street, Oxford

Another title in the series was *The Student's Dictionary of Anglo-Saxon* by Henry Sweet (1845–1912), the Oxford philologist and Reader in Phonetics. Sweet had been an acquaintance of George Bernard Shaw, with whom he corresponded on that big issue of the late Victorian and Edwardian periods: the reform of English spelling. Shaw later claimed that the irascible character of his phonetics professor Henry Higgins in *Pygmalion* (and the later *My Fair Lady*) was based, at least in part, on the phonetician Sweet. As was pointed out above, Tolkien probably used Sweet's *Anglo-Saxon Primer* when he first started to learn Old English at school; he studied the texts of Sweet's *Anglo-Saxon Reader* assiduously with his tutor Sisam at university, and used the latter book himself for his own teaching. One of several distinguished scholars who had studied with Sweet was the phonetician and historical linguist Henry Cecil Wyld, who held the Merton chair of English Language and Literature at Oxford University (Tolkien succeeded to this position on Wyld's death in 1945). Like Shaw and Sweet – and indeed sharing this interest with Bradley and Bradley's friend the poet Robert Bridges – Tolkien also used phonetic spelling systems of his own design: one he devised in the period around 1919 and referred to as 'The Alphabet of Rúmil'. The reference as we shall see is to a character in his own fiction.

Tolkien the language teacher was at the forefront in his work for *A Middle English Vocabulary*. As he put it in his prefatory note, his pedagogical purpose is to give a 'full treatment to what may rightly be called the back-bone of the language', his first point being that although Middle English resembles the modern language, and often the learner 'half-recognises' many of the words, all this can be misleading, as the words were frequently used in different ways. The needs of a learner therefore are not primarily for a list of the difficult or abstruse words. Instead the student requires a good working knowledge, which depends on 'familiarity with the ordinary machinery of expression – with the precise forms and meanings that common words may assume'.

In his *Middle English Vocabulary*, Tolkien aims to impart an ability to understand the core vocabulary, the plain concrete style of Middle English, and 'the idiomatic phrases, some fresh-minted and some worn thin, but all likely to recur again and again in an age whose authors took no pains to avoid usual or hackneyed turns of expression'. A characteristic working method and philosophy of language lie behind such statements: an appreciation of the limitations but also the expressive possibilities of medieval literature with its rootedness in time-honoured phrases and idioms. The study of Tolkien's dictionary work is a richly productive one, for it uncovers the ground of many of Tolkien's poetic words and phrases, what could be seen as the different textures and registers of his writing style.

Wight and barrow-wight

In accordance with these aims for the *Vocabulary*, Tolkien selects the essential words in all the passages of the textbook and identifies their common meanings. For each headword he gives a brief etymological note on its origin in OE, ON or OF (Old English, Old Norse and Old French) plus for difficult cases a reference to the *NED* or *New English Dictionary*, the older preferred title for the multi-volume *OED*. The etymology or origin of a word is necessary not only for historical reasons but also to identify in present-day English those words known as *homonyms* (words of the same form but a different meaning) and *homographs* (words which are unrelated in meaning but are nevertheless spelt the same). As Howard Jackson puts it: 'the basic criterion that dictionaries use to identify homographs is etymology: if two or more different origins can be identified for the same spelling, then the orthographic word is entered as many times as there are different etymologies'.[1]

A good example is Tolkien's two entries for *wight*, a word which was to appear prominently in his poetry and fiction in the form *barrow-wights*, the wraith-like creatures that inhabit the Barrow Downs north of the Old Forest where Bombadil lives. As we have seen (chapter 5), the story of Tom Bombadil and the barrow-wights goes back even earlier than the writing of *The Hobbit*, and Tolkien's first idea on beginning the sequel in 1937–8 was to retell Bombadil's story in the form of a novel.

The word *wight* is fairly common in Middle English, and back in the early 1920s, when compiling his vocabulary, Tolkien's first task was to identify all the different spellings of it as found in Sisam's textbook, along with the word class (adjective, noun etc.) to which it belonged. On the basis of etymology, he distinguished two homonyms, one deriving from ON and one from OE. He then listed references (by chapter and line number) to their occurrence in the textbook. Here is the result of his research: the two headwords – with bold, italics and punctuation as in Tolkien's original text:

> **Wight, Wyht, Wicht** (x), *adj.* valiant, X, 122, 148, XIV *b* 5 (*see* Wede): *adv.* quickly, straightway, XV *b* 36. [ON. *víg-r*, neut. *víg-t*.]
> **Wight, Wyght**, *n.* creature, person, VIII *a* 243, XVII 47, &c.: **Wyȝte**, VI 134; **Wiht**, XII *b* 77; **Wytes**, *pl.* XV *i* 19. [OE. *wiht*.]

Tolkien here identifies an *adjective* and adverb meaning 'valiant', deriving from Old Norse *vígt*, and distinguishes this headword from a *noun* going back to Old English *wiht*, which he translates as 'creature' or 'person'.

A student using the *Vocabulary* would look up passages in *Fourteenth-Century Verse and Prose* to see examples of the words in use, along with other, related words. Thus for the adjective *wight*, an example is 'wicht men armyt intill steill' (valiant men armed in steel) from John Barbour's Scots poem *The Bruce*.[2] In a special idiomatic sense the Middle English *wede*, meaning 'clothing, attire' (as in the old phrase 'widow's weeds'), is combined with *wight* in 'The Taking of Calais', an occasional poem by Laurence Minot. The occasion was an incident in 1347 during the war with France when King Edward put an end to pirate ships operating from Calais. As Tolkien notes in his *Vocabulary*, the whole collocation *wight in wede* means 'valiant' or perhaps 'valiant in arms'. This is an example of what he calls 'the idiomatic phrases, some fresh-minted and some worn thin, … usual or hackneyed turns of expression'. In fact, the whole first stanza of this poem contains a number of such phrases, which Tolkien takes pains to translate in his *Vocabulary* as follows: *to mede* (in payment, as reward), *on mold* (on earth, alive), *sall ken you youre crede* (will teach you what you ought to know), *mend you of youre misdeed* (reform your evil ways), *will ye it ken* (if you will recognise the fact):

> Calays men, now mai ye care,
> And murning mun ye have to mede;
> Mirth on molde get ye no mare,
> Sir Edward sall ken you yowre crede.
> Whilum war ye wight in wede
> To robbing rathly for to ren;
> Mend yow sone of yowre misdeed:
> yowre care is cumen, will ye it ken.

> [Men of Calais, now you have reason to sorrow, and mourning you will have in payment, you will get no more joy alive, Sir Edward will teach you what you ought to know. Formerly you were valiant in arms to run out robbing quickly; reform your evil ways: your sorrow has arrived, if you will recognise the fact!]

In this way, Tolkien's *Vocabulary* provides useful information on the idiomatic phrases as well as the individual words in the poems in the textbook. The emphasis on the phrase is important for understanding how Tolkien was to benefit from this work in his later writing of fiction.

As for the meaning of the Middle English noun *wight*, one citation is from *Piers Plowman*, William Langland's great poem about the estates of England 'Kynde Witt wolde that eche a wyght wroughte' (Natural Good Sense requires that each person should work). This use of *wight* to mean 'person' persists in dialect writing; for example, in the poems of Thomas Hardy.[3] Another of the occurrences of the noun *wight* in Sisam's textbook, however, is the plural form *wytes*, meaning 'creatures', which resembles Tolkien's later use of the word in *barrow-wights*. The passage in question occurs in a verse charm in which the speaker calls on the power of God and the saints to dispel a plague of rats, referred to as *wykked wytes*; the charm is entitled by Sisam 'Rats Away',[4] and the relevant lines (19–20) read as follows:

> God saue this place from ratones and from alle other wykked wytes,
> Bothe be dayes and nytes!

[God save this place from rats and from all other evil creatures, Both by day and by night!]

The rhythmical language is typical of the charm; it makes the verse easier to say and remember, and the rhythm seems to add weight to its effectiveness. Here are some further examples from this very functional text (lines 1–2, 8–9, 14–15, 18):

> I comawnde alle the ratones that are here abowte,
>
> That non dwelle in this place, withinne ne withowte,
>
> [...]
>
> God graunte that grace
>
> That non raton dwelle in the place
>
> [...]
>
> Be dayes and be nyght,
>
> God bad hem flen and gon out of every mannese sight.
>
> [...]
>
> I betweche thes place from ratones and from all other schame [...]

'Wicked wights' can only be dispelled by the careful and effective use of suitable language, including rhyme (*nyght, sight*) and alliteration (*withinne, withoute*). A comparable passage occurs in 'Fog on the Barrow Downs', when Bombadil uses rhythm and rhyme 'Get out you old Wight! Vanish in the sunlight' to expel the wight from its haunted barrow and send it 'far beyond the mountains'.[5] In 'Rats Away', the doublet *by day and by night* has a rhythmical fit, while the phrase *wykked wytes* alliterates on the initial consonant. This is typical of many of these medieval English formulaic phrases, such as *mirth on molde* or *wight in wede*. Tolkien was attracted enough to use such techniques in his own writing, and many examples can be found to prove the point.

Formulaic phrases in Tolkien's fiction

Alliteration was a favourite device in medieval poetry, with ancient roots in the distant past: sometimes it was combined with rhyme in poems like *Sir Orfeo* or *Pearl*; sometimes it was the major determinant feature of the metre of the poem, as in *Sir Gawain and the Green Knight* or the Old English *Beowulf*. Other Middle English alliterative phrases listed in Tolkien's *Middle*

English Vocabulary include: *neither stub no ston* ('nothing'; in the poem *Sir Orfeo*), *stylle as the ston* (firm as a rock; in *Sir Gawain*), or the phrase *by stok other ston* (anywhere), which appears in the moving line spoken by a father to his lost daughter in the visionary poem *Pearl* (line 380):

> God forbede we be now wrothe,
> We meten so selden by stok other ston.[6]

The line is surprisingly difficult to translate with the appropriate tone; in prose it might read: 'God forbid that we should be angry with each other, since we meet so rarely'; though Tolkien chose a paraphrase in his translation, a fellow philologist, Sir Israel Gollancz, merely modernised the words:

> God forbid we be now wroth!
> We meet so seldom by stock or stone.[7]

In *LOTR*, however, as Shippey has shown, Tolkien reused the formulaic phrase *by stock and by stone*, probably for its alliterative effects and resonances with the medieval poetic tradition, in a scene when Treebeard takes his leave of Galadriel and Celeborn.[8]

Apart from his consideration of the needs of the learner, therefore, Tolkien's focus on the formulaic phrases in the *Vocabulary* illustrates very well a poetic rather than pedagogical concern: his fascination with the ground and roots, the creative stock and the branches, of the English language. As Norman Blake has argued, medieval literature was originally read out loud, and uses pleonastic – deliberately superfluous – words and phrases. Such fillers provide time for the listener to assimilate what is being said; they add a formal balance, allow speakers to weigh their words, while still remaining grounded in everyday speech.[9]

The final leave-taking between Bilbo and the dying Thorin Oakenshield at the end of *The Hobbit* could be seen in this light. It is worth taking a moment to reread the short scene, located near the beginning of chapter 18, 'The Return Journey'. Many readers find this episode moving, simply because the situation is a sad leave-taking, but I wonder if the dignity of weighed word and phrase also contributes to the effect. Thorin apologises to Bilbo, and in response Bilbo thanks Thorin for giving him a chance to prove his potential; this is the force of what they say. But the actual words *thank* and *apologise* do not occur. Instead they literally say their farewells, and address each other with formal epithets 'good thief' and 'King under the Mountain' respectively. Thorin uses time-honoured expressions such as 'sit beside my fathers' or rhythmical doublets such as 'gold and silver' or 'part in friendship' or 'words and deeds'. For his part Bilbo takes up an appropriately alliterative proverb 'not a mountain of gold can amend it'. And Thorin responds in kind to the effect that it would be a merrier world if people valued food and cheer more than gold, but now, whether sad or merry, he must leave this world, and he bids his farwell.

Sir Orfeo and *The Hobbit*

As we have just seen, the idiom *wight in wede* (valiant in arms) is explained by the cross-reference to the word *wede*. Now normally *wede* means 'garment, article of attire', as in a passage cited from the poem *Sir Orfeo* about the entourage of the 'king of fairy' (here with spelling slightly modernised):

> Tho com her king also blive,
> With an hundred knightes and mo,
> And damisels an hundred also,
> Al on snow-white steeds;
> As white as milke were her wedes[10]

for which Tolkien chose to revive the word *weed* in his later poetic translation.[11]

Sir Orfeo is a Middle English poem about an abduction of a queen by the king of Faerie and the protagonist's bid to retrieve her, his aimless wandering in the Wild until quite by chance he sees his lost wife riding out to pursue the art of falconry with the ladies of Faerie. The poem was a favourite of Tolkien's, for obvious reasons: he was fascinated by its motif of 'the dim cri and blowing': the hue and cry and sounding horns of the forest hunt of the hosts of Faerie (lines 281–8):

> He might se him bisides
> Oft in hot undertides
> The king o fairy with his rout
> Com to hunt him al about,
> With dim cri and bloweing;
> And houndes also with him berking;
> Ac no best thai no nome,
> No never he nist whider thai bicome.

[He would see near him, often at hot noontide, the king of Faerie with his host, come to hunt all about, with dim cry and blowing; and also with him hounds barking; but they never caught any animal, nor did he ever know where they went.]

The image of the otherworldly hunt is later taken up to good effect in the mysterious hunting scenes in Mirkwood in *The Hobbit* (chapter 8), when the dwarves hear the 'dim blowing of horns in the wood', the barking of the hounds, and the noise of a hunt passing to the north of their path, though they see no sign of it. It should be emphasised that *Sir Orfeo* is not only a verbal influence on Tolkien's style, it also informs images, scenes and story-elements in *The Hobbit*.

Rúmil and Bilbo

Given all the philological work in which Tolkien was involved, it is clear that Tolkien nevertheless retained a sense of humour, satire and even self-parody. It is amusing to note that the second and third of the stories in *The Book of Lost Tales* are narrated by the philologist Rúmil, the same who

Fig. 14b   Path, wall and garden

is credited with inventing the Rumilian phonetic script that Tolkien had adopted for his private use in the 1920s. In the frame narrative begun in the story *The Cottage of Lost Play*, Rúmil is the aged door-keeper who first grants Eriol entry to the great house. Taking a walk the following morning after his arrival, Eriol has his first conversation with Rúmil in a lane of hazel bushes in the grounds of the house. Rúmil is preoccupied with his head bowed, and at first does not notice Eriol's presence, since he is trying to work out the meaning of a new bird-song that he has just heard. He mumbles and grumbles, complaining that languages shift and change and never stay still and it is hard for the specialist to keep track of them all.[12] Rúmil turns out to be a gentle satire of a philologist or lexicographer 'babbling of songs and words': he is a kindly but obstreperous and rather garrulous old man, like some eccentric but genial Oxford don, who walks through the college quadrangle with his head down, muttering to himself.

Is this a portrait of one of Tolkien's colleagues? Or is this a parody perhaps directed at Tolkien himself and his own philological labours, as he was to do in such later fictional works as *Leaf by Niggle*? According to an estimate by Gilliver, Marshall and Weiner, Tolkien must have spent at least nine months of full-time work on his *Middle English Vocabulary*, which is detailed, painstaking and accurate lexicography. In a letter to Elizabeth Wright, wife of his former tutor, Tolkien confessed that he 'certainly lavished an amount of time on it, which is terrible to recall'. But the hard work is necessary.

Another eccentric in Tolkien's fiction is Bilbo himself, particularly in his later years when we meet him again in *LOTR*. But even in *The Hobbit*, Bilbo stands out among his peers. The experience in the wild changes him: he becomes a poet capable of composing – almost literally on the hoof as they guide their ponies towards the Hill – the impressive final poem 'Roads go ever on' three or four pages before the end of *The Hobbit*. And Bilbo finds that his adventures in foreign parts mean that he has lost his respectability and his reputation back at home. Some locals even refuse to believe he is the real Bilbo, but the narrator tells us that Bilbo has changed so much that he does not care. He takes to writing poetry and visiting elves, and many denizens of the Hill shake their heads over 'Poor Old Baggins'. And in the sequel *LOTR*, or *The Return of the Shadow* as it was called in the late 1930s, Bilbo has become something of a scholar and the author of his adventures (the conceit is that *There and Back Again* is actually written by Bilbo himself); in Rivendell he is a bit of recluse, who likes to keep apart from the festive company and compose his own poems in the Hall of Fire.

In many ways he also resembles the old hard-working philologist Rúmil, chasing the shifts and changes of the tongues of men and women, the hard stuff out of which he will fashion his songs and tales.

Fig. 14c   A green man (based on a medieval carving)

Chapter Fifteen

Rhymes and riddles

The origin of nursery rhymes

I N HIS LECTURE *On Fairy-stories*, Tolkien argued that many fairy-stories are very ancient, since related narratives often appear in very early records. Nursery lore is a similar case; as he writes in a footnote, for the very useful folklore of tradition is passed on by the rustic child-minder to her charges, even though her supposed 'betters' have neglected it.[1] In short, Tolkien was convinced that the old folklore had been relegated to the children's play-room along with the old-fashioned furniture that the adults no longer want.

As we saw in chapter 13, Tolkien used the philological method of recon-struction when writing his fiction in order to explore the origins of old words or to revive meanings that may possibly have attached to them. The same method can be applied to nursery rhymes. In his second poem in *A Northern Venture*, for example, Tolkien turns from faery vision to nursery rhyme. 'Why the Man in the Moon Came Down too Soon' is a nursery rhyme with a difference; for Tolkien, it is a poem with a long-standing tradi-tion behind it, a case of nonsense verse reworking an old myth. In terms of purpose and humour, there are parallels here with another comic poem 'The Cat and the Fiddle', published simultaneously in a sister publication *Yorkshire Poetry*. Here in the subtitle Tolkien claims to reveal the original poem that lies behind the nursery rhyme 'Hey diddle diddle ... the cow jumped over the moon'.[2] The serious point behind the tomfoolery is that traditional texts often have a long oral history before they end up in the children's library.

'The Man in the Moon Came Down too Soon'

The traditional nursery rhyme that Tolkien had in mind runs as follows:

> The man in the moon came down too soon,
> and asked his way to Norwich,
> he went by the south and burnt his mouth
> By supping on cold plum porridge.

Much of this might be dismissed as purely nonsensical rhyming: the man came down too soon, because *soon* rhymes with *moon*; he went to *Norwich* so he had to have *porridge*. What Tolkien purports to explain in his poem 'The Man in the Moon had Silver Shoon' is the actual reason '*why* the Man in the Moon came down too soon'. In Tolkien's poem, written originally in 1915, the Man in the Moon is tired of his 'pallid minaret' (the lunar tower in which he lives) and wishes to escape his 'great white globe' of pearls and diamonds in order to be merry and free, so he fashions a staircase of filigree and slips down it towards the earth – the golden world of colour that he longs for, with its rubies and emeralds and sapphires.[3] He looks forward with anticipation to the solid meat and robust red wine that he knows the earth can provide. But then comes the mishap. He trips on a stair and falls headlong into the foaming bath of the North Sea, where he is picked up in the net of a Yarmouth fishing boat, whose amazed crew pack him off to Norwich to dry off. But although the bells of Norwich ring with the news, there is no one to greet him, for like Hugh Smith's poem about the vision of the Yorkshire shepherd, everyone else is 'abed'. In the end he has to barter his fairy cloak for a space to sit in the corner of a kitchen, where all there is to eat is a bowl of cold plum porridge, which he pays for with a priceless jewel. He has arrived much too soon on his quest 'from the Mountains of the Moon'. This then is the explanation announced in the title, and much of it reads like an extended piece of nonsense verse in the tradition of Edward Lear or Lewis Carroll.

But there are a number of mythic overtones in the poem that connoisseurs of *The Tale of the Sun and the Moon* in Tolkien's *Book of Lost Tales* will not fail to hear, though ironically it is not recorded that any contemporary readers of *A Northern Venture* had actually read that story. (Apart from the few close friends and associates in the know, Tolkien seems to have kept his private mythology to himself at this stage in his career.) In the ongoing frame narrative of the *Lost Tales*, this (eighth) story is told by Lindo, the host of the Cottage of Lost Play, in a voice 'most pleasant to hearken to of all tale-tellers'. It is a long narrative, full of rich descriptions worth reading in their own right; there is space only for the briefest of summaries here. As Lindo begins, the disastrous moment in the *Silmarillion* narrative – the killing by Morgoth and Ungoliant of the two light-bearing Trees of Valinor – has just taken place; the silmarils have been stolen, and the Noldoli have fled Valinor for the Great Lands of Middle-earth. The world is now in darkness and the Gods are making various vain attempts to revive the two defunct trees. By a combination of the hard-earned magic of the nature goddess Yavanna and the gentle love of Vána and the devotional song of Lórien, the trees are given a last lease of life, enough to bring forth the marvellous fruit and delicate rose that develop into the bright golden Sun and the lesser silver Moon. These are then placed in special vessels that can traverse the winds of the air at regular intervals, and thus the cycle of day and night is created, and the waxing and waning of the lunar month.

Along with the highly imaginative descriptions that he provides, in which the energy that is light is conceived of in mythic terms as a kind of buoyant liquid, Tolkien manages to inject unexpected drama into the mythic events. The creation of the Sun is a surprise unlooked for. The tears of Vána for the dead Tree of Gold have a reviving effect and the stock puts forth one last branch before it dies, on which golden blossoms bloom until a fruit develops like a vast golden globe, which – not without some opposition – Aulë and Tulkas divide into two halves and carry off to be fashioned into a 'vessel like a great ship broad of beam'. As for the moment when the Moon is engendered, this also is fraught with tension, for Lórien is ambitious, and yearns to produce – unaided on his own – a light equal to that of the Sun. And as the silver Rose swells into a flower of ten thousand petals it becomes too heavy for the frail branch, which snaps, causing the Rose of Sílpion to fall, losing some of its light and some of its petals.[4] Appropriately, the vessel that bears the Moon is constructed of a special substance as thin as the petal of a rose and as transparent as glass. The rose itself is placed in a crystal cup, and rods of ice rise from the vessel to serve as aëry masts, with sails held to them by slender threads.

An Old Norse mythological poem that Tolkien knew well lists the names of the moon, each appointed to a different being or race:

> THOR   What is the moon called, that men see,
>   In all the worlds there are?

ALVIS   *Moon* by men, *The Ball* by gods,
  The Whirling Wheel in Hel,
The Speeder by giants, *The Bright One* by dwarves,
  By elves *Tally-of-Years*.[5]

The passage probably provided some inspiration for Tolkien, although in his own mythology the list of names is further elaborated philologically: Rána the Moon, Sil the Rose, Isaluntë the silver shallop, Minethlos the argent isle, and Crithoscelog the disc of glass.[6]

All this (the cosmology, the elaborate descriptions, the names) forms the mythic background to Tolkien's moon poem in *A Northern Venture* (which can be read, of course, most conveniently in Tolkien's volume of verse *The Adventures of Tom Bombadil*). *The Tale of the Sun and Moon* also usefully explains some of the otherwise inexplicable details that inform the text of the poem; for instance, the mention of silver, ivory and crystal and other details of materials in the opening lines.

When the moon-man plunges into the sea, the 'shimmering wet' colours of bluey white and liquid green suggest again Tolkien's mythic, non-scientific concept of light as a precious liquid.

In his use of the old plural *shoon* for 'shoes', Tolkien perhaps remembered the lines from G.B. Smith's *Spring Harvest*, 'A Preface for a Tale I have Never Told', which ends with the lines:

A tale that shod itself with ancient shoon
And wrapped its cloak, and wandered from the west.[7]

The Cat and the Fiddle

Tolkien's *The Cat and the Fiddle* is based on a well-known nursery rhyme that exists in many versions, since it circulated orally; it was first published around 1765 in *Mother Goose's Melody* with the wording as follows:

High diddle diddle,
The Cat played the Fiddle,
The Cow jump'd over the Moon,
The little dog laugh'd to see such Craft,
And the Dish ran away with the Spoon.[8]

The great folklorist James Orchard Halliwell (1820–89) published the following version:

> Hey! diddle diddle,
> The cat and the fiddle,
> The cow jumped over the moon;
> The little dog laugh'd
> To see the sport,
> While the dish ran after the spoon.[9]

This more modern version has replaced *craft* with the more understandable *sport*; such changes in a poem transmitted by word of mouth is common, and it of course suggests that the original may well have been very different. Since the rhyme is alluded to in Thomas Preston's play *Cambyses King of Persia* (1569), it is possible that it has much older roots, and various theories have been propounded to show that it had a topical, political or even mythological significance.

Tolkien's two Man-in-the-Moon poems are closely connected, published in the same year by the same publisher, but he was not the first modern poet to link the two original nursery rhymes. As a study by Johnston has revealed, the Victorian poet and fantasist George MacDonald, whose writings Tolkien had read as a child, also wrote a Man-in-the-Moon poem.[10] It appears in the 'Another Early Bird' episode in the children's novel *At the Back of the North Wind* (1870). In an episode illustrating the truth of the proverb that the early bird catches the worm, this chapter tells how young Diamond goes out driving his father's hansom cab to earn money when his father is ill.[11] Arriving safely home, Diamond sings the song to the baby in the cradle:

> Hey! diddle diddle!
> The cat and the fiddle!
> He played such a merry tune,
> That the cow went mad
> With pleasure she had,
> And jumped right over the moon.
> But then, don't you see?
> Before that could be,
> The moon had come down and listened.
> The little dog hearkened

So loud that he barkened,
'There's nothing quite like it, there isn't.'

Like Tolkien's poem, MacDonald's Man in the Moon has descended to earth, which explains how it is possible for a cow to jump high enough to actually sail over the moon. MacDonald's poem continues in a similar rationalising vein and goes on to explain what happened to the dish and the spoon, namely that they are stolen by the Man in the Moon, who coming back too soon 'from the famous town of Norwich' finds they are just what he needs to eat his plum-porridge without burning his mouth. While Tolkien's poem does not follow this explanation, it does give a further reason why the moon is on earth – he has stayed up too late drinking fine brown ale. (A similar story written in the 'Father Christmas Letter' for 1927 sees the Man in the Moon staying too long at the North Pole, because he stays up late drinking brandy, while in his absence the dragons on the moon cause an eclipse with the smoke from their fiery breath, and the Man in the Moon has to rush back home to sort out the chaos.)

As Shippey has shown, Tolkien connected the rhyme with the Middle English poem known as 'Mon in the Mone', in which the local villagers rescue the Moon from the local jail by bribing the bailiff with drink.[12] This poem is found in a manuscript miscellany of over a hundred texts written in English, French and Latin in about the year 1340, probably in the Shropshire region in the west of England.[13] The western locality may well have appealed to Tolkien, as is argued elsewhere in this book (chapter 5), for he felt at home in the west of England and admired the dialects and literary culture of the region. It perhaps gave him his idea to use the poem in his own way in his fiction.

Outside poetry, however, the mythological concept of the moon had a limited role in Tolkien's novels. Mythological tales are one thing and novels with their realist demands are another – it is better to suggest, allude to and hint at any background mythology rather than spell it out fully. The alternative is to write a comic poem, to use it as entertainment in the manner of the Middle English 'Man in the Mone'. Accordingly, Tolkien used the poem as a comic moment in the scene at the Prancing Pony at Brill in *FR* when Frodo sings the poem as a partypiece and rather foolishly puts on his ring of invisibility at the crucial moment, to the disgust of the locals, who see it as some kind of uncanny conjuring trick that has been played on them in their crowded pub.

Anglo-Saxon riddles

In a broadly comparable way, the other two of Tolkien's four contributions to *A Northern Venture* develop further this idea of tracing back the origin of nursery rhymes. Ostensibly as editor, Tolkien here publishes two poems written in Anglo-Saxon (i.e. in Old English). Their Latin title *Enigmata Saxonica Nuper Inventa Duo*, 'Two Recently Invented Saxon Riddles', is a linguistic joke in itself, since the older meaning of *inventa* is 'discovered', and it implies that this is a traditional scholarly edition of two previously unpublished texts. Nevertheless, although they are new compositions, Tolkien's two poems imitate the format and style of the genuine Old English riddles that are to be found in the famous Exeter Book manuscript.

There are about ninety Old English riddles (the figure depends partly on where the various modern editors have placed breaks in the text), all of which explore in a poetic style the unusual or intriguing aspects of the objects, phenomena and creatures of the world, human or otherwise. Almost animistic in style (though not in their Christian religious content), the riddles frequently personify the subject of the poem and give that subject a speaking voice. Often, though not always, a line near the end of the poem declares 'Tell me what my name is – say what I am called', demanding that the reader or listener come to a decision.

Here is a sample of a genuine Old English riddle, with a solution relevant to Tolkien's 'Riddles in the Dark' chapter in *The Hobbit*:

Nis min sele swige, ne ic sylfa hlud
ymb ...... unc dryhten scop
sith ætsomne. Ic eom swiftre thonne he,
thragum strengra, he threohtigra.
Hwilum ic me reste; he sceal yrnan forth.
Ic him in wunige a thenden ic lifge;
gif wit unc gedælath, me bith death witod.

[My hall is not silent nor am I myself loud
The Lord made
our journey together. I am swifter than he,
at times stronger, while he is more persistent.
Sometimes I rest, but he must keep running.
I dwell in him for the time that I live;
If we part, I am dead for sure.][14]

Two travellers, one loud, the other quiet: the Lord made their journey together and when they part it is certain death. Is this is a poem about the soul in the body? If so, why does the soul – the speaker – describe herself as swifter and stronger, although the body is more persistent? The listener will need to rethink, a common experience when reading a riddle. The answer to this riddle is of course 'a fish in a running river'.

It is important to realise that the riddles are not always about living creatures, even if they present themselves as such. Both Tolkien's riddles follow the common pattern. His first, 'Meolchwitum sind marmanstane', may be translated as follows:

> In milk-white marblestone
> my walls are wondrously adorned;
> a soft garment is hung inside,
> most like to silk; afterwards in the middle
> a well is fashioned, water clear as glass;
> Gold glistens there, held in the running streams,
> the most beautiful of apples. No one has entry
> to my stronghold; nevertheless
> bold thieves burst in on my glorious palace
> and steal the treasure – tell me what my name is!

At first the speaker sounds like the owner of a rich house that he has hung with silk tapestries, a *thryth-ærn* or 'glorious palace' as it is later called, with its own garden where the trees drop golden apples into the clear water running from a well. But the thieves break in and take the treasure.

Is this a classical myth? Or is it another version of the Fall of Gondolin? Or perhaps the story of Thingol in his wonderful cave in Doriath, where Úrin brought the treasure of Glorund the dragon? None of these solutions fit entirely. In actual fact, the poem is designed to show the world of an egg from a different perspective: the eggshell is the marble lined with silk, the egg white is the well of clear water, the yolk is like a golden apple. Once the solution is found, the riddle can be put aside, but poems of this kind demand intense engagement and do have their serious side. For a minute or two of concentration, while the reader or listener contemplates the riddle in their mind, the everyday object takes on new life, it becomes wondrous and precious. Such is the appeal of the Anglo-Saxon riddle as 'a poem in its own right', and Tolkien captures the style very skilfully. To add to the sense of playfulness that is also characteristic of the genre, Tolkien makes the poem a version of a traditional nursery rhyme; as Rateliff demonstrates in his *History of the Hobbit*, the following nursery rhyme is the likely source of the poem:

> In marble walls as white as milk
> Lined with a skin as soft as silk,
> Within a fountain crystal-clear,
> A golden apple doth appear.
> No doors are there to this stronghold,
> Yet thieves break in and steal the gold.[15]

Tolkien's conceit is that the Saxon riddle 'Meolchwitum sind marmanstane' is the putative 'original version' of the later nursery rhyme. The rhyme 'In marble walls as white as milk' certainly might easily give the impression of being very ancient; on the whole its language is modern, but the individual words of the text have a long history, and most of them can be traced back to Old English, such as *walls*, *milk* and *white*, which come from *wagas*, *meolc* and *hwit* (riddle, line 1), notable exceptions being words like *fountain*, *clear*, *appear*, which go back to French, and entered the English language in the medieval period.

The riddle contest

As Tolkien later admitted, of course, a reduced version of the egg-riddle also appears in the episode 'Riddles in the Dark', chapter 5 of *The Hobbit*,.[16] In this episode the riddle is Bilbo's, and he uses it at a tight moment to gain time in the life-or-death riddle game that he is playing with the creature Gollum, who he thinks will easily guess this old chestnut. The solution is ever-present on Bilbo's mind: he has been day-dreaming for some time now of eggs and bacon in his kitchen at home, as the beginning of the chapter reveals, since he is lost in a dark tunnel, with no obvious way out, and with nothing to eat or drink. In fact, Gollum has spent so long brooding down in the darkness at the roots of the mountains that he has almost forgotten the outside world of wind and sunlight, birds on the wing, and eggs in a nest.

Bilbo for a moment thinks he is free, but Gollum thinks back to his earlier life (as later readers of *LOTR* will discover, Gollum was once in his earlier life a kind of hobbit), and he remembers the proverb 'teaching his grandmother

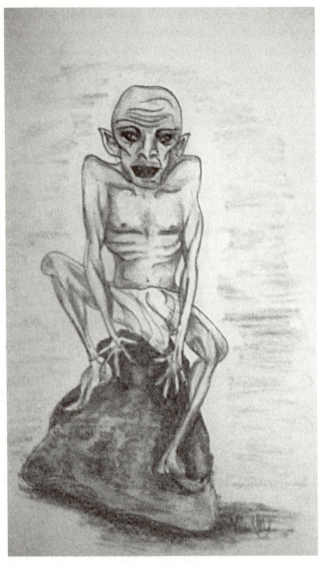

Fig. 15a 'Eggses!'

to suck – Eggses!' Responding in kind, Gollum asks a 'poser' to Bilbo about
a creature dressed in mail and always drinking, which Bilbo manages to
solve only just in time to escape Gollum's murderous grasp, when a startled
fish leaps in the lake near where he is sitting. Clearly, Gollum had also been
pondering his usual morning breakfast.

There is a dark almost pantomime humour about this riddle game, despite the life-or-death wager that Bilbo has agreed to make. Bilbo even teases Gollum when he cannot guess the egg-riddle, and when the roles are reversed and Bilbo cannot solve the fish-riddle, he objects on the grounds of fairness that Gollum should give him half a moment longer before he eats him, just as Bilbo had given Gollum plenty of time in the previous round. The dark humour may owe something to the sources Tolkien used, such as the anonymous collection of Old Norse poetry known as the *Elder Edda*. In 'The Words of the All-Wise', a poem in this collection, the god Thor, who disapproves of the dwarf Alvis, promises to give him permission to marry his daughter only if he can answer his questions about 'all the worlds there are'. So Alvis, for example, tells him the names of the *night*, among many other phenomena:

> THOR   What is night called, that Nor fathered,
>   In all the worlds there are?
> ALVIS   *Night* by men, *The Dark* by gods,
>   By holy powers *The Hood*,
>   *Unlight* by giants, by elves *Sleep-Pleasure*,
>   By dwarves *Spinner-of-Dreams*.

Thor keeps Alvis busy doling out his wisdom through all the hours of darkness until, as he discourses on the names of *ale*, the dawn breaks and the dwarf is turned back into the mountain stone out of which he was made. In *The Hobbit*, Tolkien borrowed this episode for the chapter at Trollshaws in which Gandalf tricks the three trolls into arguing and bickering until the break of day, when they too are turned into stone.

These Norse stories, which Tolkien was studying and teaching in the 1920s and 1930s, form a solid layer of influence on the invention and then writing of *The Hobbit*. Partly this is mood, and cultural background, but the influence even touches details of plot and event. Bilbo, for example, wins his riddle competition partly by luck and partly also by a kind of trick, for he touches the magic ring as he nervously puts his hand in his pocket and quite inadvertently asks out loud the question 'what have I got in my pocket?' Gollum, who had been pressing Bilbo with his 'ask us, ask us' now makes his mistake. He insists that Bilbo 'ask another question' rather than 'ask another *riddle*' (as he meant to say); in so doing he inadvertently changes the actual game they are playing. The riddle competition is sacred, says the narrator, and no one may cheat, but now the dialogue has shifted to a guessing game in which Gollum has three guesses to work out what Bilbo actually does have in his pocket. And Gollum even cheats on his third turn by delivering two guesses instead of one, neither of which is correct. Bilbo has won the game. Again there is a Norse analogue, which must have given Tolkien the idea. In 'The Lay of Vafthrudnir', also in the *Poetic Edda*, the god Odin matches his wit in a 'word-joust' with the giant Vafthrudnir, and he wins the dispute on a technicality with his final question:

> What did Odin whisper in the ears of his son
> before Baldur was borne to the pyre?

This is the one question to which only Odin, as father of the much-lamented Baldur, can know the answer. It effectively puts the game to an end.[17]

Dialogues of this kind often function as a mnemonic, a convenient and interesting narrative device for memorising and passing down traditional wisdom or the facts of cosmology or mythology. In Old English prose there are the didactic dialogues known as *Solomon and Saturn* and *Adrian and Ritheus*, in which representatives of Christian and pagan wisdom ask questions and exchange their wisdom and learning. In Old English verse there is the similarly-named *Poetic Dialogues of Solomon and Saturn*, in which the two speakers are much more clearly in some sort of dispute or competition than they are in the similarly named prose dialogue. In this game, each participant in turn is given a chance to pose a riddle, to which the other has to respond with a full explanation. The riddle on old-age in this dialogue is the likely source for Gollum's time-riddle. In the Old Norse *Saga of King Heidrek the Wise*, Odin disguised as Gestumblindi takes part in a similar riddle dispute with King Heidrek. The line 'What lives with out breath? Hverr andalauss liffir?' perhaps suggested the fish riddle that Tolkien used for *The Hobbit*. Another similarity is that Odin also 'cheats' with his final question and so wins the competition:

> What said Odin
> in the ear of Baldur,
> before he was borne to the fire?

'You alone know that, vile creature!' cried King Heidrek, and he drew Tyrfing and slashed at Odin, but he changed himself into the shape of a hawk and flew away; yet the king, striking after him, took off his tailfeathers, and that is why the hawk has been so short-tailed ever since.[18]

'Riddles in the Dark' in *The Hobbit* is Tolkien's own take on the exchange-of-knowledge or riddle competition, a common theme in early medieval dialogue literature, combining humour, danger and the memorisation of traditional lore and learning. It also shows the other aspect of the philologist's task of reconstruction: tracing back old stories and finding rational explanations of how they began in the far distant past.

Fig. 15b   Reader with gull on his head (statue)

Chapter Sixteen

Dialect matters

As Tolkien shaped and re-shaped his Shire during the writing of the first chapters of the sequel to *The Hobbit*, he began to explore further the possibilities of using dialect words and expressions. He was not a dialect speaker himself, though he knew and admired the regional speech of Western Mercia (the West Midlands), where he had been brought up. His enthusiasm for other varieties of English was not merely personal; he had a strong professional interest in dialect, particularly northern dialect, kindled not only by his residence in Leeds and acquaintance with such dialect specialists as Joe Wright and Hugh Smith, but also by his interest in Chaucer and the poet of *Sir Gawain and the Green Knight* and their two, very different, uses of northern dialect in their poetry. *The Hobbit* contains surprisingly little overt dialect speech, but, like Old and Middle English, Tolkien used dialect as a source of inspiration, from which he drew new words and ideas for his writing.

First we need a definition. What is dialect? Essentially, dialects are the other varieties of spoken English; these exist in local regions alongside the standard variety but do not derive from it. In her book *Rustic Speech and Folk-Lore* (1913), Elizabeth Wright challenged the linguistic prejudices of her day:

> Among common errors still persisting in the minds of educated people, one error which dies very hard is the theory that a dialect is an arbitrary distortion of the mother tongue, a wilful mispronunciation of the sounds, and disregard of the syntax of a standard language.[1]

Like other philologists of the late nineteenth and early twentieth centuries, such as Joseph Wright and his wife Elizabeth, Tolkien studied non-standard varieties of English, particularly country dialects, for two principal reasons. First, the dialects illustrated the life of natural language, the way the sounds of English change or develop when untrammelled by the orthography – that is, by the rules of the spelling and grammar books. Second, the dialects preserved the heritage of the English language: in dialects there remained in use older words that the standard language had long since abandoned earlier in its history. At university Tolkien perhaps read the study of the dialect of the southern counties of Scotland by James Murray, editor of the *OED*. And he certainly knew his tutor Joseph Wright's imposing *English Dialect Dictionary*, or *EDD* as he called it. As he wrote in a letter to Elizabeth Wright while teaching at the University of Leeds in the 1920s, he regarded the *EDD* as indispensable and encouraged his students to browse in it.[2] Likely enough he knew Joseph Wright's scholarly treatise on his Windhill dialect as well as the books and studies by his wife Elizabeth. And with them he no doubt believed that 'the study of our English dialects may … give us a clearer insight into the life and character of the British peasant and artisan'.

Dialect speakers in Tolkien's fiction

In scenes that came to be set in the Shire in *LOTR*, the dialogues are peppered with dialect words and usages:

drownded	'drowned'
worriting	'getting worried'
mistook	'mistaken'

The last two are spoken by Farmer Maggot, as we saw in chapter 5 an interesting and idiosyncratic local character if ever there was one. One lively specimen of his talk is to be found in the earlier version of the novel written in 1938, shortly after *The Hobbit* had been published. Here the farmer is telling the hobbits about the visit of the Black Rider to his farm. The passage needs to be quoted at length, for it is the combination of words and their repeated patterns that give the impression of a rich and colourful dialect: collocations such as 'rare memory', 'funny customer', the last with its extended use of the idea of *customer*, meaning here 'someone who wants to acquire something':

'Well now, let me see – you'll be Mr Frodo Took, Mr Folco Took's son, if I'm not mistook (and I seldom am: I've a rare memory for faces). You used to stay with young Mr Marmaduke. Any friend of Mr Marmaduke Brandybuck is welcome. You'll excuse my speaking sharp, before I recognised you. We get some strange folk in the parts at times. Too near the river,' he said, jerking back his head. 'There's been a very funny customer round here only an hour back. That's why I'm out with the dog.'[3]

In this way of talking, the dialect colour is found also in the pattern of the grammar; for instance, the adverb in 'speaking sharp' rather than *speaking sharply*, or 'an hour back' instead of the more standard *an hour ago*, this latter combined with the tense 'there's been' rather than *there was*. The past participle 'mistook' is a typical example. This is considered 'wrong' in Standard English, but as any philologist would point out it is not ungrammatical, since it simply follows a natural tendency in the language to level together past tense and past participle. For example, if we take a regular verb like *deceive* or *dupe*, the past tense and the past participle are identical, so that we find *he deceived me* and *I was deceived*, or *he duped me* and *I was duped*, are the standard forms. The logic of dialect grammar is to extend the pattern to other verbs such as *mistake* so that the past tense in *I mistook* and the past participle in *I was mistook* are identical in form.

The local vernacular adds flavour to a person's speech. It goes well with humour, for *mistook* is also a pun in the context of recognising someone with the surname Took; it also goes with hospitality 'to pass the news more comfortable' over 'a drop of good ale' (*FR* in *LOTR*, book I, chapter 4); less attractively perhaps but understandably it also goes with a liking for conventional respectability and a natural suspicion for *outlandish* characters, although this is another philological joke, since the modern extended meaning of the adjective *outlandish* is 'funny, strange' but originally it derives from Old English *utlendisc*, meaning literally 'out-landish' (i.e. 'outsider, from out of this land'). On the whole, dialect is treated with respect here; there is little sense of social snobbery in Tolkien's presentation.

An exception would be the three trolls that Bilbo and his fellow-travellers encounter in the second chapter of *The Hobbit*, for Tolkien has them speaking dialect for deliberately absurd, comic effects. The first time we hear one of the trolls speak is when he captures the hobbit in the act of theft; in fact, Bilbo is rather foolishly attempting to pick his pocket. William, otherwise known as Bill Huggins, and Bert are the quite unexpected names of two of these monsters; while the third has the similarly workaday name of Tom. Rather improbably, to judge by the question 'what are yer?', the trolls are from working-class London. Certainly, Bill Huggins's magic talking purse with its ''ere 'oo are you?' has the unmistakable Cockney h-dropping that was such a shibboleth or classic test of 'vulgar' speech in writings on language and etiquette from the second half of the nineteenth century; everyone loved to hate h-dropping.[4] As Tolkien had written in an academic paper around the same time as he wrote this chapter of *The Hobbit*: 'a sound will be dubbed uncouth by speakers of another dialect, owing to its contrast to the familiar sound. It may well be current in their own speech in another context'.[5] The phenomenon of h-dropping does occur in some contexts in standard southern speech, but when the unaccustomed sound appears in a common word the effect is 'all the more odd and laughable'.[6]

Dialect is also marked by vocabulary and choice of word. In the *OED* *lumme* is explained as 'a corruption of *Lord love me*' (an odd turn of phrase for a troll!) while 'blimey' is defined as a 'vulgar corruption of the imprecation *blind me!* or *blame me!*' Citations that the *OED* gives from the period include one from James Joyce's *Ulysses* (1922) and another from the children's author Richmal Crompton:

> 'Blimey!' said Charlemagne.
> 'Pardon him, dear,' said Miss Milton in a shaking voice. 'He doesn't often use bad language.'[7]

As Tolkien himself pointed out in a paper on Chaucer's use of dialect written in the period when he was working on *The Hobbit*, dialect used in a novel is only likely to amuse its readers if they have some actual experience of it and can laugh at their own memories of it.[8] This must be the reason for Tolkien's use of the dialect of London in *The Hobbit*; it is 'more or less intelligible', and amusing for at least two reasons. It was familiar to readers, for everyone in Britain knew about Cockney as an English accent and would have heard it on visits to the nation's capital city; moreover, there was a tradition of depicting Cockney speakers in novels, the best-known example being the writings of Charles Dickens. At the same time, Cockney would be amusing in *The Hobbit* because of the sheer element of surprise: readers do not expect to hear it here. With their h-dropping and their urban usages *blimey* and *lumme* and *cop*, the language of the trolls is the closest that Tolkien sails to 'bad language' in *The Hobbit*.

Fig. 16a *''Ere, oo are you?'*

Chaucer, *The Reeve's Tale*

Chaucer was an author Tolkien knew well – he had been involved for many years in an editing project 'the Clarendon Chaucer' that he never found time to complete, much to the exasperation of the commissioning editor, his former colleague (and former tutor) Kenneth Sisam.[9] In Chaucer's celebrated *The Canterbury Tales*, a rough-and-ready set of pilgrims en route from London to the shrine of St Thomas Becket at Canterbury pass the time by telling tales of various sorts. Famously, in each case, Chaucer devoted plenty of space to the narrative of the frame – the ride by the pilgrims to Canterbury, their boisterous conversations at the inn and their vivid and memorable characters. As was suggested in part II of this book, Chaucer's tale collection (along with the ones by Boccaccio and Snorri) perhaps helped to inspire Tolkien's own *Book of Lost Tales*.

A fact not often mentioned is that Tolkien was working on Chaucer's *The Reeve's Tale* at the same time as he was writing *The Hobbit*, in the early 1930s. Coincidentally, both stories begin in a small village with a water-mill (Middle English *melle*):

At Trumpyngtoun, nat fer fro Cantebrigge,
Ther gooth a brook, and over that a brigge,
Upon the whiche brook ther stant a melle;
And this is verray sooth that I yow telle:
A millere ther was dwellynge many a day.[10]

Did Chaucer's tale contribute to the depiction of Hobbiton in *The Hobbit*? It is certainly possible, although there is of course no hill of any height in Trumpington.

Otherwise, it must be said that, like his interest in *Babbitt*, Tolkien's interest in this text may at first sight seem surprising. *The Reeve's Tale* is a comic and decidedly bawdy and violent example of the *fabliau*. This medieval comic genre verges on a parody of the courtly romance; it has lower-status characters (rather than lords, knights and ladies) and rather foolish anti-heroes, who expend most of their efforts playing tricks and deceptions on other characters in the story. In particular, *The Reeve's Tale* relates comically the revenge taken on a thieving miller in East Anglia by two *clerkes* – that is, students – both from the north of England, who are studying at Soler Hall at the University of Cambridge. The miller cheats the students and their college out of their corn, and the two students cheat on the miller in a bedroom farce with his wife and buxom daughter. There is a kind of moral to the tale: the miller is a proud social climber, and a villain, and aggressive with it, but he ends up with a crack on the head given to him accidentally by his own wife in the dark – a case of mistaken identity – and the students beat him for good measure.

In 1934, not long after he had finished his children's novel, Tolkien published his paper 'Chaucer as a philologist: *The Reeve's Tale*', which he had read to the London Philological Society in 1931. His main purpose was linguistic: to demonstrate the accuracy of Chaucer's use of northern dialect in the story. Before considering his argument it is useful to rehearse some of the language background to Chaucer's tale.

In terms of its language, *The Reeve's Tale* is unusual in Middle English literature; aside from the Townley Shepherd's play, a medieval mystery play about Christ's Nativity, this tale is probably the first English text in which dialect is used firstly for comic effect, to make fun of another form of English, and secondly for realism, to depict realistically the speech of a character from a different region of England. In the age of the novel, particularly from the nineteenth century onwards, modern readers have become used to this; writers often put dialect into the mouths of their rustic and urban characters. But here this is a relatively new phenomenon. In the Middle Ages there was no standard form of English speech; every scribe or scrivain wrote in his or her own dialect and sometimes changed the grammatical forms and spellings of the poem they were copying to make it fit their own ways of speaking and writing. Most people spoke their regional dialect, whatever their social standing, as is still the case with German dialect speakers in modern Switzerland, and when they travelled they used their dialect in attempts to communicate, apparently to the consternation of the locality they were visiting. One southern writer, John Trevisa, in the fourteenth century complained that northern speech was 'scharp, slytting, and frotyng, and unschape',[11] but gave no examples. Chaucer took up the challenge.

Typically, Tolkien begins his discussion with the sounds of the living spoken language: one of the first prerequisites for the study of any dialect is to actually hear it spoken. Tolkien insists that the tale has to be read out loud, ideally by an accomplished renderer: Tolkien himself was suitably skilled at this (he was later commissioned by the Poet Laureate John Masefield to do a reading of Chaucer's *The Reeve's Tale* at the festival of Summer Diversions in Oxford in 1939). Here, however, he refers in passing to one accomplished performer, Henry Cecil Wyld (1870–1945), the Merton Professor of English Language and Literature at Oxford, and a well-known philologist, phonetician and historian of the English language. Tolkien was evidently on friendly terms with Wyld: the two scholars shared an interest in things Finnish, and Tolkien once recalled Wyld demolishing a table of cups, saucers and afternoon tea in an exuberant gesture as he imitated the oral performance of a Finnish bard reciting the legendary epic the *Kalevala*.[12]

A few passages will illustrate the way dialect works in the tale; the first point is the pronunciation: the use of the *a* vowel where the Southern dialect has *o*: so John says their purpose is to purchase corn and carry it 'ham' (for *home*), and Aleyn the clerk says 'this lange nyght' for *this longe nyght*, and John says he wants to watch the milling process to see 'howgates the corn gas in' for what in Southern would be to see *how the corn gooth in*. Northern grammatical forms here include the -s ending on the present tense of the verb (this has now of course become the standard modern English form). Vocabulary creates humour: John says about the college manciple 'I hope he wil be deed', where – as Tolkien points out – *hope* means to 'expect without wishing'. Chaucer used *hope* here primarily for humorous reasons. A classic example of dialect humour for Tolkien is John's soliloquy when he berates himself about his cowardice, whereas his fellow student Aleyn is boldly seizing the moment with the miller's daughter. John feels he is a 'draf-sak' (a rubbish sack) for lying in bed (lines 4207–8):

> And when this jape is tald another day,
> I sal been hald a daf, a cokenay.

As Tolkien points out, 'cokenay' used by John in his soliloquy provides the *NED* with its first quotation for the sense 'milksop' for the word *cockney*. He argues that *cokenay* must literally mean a cock's egg and that it is a loan borrowed from southern English (which used *eye, aye* for 'egg'). This bluff northerner, according to Tolkien, does not wish to be called a 'milksop' when he rejoins his fellow students back in Cambridge[13].

What Tolkien argued in his study of the earliest manuscripts was that Chaucer had a sensitive ear for northern dialect and reproduced its chief features accurately in *The Reeve's Tale*. A recent study by Simon Horobin points out that many scribes at the time also had a feel for dialect and that some of the northernisms could have been introduced by northern scribes into the manuscripts.[14] Nevertheless, generally Tolkien's case still stands.

Sir Gawain and the Green Knight

Tolkien was drawn to the West Midlands and north west of England because he felt affinities with the dialect, folklore and culture of that region. The fourteenth-century *Sir Gawain and the Green Knight* (*SGGK*), probably his favourite Middle English alliterative poem, was an example of literature written in that dialect, and he was fascinated by the connections that could be drawn between the dialect of present-day Lancashire and Cheshire and that of the older poem. Tolkien not only edited the poem with E.V. Gordon, he also lectured on the themes of the poem and made his own verse translation.

Tolkien later wrote that *SGGK* is a 'romance, a fairy tale for adults, full of life and colour' and its other virtues are good scenery, urbane and humorous dialogue, and a skilfully ordered narrative. There are many possible ways in which *SGGK* has influenced Tolkien's writing in *The Hobbit*. Most obviously, both stories treat the theme of there and back again, a journey into the wild which has a profound effect on the protagonist, who returns a changed person. The landscape of forest and mountain journey dominates both stories:

Bi a mounte on the morne meryly he rydes
Into a forest ful dep, that ferly was wylde,
Highe hilles on uche a halve, and holtwodes under
Of hore okes ful hoge a hundredth togeder. (lines 740–4)

[Over a mountain in the morning meerily he rides deep into a forest, that was
wonderfully wild, with high hills on both sides and woodlands below of tall
grey oak-trees in their hundreds together.]

Another shared theme is that of the hospitality of halls, the 'guestkindliness' that was discussed earlier in this book in chapter 7. In *SGGK* there is the character of Bertilak, the genial host of the hall, who welcomes Gawain on his quest and provides him with food and entertainment during the Christmas feast, and sends him on his way fortified (as Gawain sees it) for his fateful meeting with the Green Knight at the Green Chapel. As Marjorie Burns reminds us, Tolkien's Beorn, whom Bilbo first sees as a huge man with thick black beard and legs with knotted muscles, leaning on a large axe, is reminiscent of Bertilak, who is also a shape-changer with an alter ego as the Green Knight, another wielder of a large and fearsome axe.[15]

For an example of the qualities that Tolkien admired in *SGGK* we might turn with profit to another scene of hospitality, in many ways a scene of hospitality flaunted and refused: the Challenge, the account of the marvellous Green Knight's entry into King Arthur's hall on a wondrous green horse, which he rides right up to the dais where Arthur, Guinevere and Gawain and other knights are sitting at their New Year feast. In his hands he carries two objects of opposing significance: the holly-branch and the war-axe, one representing the season of goodwill, the other the threat of violence. For a brief moment as he describes the *holyn bobbe* holly bundle (line 206) 'that is greatest in greenery when groves are leafless',[16] the poet transports readers or listeners out of the hall into the surrounding countryside, only to bring them back with a jolt as he describes the alien cruelty and worksmanship of the axe, a 'spetos sparthe' (ruthless weapon) (209). Five descriptive stanzas serve to show the passage of time, from the moment when the green knight 'hales in at the halle dor' (136) to the point where he is described as making his way to the high table on the raised dais 'drivande to the heghe dece' (222), during which time the revellers stare in stunned surprise: feasting their eyes, as it were, on this marvel that is passing before them.

Part of the effect is the arrangement and timing of the narrative as it proceeds in stanzas, each well marked by the so-called bob and wheel, a single stressed phrase followed by four short lines of rhyme. In the next stanza, for instance, the knight does not speak until the end of his ride – and the end of the stanza – when he calls out his question, and again the narrative focusses on the manner in which he *loked* – the force of his glance, his eyes interrogating each man in turn as he searches for his intended inter-locutor, the king:

> Haylsed he never one, bot heghe he over loked.
> The first word that he warp, 'Wher is', he sayd,
> 'The governor of ths gyng? Gladly I wolde
> Se that segg in syght, and with himself speke
> > raysoun.'
> > To knyghtes he kest his yge,
> > And reled hym up and doun;
> > he stemmed and con studie
> > Quo walt there most renoun.

This is an example of the vivid if formal dialogue that Tolkien found so attractive in the work of the *Gawain* poet. Tolkien's translation is widely available and it is interesting to see how he goes about rendering the Middle English idiom into something more modern. It will be seen, for example, that he adds a metrical tag of his own, *in town*, in imitation of the medieval bob, though it does not occur at precisely this point in the original. A modern translator, Simon Armitage, on the other hand, has a jauntier paraphrase:

> 'And who,' he bellows, without breaking breath,
> 'is governor of this gaggle? I'll be glad to know.
> It's with him and him alone that I'll have
> > my say.'
> > The green man steered his gaze
> > deep into every eye,
> > explored each person's face
> > to probe for a reply.[17]

It is partly a matter of taste which translation you may prefer. Armitage's rendering 'it's with him and him alone that I'll have my say' is a nice touch, and much more direct than Tolkien's 'for gladly I would on the same set my sight, and with himself now talk in town'. On the other hand, Tolkien's 'cast his eye and rolled it up and down' preserves something of the Green Knight's wild mannerism which Armitage's 'steered his gaze' has lost in translation.

What emerges from such comparisons is the question of poetic diction, the special vocabulary that poets use.[18] Armitage as a modern poet no doubt feels free of any restriction, while Tolkien sometimes appears hampered in his choice of phrase, partly by his education and by the Victorian and Edwardian poetic legacy that shaped it. But Tolkien also has a stronger sense of the tradition in which the *Gawain* poet was working, and he makes an attempt to preserve some of that tradition in his verse rendering.

The novelist Alan Garner has also felt this pull of the tradition. Garner belongs to the next generation after Tolkien, but without claiming direct influence he has followed a similar path as a writer, beginning with children's fantasies such as *The Weirdstone of Brisingamen* and moving towards deeper and severer themes in novels such as *The Owl Service* or *The Stone Book Quartet*. Old folklore, and the myths that it sometimes preserves, is one of the sources of his creativity, as is the language or dialect that he believes pertains to the landscape and location in which it is spoken.[19] Garner, who comes from Alderley Edge in the Cheshire countryside, on the other side of the Pennine Hills from West Yorshire, and who has set much of his fiction in that region, even goes as far as to claim that the speech of the *Gawain* poet is still alive in the dialect that he grew up with.

A New Glossary of the Dialect of the Huddersfield District

Many of the poems of the medieval Alliterative Revival were written in a north-western dialect to which Tolkien was attracted as much for personal as scholarly reasons. On his arrival at Leeds in 1920 he joined the Yorkshire Dialect Society, which had been founded by his erstwhile tutor Joseph Wright, and included an impressive array of philologists on its member-ship roll. He was keen to promote and foster dialect studies while teaching at Leeds, including the dialect of West Yorkshire where he was living. A classic instance of this is the foreword he wrote for Walter Haigh's *A New Glossary of the Dialect of the Huddersfield District*.[20] Walter Haigh (1856–1931), a member of the Council of the Yorkshire Dialect Society, taught at Huddersfield Technical College, where he was head of the English and History Department from 1890 to 1918, and subsequently an Emeritus Lecturer in English.[21] There was a tradition of writing glossaries of this kind, each focussing on the speech of a small region or locality. Joseph Wright had used such studies as a basis for his lexicographical project *The English Dialect*

Dictionary, taking his example sentences from their work, marked by an abbreviation; thus 'n.Yks.1' referred to the Rev. J.C. Atkinson's *Glossary of the Cleveland District* (1868), and 'Der.2' John Sleigh's *An Attempt at a Derbyshire Glossary* (1865), and so on. Haigh himself based his work on Alfred Easther's *A Glossary of the Dialect of Almondbury and Huddersfield* (1883).

Tolkien first saw a draft of Haigh's *New Glossary* in 1923, and he provided Haigh with encouragement and assurance of the value of the work 'not only to local patriotism, but to English philology generally'.[22] There may be various reasons for Tolkien's admiration for this particular dialect study. One is the high proportion of Scandinavian words in the dialect, for which Haigh's introductory chapter explores the likely reasons. Citing the terrible harrowing of the north by William the Conqueror's troops after the rebellion at York in 1069, Haigh speculates that the population of central Yorkshire dispersed, and that groups of them fled to the southern foot-hills and valleys of the West Riding.[23] Since, as recent historical studies of the Danelaw confirm, Yorkshire had a high proportion of Danish inhabitants going back to ninth-century settlements, it is likely that the new settlers and farmers were speakers of Danish, in other words a variety of Old Norse. Haigh presumably implies that the settlers in the region were at first bilingual speakers of Old Norse and Old English, and this meant that the English dialect which came to be spoken in the region now preserves a high proportion of Norse-derived words and farming terms. As a specialist in Old Norse, Tolkien naturally found this fact of enormous interest.

Another reason why Haigh's choice of the Huddersfield District attracted Tolkien was that this region is located in the south-west corner of the West Riding of Yorkshire bordering on the region of England (the north west and west) where – broadly speaking – his own local patriotic interests lay. For instance, he cites the following entry on p. 45 of the *Glossary*:

> gruch, *w.vb.*, to grutch, grudge;
> grumble. [ME. *grucchen*, to mur-
> mur; OFr. *grouchier, groucher*.]
> The word is used in Lancashire, and
> the W. Riding borders of it. See greẹs
> (2), which is much commoner here.

Where East Lancashire has *gruch*, the West Riding mostly uses the cognate *greẹs*, meaning 'to grouse, grumble, mutter', but similarly derived from Old French *grouchier, groucher* (to murmur). Historically, Huddersfield was located at a meeting point of different dialects; 'the scene of the swaying fortunes of different types of English since very early times', as Tolkien puts it.[24]

What Tolkien liked in a dialect dictionary was the selection of a limited geographical area and then a full coverage of all the words spoken in the dialect in that area. As his review of dialect studies in 1923 put it, there exists 'the illusion that only words not now present in the standard English are the ones that are worth recording or have an interest for philology'.[25] Tolkien felt that Haigh's *New Glossary* observed the principle of full coverage, and it was instructive for the philologist to see the form in which a standard word takes when spoken naturally in the dialect. A good example of what he means, taken at random, is the first page of the *New Glossary*, where there are twenty-three items, of which on my count at least eleven exist also in standard southern English:

> Huddersfield dialect: æv, æch, æftẹr, æk, ækẹrin, ækkẹr, æks, ækt, æktli, ælẹdi, æm
>
> Southern English: have, hatch, after, hack, acorn, acre, ask, act, actually, holiday, am.

In a glossary covering only exotic local words, the eleven items could well have been omitted, but their actual spoken forms and meanings differ greatly from the standard language; for example, *ækkẹr* means 'field' rather than simply 'acre', and *æktli* means 'really?', expressing surprise. Such words are part-and-parcel of the spoken language of the region, often with different idiomatic usages that could not and should not be ignored.

Linked to this was the gui de to pronunciation. Tolkien must have approved of the phonetic notation that Haigh had used to represent the words, rather than the traditional dialect spellings as used, for example, by novelists of the north of England such as Mrs Gaskell or the Brontë sisters. Thus, for example, the word *gradely*, 'fine, good', is spelt phonetically as *grēdli*. The tradition of using phonetics in dialectology went back to the Victorian philologists Henry Sweet and J.A.H. Murray, as well as to the great dialect lexicographer (and Tolkien's Oxford tutor) Joseph Wright, whom Haigh cites as a model. The advantage of the phonetic script was twofold: it not only gave a more accurate representation of the sounds, it also allowed for scientific comparison with other dialects or even with other periods in the history of the language.

Tolkien picks out for special mention the fact that history had appeared to repeat itself in some of the changes in the pronunciation of the vowels of the region; a similar sound change had occurred in Old English:

The pronunciation of Anglo-Saxon *ā, eā* was in all probability very similar indeed to the sounds that Mr. Haigh has represented by *au, eę*.[26]

Such a theoretical approach is found for instance in the writings of Sweet and Wright; philology is held to be scientific, like geology, and if processes of change – whether they are geomorphic shifts or slight changes in the articulation of certain vowel sounds or diphthongs – can be observed as taking place in the present time, then it is reasonable to extrapolate that under the same conditions the same changes must have also taken place in the past.

There was a sociological interest to the *Glossary*, which Tolkien the storyteller and future writer of 'Hobbitry' also enjoyed: the 'colloquial instances' that bring to life the speech of the region (p. xiv), the fact that Haigh includes short phrases and snatches of speech, or even monologues and dialogues to illustrate the use of words and expressions. The entry *ænt*, for instance, explains briefly that *aunt* has two separate forms in the dialect: the 'polite form' *ænt* and the more general *nont*, contracted from *an aunt*, just as *notch* is a contraction derived from *an* + Old French *oche*, 'a nick, a cut on a tally stick' (p. 75). Tolkien finds particularly amusing Haigh's example, a monologue of a father teasing his daughter, listed under 'aunt' (p. 4):

> 'Tha thinks thi *nont* Sally'll bāū thi ę niu frok if thæ tōks fāūn to ęr – imitating her – "*ænt* Sarah are yǫ goin' out? au'll mind th'ouse for yǫ wāūl yǫ kum back". It's "*ænt* Sarah" this ęn' "ænt Sarah" t' uther [...]'

> My translation: 'You think your *nont* Sally will buy you a new frock if you talk fine [polite] to her. (Then, imitating her:) "Aunt Sarah, are you going out? I'll mind your house for you until you come back." It's "Aunt Sarah" this and "Aunt Sarah" the other.'

There may be a printing error in the above passage, since *back* should be spelt *bæk* in the phonetic notation. The masculine form of *nont* is *nuncle*, a dialect word for 'uncle', which Tolkien uses in his darkly comic poem 'The Stone Troll' in *The Adventures of Tom Bombadil*.

Yorkshire dialect and *The Hobbit*

It is likely that the English of Yorkshire in general and Haigh's *New Glossary* in particular influenced Tolkien's creative writing in various ways. As Shippey first pointed out in *The Road to Middle-earth*, a well-known

Tolkienian word in Haigh's Glossary is the noun *bæggin*, defined as 'tea' in the northern English sense – that is, the evening meal (p. 6):

> bæggin, a meal, now usually 'tea',
> but formerly any meal; a bagging.
> Probably so called because workers
> generally carried their meals to
> their work in a bag of some kind.
> [Scand.: cp. OIcel. *baggi*, a bag,
> particularly used for provisions, as
> in *nest-baggi*, food-bag.]

The name Baggins is rich in connotations: it suggests love of food, and coincides nicely with the fact that around this time Tolkien's aunt Jane Neave was living in a farm called Bag End. This connects with the Old Norse/Scandinavian etymology that Haigh identifies for the word *baggin*, as well as with Tolkien's witty pun on the social pretensions of Bilbo's cousins the Sackville-Bagginses. These noisome relatives have clearly added a French-derived synonym (*sac* = bag + *ville* = town) to form their double-barrelled surname.

Following Shippey's lead, the *Glossary* is well worth systematic searches for other connections to Tolkien. One Shire-related example, this time recalling Frodo's friend Samwise the gardener, is the entry *sæmmi*, 'a dull, foolish, half-witted person', which Haigh compares to the early English prefix *sam-* or *sæm-* with the meaning 'bad, weak, semi-, or half-', as in *sām-wīs*, 'foolish, half-witted'.

One indirect effect is the name Tolkien gives to the four divisions of his Shire, for the obvious model is the word *riding*, which despite appearances has nothing to do with travel on horseback. From early times right up to the county reshuffle of the 1970s, the huge north-eastern county of Yorkshire was divided into three separate parts, the Ridings, the term *riding* in fact derived by phonetic assimilation from an older word *thridding*, meaning 'a third' from Old Norse *thrithjungr*. The change came about since historically each of the three names was pronounced and spelt as one word: Norththriding, Westtriding and Easttriding. On this pattern, Tolkien later divided his fictional Shire into four Farthings, *farthing* meaning 'a fourth'; the wordplay would have been more obvious when *LOTR* was first published, since in the old pre-decimal currency in general everyday use in 1950s Britain (the system of pounds, shillings and pence) the word *farthing* meant a coin of the value of quarter of a penny.

Haigh's *Glossary* and indeed Wright's huge *English Dialect Dictionary* are both well worth further study, since it is clear that Tolkien borrowed words from them to use in his fiction. A case in point is the origin of the word *hobbit*, which has already been discussed with regard to the folklore creature the *hob* (see chapters 1 and 5); in fact, dialect sources throw further light on the name Hob and its derivatives. As Wright's entry for *Hob* reveals, the *hob* had the reputation of living in a hole or cave such as 'Obtrush Rook, as well as Hob Hole and the Cave at Mulgrave' or 'Hob of the cave at Runswick', all of which recalls the opening words of *The Hobbit*. Another example concerned the names of two hobs and their reputed haunts at 'Knott Hill Hob' and 'Narr Hob' in the region near Saddleworth in West Yorkshire; one of them was reported to have lived there even in the reign of Canute (or Cnut), the Danish king who conquered and ruled England from 1016 to 1035:

> Hob of Knott Hill ... was so designated on account of his having stood on that eminence on the approach of King Canute (Cnut or Knut), and ordered that monarch to march his army up the valley to the attack of Castleshaw.[27]

Another of Wright's examples from Derbyshire (he cites Verney, *Stone Edge*, 1868, ix), gives more reminders of *The Hobbit:* 'The Hobb niver was knowed to come beyont the Dale ... T'other hole, where Hobb has his lodging.'

Rather different entries can be found in the *EDD* under the headword *hobthrust* or *hobthrush*, defined as 'a hobgoblin having the repute of doing much useful work unseen and unheard during the night, if not interfered with'.[28] Elizabeth Wright, in her book on dialect and folklore, comments:

> If the farmer or any of his servants had spoken disrespectfully of the hobthrush, they would presently find cream-pans smashed to atoms, horses and cattle turned loose and driven into the woods, and the housewife's churning would produce no butter.[29]

Amusingly, in *The Hobbit*, it is not Bilbo Baggins who behaves, or threatens to behave like this, but the dwarves, who whisk away the cups and plates to the stone sink to wash them, singing, to Bilbo's alarm, nonsense rhymes about chipping the glasses and cracking the plates, for 'that's what Bilbo Baggins hates' (*The Hobbit*, chapter 1). Feeling 'positively flummoxed' by all the extra domestic work his visitors are causing him, Bilbo begins to get irritated, grumbling to himself 'confusticate and bebother these dwarves!' Such words as 'flummoxed', 'confusticate' and 'bebother' are inspired by dialect usage: the blends of words, the use of unusual prefixes and suffixes in order to create new words out of old. Not surprisingly there are entries in the *EDD* for *flummox* and one for *confuscated*, a Lincolnshire word for 'perplexed, confounded', clearly a near synonym of Tolkien's *confusticate*. The noun *staggerment*, employed in the scene when Bilbo first sets eyes on the fabulous treasure, is surprisingly not listed in the *EDD*. But a similar-sounding word *baggerment* does in fact occur; Wright defines it as: (1) nonsense, worthless talk; and (2) rubbish, worthless things.[30] Frequently, then, Tolkien disguised these borrowings by adapting their spelling and adopting them into the more-or-less standard English in which he had composed the story.

'Nobot an olde cave': Dialect and landscape

In the end, Tolkien finds that the most compelling reason for studying regional vernacular speech is its preservation of older styles and usages. For Tolkien, the north-west in the fourteenth century was 'the centre of a revival of writings in vernacular speech of which the most interesting examples preserved are poems in an alliterative metre descended from the old verse of Anglo-Saxon times' (p. xvi). These poems are, as we have seen, full of riches for those who take the trouble to learn to tread their paths, and dialect study assists in that process. One instance already cited is the word *gruch*, which occurs in both modern Huddersfield dialect and in *SGGK*. Another is the fact that the form *dōnjęr* and the two forms of the word *dōns* and *dons* in Huddersfield preserve the Anglo-French and Middle English *aun* of *daungere* and *daunce*, which have very different sounds and spellings in modern standard English *danger* and *dance*. Similarly, the word *nont*, other- wise spelt *naunt* meaning 'aunt', also occurs in *SGGK*, line 2467: 'therefore I ethe [implore] the ... to come to thy naunt'.

For another example, the Huddersfield *nāūbęt*, with contracted forms *nobbęt* or even *nāūt*, may be compared with SGGK *nobot*, glossed by both Haigh and Tolkien as a conjunction meaning 'only' and deriving from *noght* 'not, nothing' + *bot* 'but', ultimately from Old English. In Haigh, the expression is illustrated with a colloquial anecdote of 'a hillside man owing £5 to a shopkeeper' who goes down and pays him £1, with the remark 'Au'v *nāūbęt* foęr muęr tę pe, neę' ('I've only four more to pay now'), to which the shopkeeper responds that he has '*nāūbęt, nobbęt, nāūt* paid one'!

In *SGGK* the word *nobot* occurs in a passage describing the fabled Green Chapel, the eerie location in the wilds where Gawain has agreed to meet the

Green Knight for the return bout of the Beheading Contest. The passage is an immaculate piece of 'northern' poetic scene setting, but what is also remarkable in this respect is that – for those of us who are familiar with the region and the dialect – even after the passage of several centuries the language of *SGGK* sounds northern and contemporary, as though it is spoken by one of Haigh's 'hillside men' (lines 2178–84):

> Thenne he bowes to the berwe, aboute hit he walkes
> Debatande with himself quat hit be might.
> Hit hade a hole on the ende and on ayther side,
> And overgrowen with gresse in glodes aywhere;
> And al was holw inwith, nobot an olde cave,
> Or a crevisse of an olde cragge – he couthe hit noght deme
>   With spelle.

[Then going up to the mound, he walked round it, deliberating with himself as to what it could be. It had a hole at one end and one at each side, and was all overgrown with patches of grass, and quite hollow inside, nothing but an old cave, or a fissure in an old crag – he could not say what it was.][31]

Though it looks as if it is *nobot an olde cave* (nothing but an old cave), the Chapel seems also to be an ancient and mysterious mound, with a stream or burn running by its side. The poet uses two words to describe it: *berw* (also spelt *bergh*) and *lawe*, both words denoting 'mound' or 'knoll', with connotations of ancient customs. The first, *berw*, is the modern word 'barrow' deriving from OE *beorg* (*beorh*), meaning 'hill, cliff, mound, barrow'; the second, *lawe* (from OE *hlæw*), occurs in place names such as Taplow, a *low* or barrow in which the treasure of a great chieftain (no doubt the man Tappa) was discovered (the treasure was subsequently put on display in the British Museum). The same two words recur elsewhere in a comparable setting at the end of the poem *Beowulf*. The dying king's last request is that 'Beowulf's Barrow' (OE *Biowulfes biorh*) should be constructed, and his wish is fulfilled: 'the people built [*ge-worhton*] the mound on a headland [*hlæw on hoe*]' where it is widely seen by seafarers on the ocean; here Beowulf's treasure is interred, and twelve warriors 'rode round the low [*ymbe hlæw ridon*]' and sing his eulogy.[32] The Green Chapel is certainly mysterious and oddly ancient and the fact that the fourteenth-century *Gawain* poet seems to be aware of the antique connotations of the words he is using – and also at the same time revived or reused old poetic diction – was a source of endless fascination to Tolkien as a philologist.

Fig. 16b   Mound on headland

The above description of the Green Chapel from *SGGK* contains three words that have been discussed already with regard to *The Hobbit*: the landscape features *hole*, *cave* and *hollow*. In his *Middle English Vocabulary* and his edition of *SGGK*, Tolkien glosses *hole* as 'hole' and derives it from OE *hol*, whereas he translates *holw* as 'hollow', from OE *holh*. The synonyms *hole* and *cave* are met frequently in *The Hobbit*: the dwelling-place of the hobbit, the *holbytla* or 'hole-builder', is a 'hole in the ground'; and on his journey through the mountains there is the great 'thunderbattle' which reverberated in every 'cave and hollow'. The goblins, the elves, the dragon, the dwarves all make their homes in *caves*. As we know, Tolkien takes care in his distinctions of meaning in *The Hobbit* between different types of *hole*, and different types of *cave*. In the famous opening passage some holes are described as wet, others dry and comfortable. Caves divide into suspicious ones, like the goblin cave, and 'wholesome' ones, like the cave at the bottom of the Carrock where the company rests before making their visit to Beorn, or the great cave of the Elvenking which is 'lighter and more wholesome than any goblin-dwelling and neither so deep nor so dangerous' (chapter 8).

Later in the same final section of the poem, the *Gawain* poet again uses the word *hole*, in the famous passage where Gawain hears a noise like a grindstone on the edge of a scythe or the rushing of water in a mill-race: the Green Knight sharpening his axe on a whetstone somewhere among the crags on the hillside opposite the mound where Gawain is standing. As Gawain calls on him to show his face he suddenly appears out of a hole with his great axe:

> And sythen he keveres bi a cragge and comes of a hole,
> Whyrlande out of a wro with a felle weppen
> A denez ax nwe dyght (lines 2221–2)

[And then he makes his way down by the side of a crag and comes out of a hole, whirling out of a nook with a terrible weapon, a Danish axe newly prepared.]

The Green Knight is here in his element; he emerges from out of the landscape, a creature of the crag, a denizen of the *hyghe hil* and the *harde roche* (line 2199). And Tolkien perhaps also remembered the above description of the Green Knight whirling out of his hole when he invented Beorn, denizen of the great rock the Carrock, who lives in a great hall as a man but perhaps dwells also in the wholesome cave at the foot of the Carrock when he is in his bear-shape. In a conversation between Gandalf and Bilbo that has been cited a number of times with regard to Tolkien's approach to names, this intimate connection between place and name is emphasised:

Fig. 16c   Nobot an old cave

He called it the Carrock, because carrock is his word for it. He calls things like that carrocks, and this one is *the* Carrock because it is the only one near his home and he knows it well.

As the anthropologist David Abram has written:

If we listen, first, to the sounds of an oral language – to the rhythms, tones and inflections that play through the speech of an oral culture – we will likely find that these elements are attuned, in multiple and subtle ways, to the contour and scale of the local landscape, to the depth of its valleys or the open stretch of its distances, to the visual rhythms of the local topography.[33]

We are back with Laurence Durrell's reflections on character as a function of landscape. In J.R.R. Tolkien's work, the names reflect the places and the landscapes, and the characters who live in these landscapes speak appropriately, according to the way the landscape and its language has shaped them.

Epilogue

There ben manye other diverse contrees and manye other merveyles beyonde, that I have not seen: wherefore of hem I can not speke properly, to tell you the manere of hem. And also in the contrees where I have ben, ben manye mo dyversitees of many wondirfull thinges than I make mencioun of, for it were to longe thing to devyse you the manere. And therfore that that I have devised you of certeyn contrees, that I have spoken of before, I besche your worthi and excellent noblesse that it suffise to you at this tyme. For yif that I devised you all that is beyonde the see, another man peraunter, that wold peynen him and travaylle his body for to go into tho marches for to encerche tho contrees, myghte ben blamed be my wordes, in rehercynge many straunge thinges; for he myghte not seye no thing of newe, in the which the hereres haven other solace or desport or lust or lykyng in the herynge. For men seyn allweys that newe thinges and newe tydynges ben plesant to here. Wherfore I wole holde me stille, withouten ony more rehercyng of dyversitees or of mervaylles that ben beyonde, to that entent and ende that whoso wil gon into tho contrees, he schall fynde ynowe to speke of, that I have not touched of in no wyse.[1]

ONE OF THE passages chosen by Kenneth Sisam for *Fourteenth-Century Verse and Prose*, his textbook jointly authored with Tolkien, is a part-fictional travelogue told by John Mandeville about his journeys in the Holy Land and in Asia, where he 'passed many londes and manye isles and contrees, and cerched manye full strange places'.

Here in *Mandeville's Travels* is a reminder of Bilbo in *The Hobbit*, who travelled there and back again, and wrote 'a non-sensical account of it' on his return. Here also is an echo of the fact that Bilbo had 'many adventures and hardships before he got back', just like Sir Gawain, and there is no time or space to tell of them:

> Ofte he herbered in house and ofte al theroute,
> And mony aventure in vale, and venquyst ofte,
> That I ne tyght at this tyme in tale to remene.

> [Often he sheltered in a house and often found no shelter whatsoever, having many adventures by the way, and many victories, which at this point in the tale I do not intend to recount.][2]

Here again is a reminder of the traveller Eriol, in the frame tale of *The Book of Lost Tales*, otherwise known as Ælfwine – 'elf-friend' being another of the titles bestowed on Bilbo Baggins at the end of *The Hobbit* – with his curiosity to see 'many secrets of old and wonderful and beautiful things'. Though it is never stated in so many words, exactly that is one of the motivations behind Tolkien's study of philology and the history of language, the groundwork for his writing of *The Hobbit*.

Appendix One

A selection of poems from Geoffrey Bache Smith, *A Spring Harvest* (London: Erskine Macdonald, 1918)

THE VOLUME WAS arranged and put together by J.R.R. Tolkien and Christopher Wiseman, and Tolkien supplied a short introductory note. For discussion of these poems see chapter 11 above. A new edition of *A Spring Harvest* is forthcoming, edited by Douglas A. Anderson.

p. 24

RIME

O SCHOLAR grey, with quiet eyes,
Reading the charactered pages, bright
With one tall candle's flickering light,
In a turret chamber under the skies;
O scholar, learned in gramarye,
Have you seen the manifold things I see?

Have you seen the forms of tracèd towers
Whence clamorous voices challenge the hours:
Gaunt tree-branches, pitchy black
Against the long, wind-driven wrack

Of scurrying, shuddering clouds, that race
Ever across the pale moon's face?

Have you heard the tramp of hurrying feet,
There beneath, in the shadowy street,
Have you heard sharp cries, and seen the flame
Of silvery steel, in a perilous game,
A perilous game for men to play,
Hid from the searching eyes of day?

Have you heard the great awakening breath,
Like trump that summons the saints from death,
Of the wild, majestical wind, which blows
Loud and splendid, that each man knows
Far, O far away is the sea,
Breaking, murmuring, stark and free?

All these things I hear and see,
I, a scholar of gramarye:
All are writ in the ancient books
Clear, exactly, and he that looks
Finds the night and the changing sea,
The years gone by, and the years to be:
(He that searches, with tireless eyes
In a turret-chamber under the skies)
Passion and joy, and sorrow and laughter,
Life and death, and the things thereafter.

p. 29

A PREFACE FOR A TALE I HAVE NEVER TOLD

HEREIN is nought of windy citadels
Where proud kings dwell, that with an iron hand
Deal war or justice: here no history
Of valiant ships upon the wine-dark seas
Passing strange lands and threading channels strait

Between embalmed islands: here no song
That men shall sing in battle and remember
When they are old and grey beside the fire:
Only a story gathered from the hills
And the wind crying of forgotten days,
A story that shall whisper, 'All things change –
For friends do grow indifferent, and loves
Die like a dream at morning: bitterness
Is the sure heritage of all men born,
And he alone seeks truly, who looks out
From some huge aery peak, considering not
Fast-walled cities, or the works of men,
But turns his gaze unto the mountain-tops
And the unfathomable blue of heaven
That only change not with the changing years' –
A tale that shod itself with ancient shoon
And wrapped its cloak, and wandered from the west.

p. 30

A SONNET

THERE is a wind that takes the heart of a man,
    A fresh wind in the latter days of spring,
    When hate and war and every evil thing
That the wide arches of high Heaven span
Seems dust, and less to be accounted than
    The omened touches of a passing wing:
    When Destiny, that calls himself a king,
    Goes all forgotten for the song of Pan:
For why? Because the twittering of birds
    Is the best music that was ever sung,
Because the voice of trees finds better words
    Than ever poet from his heartstrings wrung:
Because all wisdom and all gramarye
Are writ in fields, O very plain to see.

p. 31

IT WAS ALL IN THE BLACK COUNTREE

IT was all in the Black Countree,
What time the sweet o' the year should be,
I saw a tree, all gaunt and grey,
As mindful of winter's day;
And that a lonely bird did sit
Upon the topmost branch of it,
Who to my thought did sweeter sing
Than any minstrel of a king.

p. 38

O THERE BE KINGS WHOSE TREASURIES

O THERE be kings whose treasuries
 Are rich with pearls and gold
And silks and bales of cramasy
 And spices manifold:
Gardens they have with marble stairs
 And streams than life more fair,
With roses set and lavender
 That do enchant the air.

O there be many ships that sail
 The sea-ways wide and blue,
And there be master-mariners
 To sail them straight and true:
And there be many women fair
 Who watch out anxiously,
And are enamoured of the day
 Their dear ones come from sea:

But riches I can find enow
 All in a barren land,

Where sombre lakes shine wondrously
    With rocks on either hand:
And I can find enow of love
    Up there alone, alone,
With none beside me save the wind,
    Nor speech except his moan.

For there far up among the hills
    The great storms come and go
In a most proud processional
    Of cloud and rain and snow:
There light and darkness only are
    A changing benison
Of the old gods who wrought the world
    And shaped the moon and sun.

p. 55

O, ONE CAME DOWN FROM SEVEN HILLS

O, ONE came down from seven hills
    And crossèd seven streams:
All in his hands were thyme and grass
    And in his eyes were dreams:
He passèd by a seven fields
    With early dews all grey
And entered in the stricken town
    About the break of day.

'O you old men that stand and talk
    About the market-place,
There is much trouble in your eyes
    And anguish in your face:
O woman in a silent room
    Within a silent house,
There is no pleasure in your voice
    Or peace upon your brows.'

'O how should such as we rejoice
    Who weep that others die,
Who quake, and curse ourselves, and watch
    The vengeful hours go by?
O better far to fly the grief
    That wounds, and never kills;
O better far to fly the town
    And seek the seven hills—'

'I will go pray the seven gods
    Who keep the seven hills
That they do grant your city peace,
    And easement of her ills.'
'Nay, rather pray the seven gods
    To launch the latest pain;
For there be many things to do
    Ere we see peace again.'

'Then I'll go praise the seven gods
    With hymns and chauntings seven,
Such as shall split the mountain-tops
    And shrivel up blue heaven:
That there be men who mock at threats
    And wag their heads at strife,
Love home above their own hearts' blood
    And honour more than life.'

p. 66

OVER THE HILLS AND HOLLOWS GREEN

Over the hills and hollows green
    The springtide air goes valiantly,
Where many sainted singing larks
    And blessed primaveras be:

But bitterly the springtide air
    Over the desert towns doth blow
About whose torn and shattered streets
    No more shall children's footsteps go.

p. 78 (final page)

SO WE LAY DOWN THE PEN

So we lay down the pen,
So we forbear the building of the rime,
And bid our hearts be steel for times and a time
    Till ends the strife, and then,
When the New Age is verily begun,
God grant that we may do the things undone.

Appendix Two

A selection of poems from *A Northern Venture: Verses by Members of the Leeds University English School Association* (Leeds: Swan Press, 1923)

THE FOUR POETS here selected from the volume were former pupils and colleagues with whom Tolkien stayed in contact after his time at Leeds. For discussion, see chapter 12 above.

pp. 4–5, W.R. Childe

FAIRY TALES

WHEN amid narrow streets of ancient towns,
The Child was wiser than his heart was ware:
A certain Presence brooded everywhere,
And images with alabaster crowns
Spoke to him of a world more permanent
Than he was used to; he looked up to find
Calm statues withering gently in the wind
Upon the crest of some carved monument,
An aery steeple lone amid the blue,
Round which doves circled, and their gracious speech

Of solitary dumbness made to him
More sweet appeal than most things wont to do:
His blue eyes burned with love and he would reach
Visions most welcome to the Seraphim …

THE SUMMER CREEK

THE white convolvulus invites us down
To the little narrow and strange sea-shipman's-town,
Where scarlet roofs against the sea's soft blue
Recall the fierce geranium's fiery hue,
And the bay opens on an infinite hour
Its simple sweet cerulean like a flower…

Blessed too are they who never knew the sting
Of shame's corrosion, nor the sunsetting
Of shadowy hope amid the brazen steeples
Of monstrous Babel with her swarming peoples,
Revering amid loneliness alone
The sanctity of water, seeds and stone…

For here, amid red gables and the wild
Increase of coloured herbs, man like a child,
Catches again the golden string's lost end,
Knowing that all things mortal need a friend,
Proclaimed in silence and the far off line
Of innocent serenities divine…

pp. 6–7, E.V. Gordon

A SKALD'S IMPROMPTU

A Norse verse composed by Skuli, Earl of the Orkneys (in the twelfth century), while launching his ship at Grimsby.

Edited and translated into skaldic metre by E.V. Gordon.

Ver hofum vadnar leirur
vikum fimm megingrimmar –
saur's eigi vant thar's vórum
vidr í Grimsbœ midjum.
Nú's that's más of myri
meginkátliga látum
branda elg á bylgjur
Bjorgynjar til dynja.

Grumblingly at Grimsby
Grievous weeks we eked out,
Five weeks full ere leaving,
Flound'ring in mud boundless.
Launch, then, launch our beaked bird,
Light for flight o'er billows –
Like the mew from mudbank –
Merrily to Bergen.

E.V. Gordon

'THEY SAT THERE'
'They sat there, they two ...'

A rendering of Ibsen's *De sad der, de to* – A theme afterwards expanded into the drama, *Bygmester Solness* (*The Master Builder*).

They sat there, they two, in so cosy a house,
    The autumn and winter weather.

Then the house burned down. All is fallen in ruin.
    The two search the ashes together.

For under them lies a precious jewel,
    A jewel can never be burned;
Let them rake and grope, still may a jewel
    From ashes be lightly upturned.

But they find never, the homeless two,
    The unburnt jewel, for all distress;
She finds never her faith that is burned,
    He never his burnt happiness.

pp. 12–14, A.H. Smith

[In the two dialect poems below, Smith's glosses are placed in italics in the margin next to the line to which they refer.]

SPRING

FIVE hundred gnats wi' t' gowden sun
Their short spring life ha' now begun:
Five hundred gnats 'll dee toneet,
When t' mooin o' May shines siller-breet.   [*silver-bright*]

Young crows are beating t' clouds around,
Frae t' sky them skylarks fall to t' ground,
To t' ground new donned i' green gers shawls   [*grass*]
Wi' daisies white 'at t' saisin calls.

Gert planes are brustin' into leaf
An' t' sycamores an' t' poplars chief.
Then far in t' woods aneath t' new shade
Blue bells are painting t' spring-time glade.

Through t' midst o' t' dale, o' peaty brown
A saumy stream winnds lazy down: [*dreamy*]
It's ruffled here an' there wi' rings
O' t' scunning trout, or t' curlews' wings.   [*darting*]

It shooits ower t' foss wi' clattering sang:
Wi' t' grey rock bed it sooin gets thrang.   [*busy*]
Its spray lecks t' blooming beds o' moss   [*sprinkles*]
What lap up t' blocks o' limestooan dross.   [*enfold*]

An' to this freshening pebbly sike   [*brook*]
Frisky gimmers coom down frae t' pike.   [*ewe-lambs*] [*hill-top*]
Like t' lute in t' band all birds do sing:
No Winter bass! for now it's Spring!

A.H. Smith

A VISION

T'ɴᴇᴇᴛ war dark an' stormy.
   A yowe-lamb up on t' fell.
Wheear t' winds blow hask and canty   [*keen and strong*]
   Sooin after th' harvest mell.   [*feast*]
Eight miles o' silent trapsin'   [*tramping*]
   O'er clarty, sumpy fields!   [*muddy*] [*wet*]
While Bastile* Chaps seik shelter,   [*Workhouse*]
   Us farmers leave wer bields.   [*dwellings*]

On t' brest o' t' fell I'm wankle,   [*dizzy*]
   An' unkerd seets I see,   [*strange*]
I cannot fuggle t' noises   [*avoid*]
   What mak me shak weantly.   [*strangely*]
My een bulge out like bulls do
   To see sich men in t' roke,   [*mist*]
Wi' armour, spikes, an' eagles,
   Huggered up like pigs in t' poke.   [*crowded together*] [*sack*]

Mebbe Roman sowdgers,
 Marchin' on t' Roman roads,
Have coom to t' fields o' battle
 An' the hostile Celts' abodes
What sossed ya gill o' sorrow   [*drank the tankard*]
 When t' cobby Romans coom   [*active*]
An' fell stark deead on t' fell tops –
 But t' mist aggean grows toom.   [*empty*]

Then out ' t' roke reit awfish   [*fairy-like*]
 Wi' slivers dance yon elves,   [*twigs*]
An' fill my heart wi' sweet sangs,
 Then dwine away in t' delves.
An' kye an' wye an' gimmers,   [*cows*] [*heifers*] [*ewe-lambs*]
 As at a cattle show,
Stond more like groups o' statties
 Nor t' livin' beasts we grow.

All t' yowe-lambs lowp about me,
 An' leik like bits o' fluff
Scattered by t' saft spring breezes,
 An' lick my hands reit chuff;   [*proud*]
I speik to 'em but rowpy: [*hoarsely*]
 I'm swaimish in this place.   [*my head swims*]
I waken up i' t' delf-hoil;
 T' lost gimmer licks my face.

Notes

Chapter One   'We must away ere break of day'

1 J.R.R. Tolkien, *The Hobbit*, 2nd edition (London, 1951); in view of the many reprints, all references to *The Hobbit* will be by chapter rather than by page.

2 John D. Rateliff, *The History of the Hobbit. Part One: Mr Baggins* (London, 2007), pp. xi–xx.

3 G. Ronald Murphy, *The Owl, The Raven, and the Dove: The Religious Meaning of the Grimms' Magic Fairy Tales* (Oxford, 2000), p. 5.

4 Lawrence Durrell, 'Landscape and Character', in *Spirit of Place: Letters and Essays on Travel*, ed. Alan G. Thomas (London, 1969), pp. 156–63.

5 Robert S. Blackham, *The Roots of Tolkien's Middle-earth* (Stroud, 2006).

6 Priscilla Tolkien, ed., *The Tolkien Family Album* (London, 1992), p. 20.

7 Christopher Tolkien, ed., *Pictures by J.R.R. Tolkien* (London, 1979), no. 1.

8 Humphrey Carpenter, *J.R.R. Tolkien: A Biography* (London, 1977), p.175.

9 *The Letters of J.R.R. Tolkien*, ed., Humphrey Carpenter (London: George Allen & Unwin, 1981), p. 308.

10 Tolkien, *Letters*, pp. 308–11, 316–17, 319–22, 377; for biographical information on Jane Neave, see Andrew H. Morton and John Hayes, *Tolkien's Gedling: The Birth of a Legend* (Studley, Warwickshire, 2008).

11 Tolkien, *Letters*, p. 210.

12 Kenneth Grahame, *The Wind in the Willows* (London, 1908).

13 Peter Gilliver, Jeremy Marshall and Edmund Weiner, *The Ring of Words: Tolkien and the Oxford English Dictionary* (Oxford, 2006), pp. 142–52.

14 Rateliff, *History of the Hobbit*, p. 844.

15 James M. Hutchisson, *The Rise of Sinclair Lewis 1920–1930* (University Park, 1996).

16   Sinclair Lewis, *Babbit* (New York and London, 1922).

17   Carpenter, *Biography*, pp. 45–6.

18   Cited in Christina Scull and Wayne G. Hammond, *The J.R.R. Tolkien Companion and Guide: Reader's Guide* (London, 2006), p. 1130.

19   Tolkien, *Letters*, p. 215.

20   E.A. Wyke Smith, *The Marvellous Land of Snergs* (London, 1927), pp. 10, 24–5.

21   Hugh Lofting, *Doctor Dolittle: Being the History of his Peculiar Life at Home, and Astonishing Adventures in Foreign Parts* (London, 1922), p. 17.

22   Rateliff, *History of the Hobbit*, pp. 266–8, 286–7.

23   The word *little* in 'a little old man' occurs only in the draft: Rateliff, *History of the Hobbit*, p. 30.

24   J.R.R. Tolkien, *Roverandom*, ed. Christina Scull and Wayne G. Hammond (London, 1998), p. 76.

25   Wayne G. Hammond and Christina Scull, *J.R.R. Tolkien: Artist and Illustrator* (London, 1998), pp. 56, 58, figs 52, 54; J.R.R. Tolkien, *The Book of Lost Tales, Part II*, ed. Christopher Tolkien, *The History of Middle-earth, II* (London, 1984), p. 76.

26   Christopher Tolkien, ed., *Pictures by J.R.R. Tolkien* (London, 1992), no. 37.

27   Tolkien, *Roverandom*, p. 1.

28   Edith Nesbit, *Five Children and It* (London, 1902).

29   Gillian Avery, 'Introduction and Notes' to E. Nesbit, *Five Children and It* (New York, 2005).

30   Tolkien, *Roverandom*, p. 95.

31   J.R.R. Tolkien, *Return of the Shadow*, ed. Christopher Tolkien (London, 2002), pp. 78–9; in this draft, written by 1938, Tolkien described Gollum as 'of hobbit-kind'.

32   Rateliff, *History of the Hobbit*, pp. 867–8.

33   Snorri Sturluson, *Edda*, trans. Anthony Faulkes (London, 1987), p. 16.

34   Ursula Dronke, ed., *The Poetic Edda Volume II: Mythological Poems* (Oxford, 1997), pp. 9–11.

35   Jacob Grimm and Wilhelm Grimm, *Selected Tales*, ed. and trans. David Luke (Harmondsworth, 1982), p. 75.

Chapter Two   *Fairy-stories and animal fables*

1   J.R.R. Tolkien, *A Middle English Vocabulary* (Oxford, 1922).

2   Gerard Manley Hopkins, *Poems and Prose*, ed. W.H. Gardner (Harmondsworth, 1953).

3   Martianus Capella, cited in C.S. Lewis, *The Discarded Image: An Introduction to Medieval and Renaissance Literature* (Cambridge, 1964), p. 122.

4   J.R.R. Tolkien, *The Book of Lost Tales, Part I*, ed. Christopher Tolkien, *The History of Middle-earth, I* (London, 1983), p. 66.

5   Carpenter, *Biography*, p. 48.

6   J.R.R. Tolkien, *On Fairy-stories*, expanded edition, ed. Verlyn Flieger and Douglas A. Anderson (London, 2008), p. 35.

7   Tolkien, *Return of the Shadow*, p. 51.

8   Rateliff, *History of the Hobbit*, p. 73.

9   T. Shippey, *The Road to Middle-earth* (London, 1982), pp. 170–1; Tolkien, *Letters*, p. 333.

10   Gilliver *et al.*, *The Ring of Words*, pp. 141–2.

11   Tolkien, *Lost Tales II*, p. 10.

12   Tolkien, *Lost Tales II*, pp. 11–12.

13   'Scarborough Fair', in the anthology by Michael Raven, ed., *The Guitarist's Good Book* (Manchester, 1977), p. 97.

14   Jesse L. Byock, trans., *The Saga of King Hrolf Kraki* (London, 1998).

15   E.V. Gordon, *An Introduction to Old Norse* (Oxford, 1927), p. 28.

Chapter Three   *'A green great dragon'*

1   Tolkien, *Letters*, p. 214.

2   Tolkien, *Letters*, p. 377; Carpenter, *Biography*, p. 377.

3   J.R.R. Tolkien, *The Legend of Sigurd and Gudrún* (London, 2010), pp. 16–17.

4   J.R.R. Tolkien, *The Monsters and the Critics and Other Essays* (London, 1983), p. 17.

5   Edward Thomas, *Norse Tales* (Oxford, 1912), pp. 138–9.

6   Tolkien, *Legend of Sigurd and Gudrún*, p. 108.

7   Andrew Lang, 'The Story of Sigurd', in *The Red Fairy Book* (London: Longmans, Green and Co., 1890), p. 360.

8   For Tolkien's dragon paintings, see Hammond and Scull, *Artist and Illustrator*, pp. 51, 52, 140, figs 47, 48, 49, 133.

9   Lang, *Red Fairy Book*, p. 359; the illustration is reproduced and discussed in Rachel Hart, 'Tolkien, St Andrews, and Dragons', in Trevor Hart and Ivan Khovacs, eds, *Tree of Tales: Tolkien, Literature, and Theology* (Waco, Texas, 2007), pp. 1–11, at p. 10.

10   Hammond and Scull, *Artist and Illustrator*, p. 140, fig. 133.

11   Tolkien, *On Fairy-stories*, p. 55.

12   Christina Scull and Wayne G. Hammond, *The J.R.R. Tolkien Companion and Guide: Chronology* (London, 2006), p. 12.

13   R.D. Fulk, ed. and trans., *The Beowulf Manuscript* (Cambridge MA and London, 2010), p. 237.

14   J.R.R. Tolkien, 'Beowulf: The Monster and the Critics', in *The Monsters and the Critics*, pp. 5–48.

15   A well-used modern verse translation of *Beowulf* is by Seamus Heaney. Tolkien endorsed the classic prose translation by Clark Hall, which he saw as a useful aid to learning the language of the poem; he wrote an introduction on metre for the 1940 reprint of this translation.

16 Henry Sweet, *A New English Grammar, Part II* (Oxford, 1898), p. 8.

17 Tolkien, *On Fairy-stories*, pp. 41, 61, 111.

18 Jaqueline Simpson, *British Dragons* (London, 1980), pp. 91–107.

19 Lord Dunsany, E.J.M.D. Plunkett (1878–1957), was a prolific fantasy writer in this period, who wrote novels and collections of myths; see Sandra Kemp *et al.*, *Edwardian Fiction* (Oxford and New York, 1997), pp. 38–9, 110–11.

20 Christina Scull, 'Dragons from Andrew Lang's Retelling of Sigurd to Tolkien's Chrysophylax', in *Leaves from the Tree: J.R.R. Tolkien's Shorter Fiction* (London, 1991), pp. 49–62.

21 Edward Thomas, 'Winter Music', in *Light and Twilight* (London, 1911), at pp. 94–5.

22 J.R.R. Tolkien, 'The Dragon's Visit', *Oxford Magazine*, vol. 55, no. 11 (4 February 1937), p. 342; reprinted in Douglas A. Anderson, *The Annotated Hobbit*, 2nd edition (London, 2003), pp. 309–11.

23 K. Bagpuize, 'Progress in Bimble Town', *Oxford Magazine*, vol. 50, no. 1 (15 October 1931), p. 22.

24 Tolkien, *Return of the Shadow*, p. 19.

25 The standard biographical study is Humphrey Carpenter, *The Inklings: C.S. Lewis, J.R.R. Tolkien, Charles Williams and their Friends* (London, 2006). For a survey of the group with many evocative photographs of their Oxford location, see Harry Lee Poe and James Ray Veneman, *The Inklings of Oxford: C.S. Lewis, J.R.R. Tolkien and their Friends* (Grand Rapids, 2009).

26 C.S. Lewis, *All My Road before Me: The Diary of C.S. Lewis 1922–27*, ed. Walter Hooper (London, 1991), p. 392.

27 C.S. Lewis, *Rehabilitations and Other Essays* (London, 1939).

28 Carpenter, *The Inklings*, p. 58.

29 'Inside Information', *The Hobbit*, chapter 12.

30 Rateliff, *History of the Hobbit*, p. 523, n. 33.

31 Job chapter 41, verses 5–6, 12–13, 15, 17; *The Holy Bible. Douay Version* (London, 1956).

32 Murphy, *The Owl, the Raven, and the Dove*, p. 3.

33 Carpenter, *The Inklings*, pp. 42–4.

34 C.S. Lewis, *An Experiment in Criticism* (Cambridge, 1961), p. 57.

35 Tolkien, *Lost Tales II*, p. 97.

Chapter Four *'The Heart of the Mountain'*

1 J.R.R. Tolkien, *The Adventures of Tom Bombadil* (London, 1962), poem no. 14.

2 J.R. Clark Hall, *Beowulf and the Finnesburg Fragment* (London, 1940), p. 158.

3 For extensive discussion see Rateliff, *History of the Hobbit*, pp. 595–609.

4 The original chapter may be read in Rateliff, *History of the Hobbit*, pp. 153–63; a classic discussion of the changes introduced in the second edition of *The Hobbit*

is Bonniejean Christensen, 'Gollum's Character Transformation in *The Hobbit*', in Jared Lobdell, ed., *A Tolkien Compass*, 2nd edition (Chicago, 2003), pp. 7–26.

5 Tolkien, *Lost Tales II*, p. 95.

6 Tolkien, *Lost Tales II*, p. 9.

7 Thomas, *Norse Tales*, p. 135; cf. Tolkien's version in *Legend of Sigurd and Gudrún*, p. 69.

8 Thomas Pennant, *A Tour in Scotland*, 4th edition (London, 1776), p. 115.

9 John Rateliff discusses the relationship between the two elf-kings in *History of The Hobbit*, pp. 408–16.

10 C.S. Lewis, 'On Stories', in *Essays Presented to Charles Williams* (London, 1947), pp. 90–105; Paul Edmund Thomas, 'Some of Tolkien's Narrators', in Verlyn Flieger and Carl F. Hostetter, eds, *Tolkien's Legendarium: Essays on the History of Middle-earth* (Westport, 2000), pp. 161–81, at pp. 178–9.

11 J.R.R. Tolkien, *The Quest of Erebor*, in his *Unfinished Tales of Númenor and Middle-Earth* (London, 1980), at p. 326.

12 Shippey, *Road to Middle-earth*, p. 70.

13 Shippey, *Road to Middle-earth*, pp. 90–2.

14 Tolkien translated *silmaril* into Old English *eorclanstan*, as Anderson points out in *The Annotated Hobbit*, pp. 293–4.

15 Tolkien, *On Fairy-stories*, p. 37.

16 Grimm and Grimm, *Selected Tales*, pp. 348–50.

17 George MacDonald, *The Giant's Heart*, in his *The Complete Fairy Tales*, ed. U.C. Knoepflmacher (London, 1999).

Chapter Five *Return to Bag End*

1 Shippey, *Road to Middle-Earth*, p. 72.

2 Tolkien, *Return of the Shadow*, p. 13.

3 Rateliff, *History of the Hobbit*, p. 768.

4 Eilert Ekwall, *English Place-Names in -ing* (London, 1923).

5 J.R.R. Tolkien, 'Philology: General Works', in *The Year's Work in English Studies*, vol. 4 (1923), ed. Sidney Lee and F.S. Boas (Oxford, 1924), pp. 20–44; the discussion of place-names is at pp. 30–2.

6 Margaret Gelling, *Place-names in the Landscape* (London, 1984).

7 *Oxford Mail* (3 August 1966), p. 4, cited in Scull and Hammond, *Guide*, p. 873.

8 See also Tolkien, *Family Album*, p. 20.

9 Tolkien, *Letters*, p. 390.

10 Angela Gardner, ed., *Black and White Ogre Country: The Lost Tales of Hilary Tolkien* (Moreton-in-Marsh, 2009), p. 4.

11 Tolkien, *Return of the Shadow*, p. 296, n. 6.

12 Tolkien, *Return of the Shadow*, p. 297, n. 13.

13 'A Shortcut to Mushrooms', *LOTR*, book I, chapter 4.

14 Tolkien, *Letters*, p. 26.

15 'In the Old Forest', *LOTR*, book I, chapter 6.

16 The poem 'The Adventures of Tom Bombadil' was published in *Oxford Magazine*, vol. 52, no. 13 (15 February 1934), pp. 464–5; it is reprinted in Wayne G. Hammond and Christina Scull, *The Lord of the Rings: A Reader's Companion* (London, 2008), pp. 124–7.

17 Carpenter, *Biography*, p. 162.

18 Tolkien, *Return of the Shadow*, p. 115.

19 The two Bombadil poems were revised and published in *The Adventures of Tom Bombadil* in 1962.

20 J.R.R. Tolkien, 'The Adventures of Tom Bombadil', in *Reader's Companion*, p. 127.

21 Lawrence Durrell, 'Landscape and Character', in *Spirit of Place: Letters and Essays on Travel*, ed. Alan G. Thomas (London, 1969), pp. 156–63.

22 Tolkien, *Fellowship of the Ring*, in *LOTR*, book I, chapter 7.

23 Edward Thomas, *The Icknield Way* (London, 1913), p. 22.

24 Peter Gilliver, Jeremy Marshall and Edmund Weiner, *The Ring of Words: Tolkien and the Oxford English Dictionary* (Oxford, 2006), pp. 49–51.

25 Edward Thomas, 'Lob', in *The Annotated Collected Poems*, ed. Edna Longley (Tarset, Northumberland, 2008), pp. 76–9, with extensive notes on the poem at pp. 211–24.

26 Rudyard Kipling, *Puck of Pook's Hill* and *Rewards and Fairies*, ed. Donald Mackenzie (Oxford, 1993).

27 See the detailed discussion of rural nostalgia in inter-war Britain in Anna Vaninskaya, 'Tolkien: A Man of his Time?', in Frank Weinreich and Thomas Honegger, eds, *Tolkien and Modernity*, 2 vols (Zurich, 2006), vol. 1, pp. 1–30, esp. pp. 16–22.

28 Ronald Blythe, *Akenfield: Portrait of an English Village* (London, 1972), p. 313.

Chapter Six   *The English country house and its myths*

1 Tolkien, *Letters*, p. 445.

2 J.R.R. Tolkien, *The Cottage of Lost Play*, in *Lost Tales I*, chapter 1.

3 Thomas Hardy, *Under the Greenwood Tree* (1872), chapter 1.

4 J.R.R. Tolkien, 'Kortirion among the Trees', lines 33–42; the poem is printed in *Lost Tales I*, p. 33.

5 The poem 'The Lonely Isle' is printed in John Garth, *Tolkien and the Great War: The Threshold of Middle-earth* (London, 2004), p. 145.

6 Tolkien, *Lost Tales II*, pp. 289–93.

7 Tolkien, *Lost Tales I*, p. 26.

8 George J. Zytaruk and James T. Boulton, eds, *The Letters of D.H. Lawrence. Volume II. June 1913–October 1916* (Cambridge, 1981), pp. 431–2.

9   John Lucas, 'The Sunlight on the Garden', in Carola M. Kaplan and Anne B. Simpson, eds, *Seeing Double: Revisioning Edwardian and Modernist Literature* (London, 1996), pp. 59–77, at p. 62.

10 For more discussion of the idea that many authors were influenced by the *Zeitgeist* and were thinking very often in close analogous terms, see Vaninskaya, 'Tolkien: A Man of his Time?'.

Chapter Seven   *William Guest*

1   Tolkien's designs are reproduced in Hammond and Scull, *Artist and Illustrator*, pp. 186–98, figs 183–96.

2   Richard Mathews, *Fantasy: The Liberation of the Imagination* (New York and London, 2002), pp. 85–95.

3   William Morris, *The Roots of the Mountains* (London, 1890; reprinted London, 1979), chapter 6.

4   William Morris, *News from Nowhere* (1890), reprinted in *Selected Writings* (London, 1946).

5   Fiona MacCarthy, *William Morris* (London, 1994), figs iii and iv.

6   Tolkien, *LOTR*, book II, chapter 1.

7   Morris, *The Roots of the Mountains*.

8   Tolkien, *Lost Tales I*, p. 17.

9   J.R.R. Tolkien, 'Many Meetings', *FR, LOTR*, book II, chapter 1.

10 Marcus Waithe, *William Morris's Utopia of Strangers: Victorian Medievalism and the Ideal of Hospitality* (Cambridge, 2006).

11 The amalgamated volume is available as Kenneth Sisam, ed., *Fourteenth-Century Verse and Prose* (Oxford, 1978); Tolkien's *Middle English Vocabulary* (1923) appears at pp. 293–454.

12 Francis Thompson, *Poems*, ed. Brigid M. Boardman (London and New York, 2001).

13 Tolkien, *The Silmarillion* (London, 1977), chapter 1.

Chapter Eight   *'The lonely sea and the sky'*

1   'The Field of Cormallen', in *The Return of the King, LOTR*, book VI, chapter 4.

2   On Masefield, see *Collected Poems* (London, 1938) and Constance Babington Smith, *John Masefield: A Life* (Oxford, 1978).

3   Tolkien, *Return of the Shadow*, p. 41.

4   Carpenter, *Biography*, p. 11.

5   Carpenter, *Biography*, p. 15.

6   Tolkien, *Family Album*, p. 18.

7   Scull and Hammond, *Guide*, p. 879.

8   Details of the text of 'The Tides' are given in J.R.R. Tolkien, *The Shaping of Middle-earth*, ed. Christopher Tolkien (London, 2002), p. 214.

9   Carpenter, *Biography*, p. 70.

10 Hammond and Scull, *Artist and Illustrator*, pp. 24–5, figs 20, 21.

11 For the text and history of the poem see Tolkien, *Shaping of Middle-earth*, pp. 213–18.

12 Scull and Hammond, *Chronology*, p. 62.

13 Hammond and Scull, *Artist and Illustrator*, p. 46, fig. 42.

14 Scull and Hammond, *Chronology*, p. 60.

15 Tolkien, *Lost Tales II*, p. 155.

16 Scull and Hammond, *Guide*, p. 1134.

17 Edward Burnett Tylor, *Primitive Culture*, 2 vols (London, 1871), vol. 1, p. 258.

18 E.B. Tylor, *Anthropology: An Introduction to the Study of Man and Civilisation* (London, 1881), pp. 289–90.

19 Andrew Lang, 'Edward Burnett Tylor', in W.H.R. Rivers, ed., *Anthropological Essays Presented to Edward Burnett Tylor* (Oxford, 1907), pp. 1–15, at p. 6.

20 Friedrich Max Müller, *Lectures on the Science of Language*, 2 vols, 6th edition (London, 1871), vol. 1, p. 434.

Chapter Nine   *'Far over the Misty Mountains cold'*

1   Letter to Michael Tolkien in *Letters*, p. 393.

2   Tolkien, *Letters*, pp. 391–6, at p. 392; see also 'Switzerland', in Scull and Hammond, *Guide*, pp. 992–5.

3   Tolkien, *Letters*, p. 393.

4   Tolkien, *Letters*, pp. 308–9.

5   Tolkien, *Letters*, p. 309.

6   Tolkien, *Letters*, p. 393.

7   'The Ring Goes South', in *LOTR*, book II, chapter 3.

8   Hammond and Scull, *Artist and Illustrator*, p. 208, fig. 200.

9   Hammond and Scull, *Artist and Illustrator*, p. 61, fig. 58.

10 Hammond and Scull, *Artist and Illustrator*, p. 51, fig. 47.

11 'Of Tuor and his Coming to Gondolin' is the title of a late piece of fiction by Tolkien which covers the same narrative sequence in much greater detail, written in the novelistic style of *LOTR*; see Tolkien, *Unfinished Tales*, chapter 1.

12 Tolkien, *Lost Tales II*, p. 158.

13 Hammond and Scull, *Artist and Illustrator*, p. 61, fig. 58.

14 Tolkien, *Lost Tales II*, p. 160.

15 Tolkien, *Lost Tales II*, p. 192.

16 Tolkien, *Lost Tales II*, p. 192.

17 Tolkien, *Unfinished Tales*, p. 4.

18 Tolkien, *Lost Tales II*, p. 158.

Chapter Ten   *Goblin wars*

1   Rateliff, *History of The Hobbit*, p. 115.
2   'Father Christmas Letter, December 23rd, 1932', in J.R.R. Tolkien, *Letters from Father Christmas*, ed. Baillie Tolkien (London, 2004), pp. 50–2.
3   The story of Rumpelstiltskin is widely available; for example, in Grimm and Grimm, *Selected Tales*.
4   Margaret Hunt, *Grimm's Household Tales*, 2 vols (London, 1884).
5   Tolkien admitted to the novelist Naomi Mitchison that MacDonald had influenced his depiction of goblins; see Tolkien, *Letters*, p. 178.
6   Gilliver *et al.*, *Ring of Words*, pp. 137–8.
7   Tom Shippey, 'Orcs, Wraiths, Wights: Tolkien's Images of Evil', in George Clark and Daniel Timmons, eds, *J.R.R. Tolkien and his Literary Resonances* (Westport, 2000), pp. 183–98.
8   Tolkien, *Letters*, pp. 78, 82, 115.
9   Diane Purkiss, *Troublesome Things: A History of Fairies and Fairy Stories* (London, 2000).
10 John Garth, *Tolkien and the Great War: The Threshold of Middle-earth* (London, 2004).
11 Tolkien, *Lost Tales II*, p. 170.
12 Tolkien, *Lost Tales II*, p. 184.

Chapter Eleven   *Literary myth and the Great War*

1   Robert Graves, *Fairies and Fusiliers* (London, 1917), pp. 14–15, 18, 19, 34, 50, 57, 79.
2   Tolkien, *On Fairy-stories*, p. 56.
3   Paul Fussell, 'Myth, Ritual, and Romance', in his *The Great War and Modern Memory* (Oxford, 1977), pp. 114–54.
4   Fussell, 'Myth, Ritual, and Romance', p. 136.
5   William Morris, *The Well at the World's End* (1896), book III, chapter 18 (reprinted New York, 1979).
6   Hugh Quigley, *Passchendaele and the Somme: A Diary of 1917* (London, 1928), pp. 128–9, p. 159.
7   Geoffrey Bache Smith, *A Spring Harvest* (London, 1918).
8   Carl Phelpstead, *Tolkien and Wales: Language, Literature and Identity* (Cardiff, 2011), pp. 60, 74.
9   Thomas Honegger, 'The Passing of the Elves and the Arrival of Modernity: Tolkien's "Mythical Method"', in Thomas Honegger and Frank Weinreich, *Tolkien and Modernity* (Zurich, 2006), vol. 2, pp. 213–32, at p. 216; T.S. Eliot, *Selected Prose of T.S. Eliot*, ed. Frank Kermode (London, 1975).
10 David Jones, *In Parenthesis* (London, 1963).

11 Paul B. Taylor and W.H. Auden, trans., *The Elder Edda* (London, 1973), p. 56.

12 Robert Graves, *The White Goddess: A Historical Grammar of Poetic Myth*, 3rd edition (London, 1952).

13 Fussell, 'Myth, Ritual, and Romance', p. 131.

Chapter Twelve *Visions of peace*

1 *The Stapeldon Magazine*, vol. 5, no. 25 (December, 1919).

2 *The Stapeldon Magazine*, vol. 5, no. 25 (December, 1919), p. 2.

3 *The Stapeldon Magazine*, vol. 5, no. 26 (June, 1920), p. 87. The comparison of *The Fall of Gondolin* with the works of Lord Dunsany was an apt one; Dunsany was the author of similar mythologies in *The Gods of Pegana* (1905) and *The Book of Wonder* (1912).

4 Wayne G. Hammond, with the assistance of Douglas A. Anderson, *J.R.R. Tolkien: A Descriptive Bibliography* (Winchester, 1993), p. 345.

5 Tolkien, *Lost Tales II*, p. 273.

6 *The Stapeldon Magazine*, vol. 5, no. 26 (June, 1920), p. 69; cf. Tolkien, *Lost Tales II*, pp. 273–4.

7 *A Northern Venture*, verses by members of the Leeds University English School Association (Leeds: At the Swan Press, 1923); 'Tha Eadigan Sælidan' ('The Happy Mariners') appears at pp. 15–16.

8 Scull and Hammond, *Guide*, p. 937.

9 Albert Hugh Smith, *The Merry Shire: Poems in the Yorkshire Dialect* (Leeds: At the Swan Press, 1923).

Chapter Thirteen *Early lessons in philology*

1 Shippey, *Road to Middle-Earth*, p. 31.

2 Tolkien, *Letters*, p. 13.

3 Judith Priestman (ed.) *J.R.R. Tolkien, Life and Legend: An Exhibition to Commemorate the Centenary of the Birth of J.R.R. Tolkien (1982–1973)* (Oxford: Bodleian Library, 1992) p. 16.

4 Christopher Stray, *Classics Transformed: Schools, Universities, and Society in England, 1830–1960* (Oxford, 1998).

5 Tolkien, *Letters*, p. 172.

6 Henry Bradley, *The Making of English* (London, 1904), p. 1.

7 Bradley, *The Making of English*, p. 3.

8 J.R.R. Tolkien, 'Henry Bradley, 3 Dec. 1845–23 May, 1923', *The Bulletin of the Modern Humanities Association* (October, 1923), pp. 4–5.

9 Henry Sweet, *First Steps in Anglo-Saxon* (Oxford, 1897).

10 Henry Sweet, *An Anglo-Saxon Primer* (Oxford, 1882).

11 Tolkien, *The Return of the Shadow*, p. 60.

12 Henry Sweet, 'Some of the Sources of the Anglo-Saxon Chronicle', *Englische Studien*, 2 (1879), 310–12.

13 Maria Artamonova, 'Writing for an Anglo-Saxon Audience in the Twentieth Century: J.R.R. Tolkien's Old English Chronicles', in David Clark and Nicholas Perkins, eds, *Anglo-Saxon Culture and the Modern Imagination* (Cambridge, 2010), pp. 71–88.

14 For Tolkien's language-aesthetic, see Dimitra Fimi, *Tolkien, Race and Cultural History: From Fairies to Hobbits* (London, 2009), pp. 76–92; Ross Smith, 'Fitting Sense to Sound: Linguistic Aesthetics and Phono-semantics in the Work of J.R.R. Tolkien', *Tolkien Studies*, 3 (2006), pp. 1–21.

15 J.R.R. Tolkien, 'Valedictory Address', in Mary Salu and Robert T. Farrell, eds, *J.R.R. Tolkien: Scholar and Story Teller* (Ithaca and London, 1979), p. 31.

16 J.R.R. Tolkien, '"The Story of Kullervo" and Essays on *Kalevala*', ed. Verlyn Flieger, *Tolkien Studies*, 7 (2010), pp. 211–78, at p. 251.

17 Tolkien, *Letters*, p. 214.

18 Friedrich Max Müller, 'Lecture VIII: Morphological Classification', in his *Lectures on the Science of Language*, vol. 1, 2nd edition (London, 1862), p. 310.

19 Edward Burnett Tylor, *Primitive Culture*, 2 vols (London, 1871). Reprinted in 2 vols: *The Origins of Culture and Religion in Primitive Culture* (New York, 1958), vol. 1, p. 195.

20 Gerard Manley Hopkins, *Poems and Prose*, ed. W.H. Gardner (Harmondsworth, 1953), p. 90.

21 Verlyn Flieger, 'Meaning and Myth in Owen Barfield', *Poetic Diction: A Study in Meaning* (Faber and Gwyer, 1928), pp. 59–81; Verlyn Flieger, *Splintered Light: Logos and Language in Tolkien's World*, 2nd edition (Kent, OH, 2002), pp. 33–44.

22 David Abram, *The Spell of the Sensuous: Perception and Language in a More-than-Human World* (New York, 1999), p. 75. Abram's ideas, based in anthropology and phenomenology, are related to Barfield and Tolkien by Ross Smith, 'Fitting Sense to Sound: Linguistic Aesthetics and Phono-semantics in the Work of J.R.R. Tolkien', *Tolkien Studies*, 3 (2006), pp. 1–21.

23 Carpenter, *Biography*, p. 64.

24 Clive Tolley, 'Old English Influence on *The Lord of the Rings*', in Richard North and Joe Allard, eds, *Beowulf and Other Stories* (Edinburgh, 2007), pp. 38–62, at pp. 57–9; see also Carl F. Hostetter, 'Over Middle-earth Sent unto Men: On the Philological Origins of Tolkien's Eärendel Myth', *Mythlore*, vol. 17, no. 3, whole no. 65 (spring, 1991), pp. 5–10.

25 Tolkien, *Letters*, p. 385.

26 Henry Sweet, *Anglo-Saxon Reader*, 8th revised edition (Oxford, 1908).

27 Mark Atherton, 'Priming the Poets: The Making of Henry Sweet's *Anglo-Saxon Reader*', in Clark and Perkins, *Anglo-Saxon Culture and the Modern Imagination*, pp. 31–49.

28 S.A.J. Bradley, trans., *Anglo-Saxon Poetry* (London, 1995).

29 Anderson, in *The Annotated Hobbit*, pp. 293–4.

30 Gilliver *et al.*, *Ring of Words*, pp. 89–224.

31 *The Dream of the Rood*, lines 30–3. The text is chapter 25 of Sweet, *Anglo-Saxon Reader* (1908); the poem is found in numerous anthologies of Old English poetry.

32 Tolkien, *Letters*, p. 381; Gilliver *et al.*, *Ring of Words*, pp. 206–7.

33 Fimi, *Tolkien, Race and Cultural History*, pp. 93–115.

34 For learning Old English, with texts and a CD of sound recordings, see Mark Atherton, *Complete Old English* (London, 2010).

35 Tolkien's idiosyncratic spelling and pronunciation *dwarves* is discussed by Gilliver *et al.*, *Ring of Words*, pp. 104–8.

36 Sweet, *Reader*, line 23.

37 Tolkien, *On Fairy-stories*, pp. 43–4, 182.

Chapter Fourteen *Tolkien as word-collector*

1 Howard Jackson, *Lexicography: An Introduction* (London, 2002), p. 87.

2 Sisam, *Verse and Prose*, chapter 10, line 122.

3 Gilliver *et al.*, *Ring of Words*, pp. 214–16.

4 Sisam, *Verse and Prose*, chapter 15, *i*.

5 In 'Fog on the Barrow-Downs', *LOTR*, book I, chapter 8.

6 Sisam, *Verse and Prose*, chapter 2, line 346; chapter 5, line 225; chapter 6, line 20.

7 Israel Gollancz, *Pearl: An English Poems of the Fourteenth Century Re-set in Modern English* (London, 1918), stanza 32.

8 Shippey, *Road to Middle-earth*, p. 136.

9 Norman Blake, *The English Language in Medieval Literature* (London, 1977).

10 Sisam, *Verse and Prose*, chapter 2, lines 143–6.

11 J.R.R. Tolkien, trans., *Sir Gawain and the Green Knight, Pearl, and Sir Orfeo* (London, 1975).

12 Tolkien, *Lost Tales I*, p. 47.

Chapter Fifteen *Rhymes and riddles*

1 Tolkien, *On Fairy-tales*, p. 50.

2 J.R.R. Tolkien, 'The Cat and the Fiddle: A Nursery Rhyme Undone and its Scandalous Secret Unlocked', the new poem heading the issue in *Yorkshire Poetry*,

vol. 2, no. 19 (20 October 1923) (Leeds: At the Swan Press, 1923), pp. 1–3. A revised version was later published as 'The Man in the Moon Stayed up too Late' in Tolkien's *Adventures of Tom Bombadil*.

3   The Man in the Moon moving earthwards on his bridge of filigree is pictured in a watercolour by Tolkien; see Hammond and Scull, *Artist and Illustrator*, p. 49, fig. 45.

4   Tolkien, *Lost Tales I*, p. 191.

5   Taylor and Auden, *Elder Edda*, p. 80.

6   Tolkien, *Lost Tales I*, p. 192.

7   Smith, *Spring Harvest*, p. 29.

8   I. Opie and P. Opie, *The Oxford Dictionary of Nursery Rhymes*, 2nd edition (Oxford, 1997), pp. 203–4.

9   J.O. Halliwell, *The Nursery Rhymes of England*, 5th edition (London, 1970), p. 170.

10   George Burke Johnson, 'The Poetry of J.R.R. Tolkien', *Mankato State University Studies*, 2 (February 1967), pp. 63–75.

11   George MacDonald, *At the Back of the North Wind* (London, 1956), pp. 191–3.

12   Shippey, *Road to Middle-earth*, pp. 29–30.

13   London, British Library, manuscript Harley 2253, ff. 114–15.

14   Translation by the author. For a convenient edition, see John Porter, ed. and trans., *Anglo-Saxon Riddles* (Hockwold-cum-Wilton, 2003).

15   Opie and Opie, *The Oxford Dictionary of Nursery Rhymes*, p. 152; quoted in Rateliff, *History of the Hobbit*, p. 171.

16   There is a full discussion of the egg-riddle and its sources in Rateliff, *History of the Hobbit*, pp. 168–74.

17   Taylor and Auden, *The Elder Edda*, pp. 71, 78, 82–3.

18   For the texts cited, see Christopher Tolkien, ed., *The Saga of King Heidrek the Wise* (London, 1960), pp. 44 and 80.

Chapter Sixteen   *Dialect matters*

1   Elizabeth Wright, *Rustic Speech and Folk-Lore* (London, 1913), p. xix.

2   Tolkien, *Letters*, p. 11.

3   Tolkien, *Return of the Shadow*, p. 94.

4   Lynda Mugglestone, *Talking Proper: The Rise of Accent as Social Symbol* (Oxford, 2003).

5   J.R.R. Tolkien, 'Chaucer as Philologist: *The Reeve's Tale*', *Transactions of the Philological Society* (1934), pp. 1–70, at p. 9, n.1.

6   Tolkien, 'Chaucer as Philologist', p. 9.

7   Richmal Crompton, *William and the Moon Rocket* (London, 1954), chapter viii.

8   Tolkien, 'Chaucer as Philologist', p. 5.

9   Scull and Hammond, *Guide*, pp. 153–6.

10   Chaucer, *The Canterbury Tales*, lines 3921–5; Larry D. Benson, ed., *The Riverside Chaucer*, 3rd edition (Oxford University Press, 1988).

11 Sisam, *Verse and Prose*, chapter 13.

12 J.R.R. Tolkien, 'Valedictory Address', in Mary Salu and Robert T. Farrell, *J.R.R. Tolkien, Scholar and Storyteller: Essays in Memoriam* (Ithaca and London, 1979), pp. 31–2.

13 Tolkien, 'Chaucer as Philologist', p. 53.

14 Simon Horobin, 'J.R.R. Tolkien as a Philologist: A Reconsideration of the Northernisms in Chaucer's Reeve's Tale', *English Studies*, 82 (2001), pp. 97–105.

15 Marjorie Burns, *Perilous Realms: Celtic and Norse in Tolkien's Middle-earth* (Toronto, 2005), pp. 34–6.

16 Tolkien, *Sir Gawain* trans., p. 19.

17 Simon Armitage, trans., *Sir Gawain and the Green Knight* (London: Faber and Faber, 2007), p. 14.

18 For a history of English poetic diction theory since the Renaissance, see Emerson R. Marks, *Taming the Chaos* (Detroit, 1998).

19 Alan Garner, *The Voice that Thunders: Essays and Lectures* (London, 1997), pp. 47–9.

20 Walter E. Haigh, *A New Glossary of the Dialect of the Huddersfield District* (London, 1928), pp. xii–xviii.

21 Janet Brennan Croft, 'Walter E. Haigh, Author of *A New Glossary of the Dialect of the Huddersfield District*', *Tolkien Studies*, 4 (2007), pp. 184–8.

22 Haigh, *New Glossary*, p. xiii.

23 Haigh, *New Glossary*, p. xxii.

24 Haigh, *New Glossary*, p. xv.

25 J.R.R. Tolkien, 'Philology: General Works' in The Year's Work in English Studies, vol. 4 (1923), pp. 20–44, at p.00.

23 Haigh, *New Glossary*, p. xviii.

24 Joseph Wright, *The English Dialect Dictionary*, vol. 3 (London: Henry Frowde, 1902), p. 183, citing the journal *Notes & Queries*, 4th series, 5 (1870), p. 156.

25 Wright, *EDD*, vol. 3, p. 189.

26 Elizabeth Mary Wright, *Rustic Speech and Folk-Lore* (London, 1913), p. 202.

27 Wright, *EDD*, vol. 1, p. 130.

28 W.R.J. Barron, ed., *Sir Gawain and the Green Knight* (Manchester, 1974), p. 145.

29 *Beowulf*, lines 2807, 3155–6, 3169. A useful edition of the poem with explanations of vocabulary provided in the margins of the text is George Jack, ed., *Beowulf: A Student Edition* (Oxford, 1994).

30 Abram, *Spell of the Sensuous*, p. 140.

Epilogue

1 From *The Voiage and Travaile of Sir Iohn Maundevile, Kt.*, in Sisam, *Verse and Prose*, p. 104.

2 Barron, *Sir Gawain and the Green Knight*, pp. 160–1.

Bibliography

THE BIBLIOGRAPHY COVERS literary, biographical, historical, cultural and linguistic themes relevant to *The Hobbit*. It aims to bring together in a convenient form most of the books and articles consulted during the writing of this study. It also provides a quick guide to some major writings on Tolkien that have appeared since the early 2000s. In addition, the bibliography provides recommendations for further reading, to show readers where to go next. For a first orientation, readers would do well to look at the two studies by Tom Shippey, which each take respectively two different but complementary approaches to the study of Tolkien: in linguistic terms, the diachronic (historical development) and the synchronic (the study of a writer in the context of his own time). Thus Shippey's *The Road to Middle-earth* deals with philology, the historical focus that considers Tolkien's sources: the languages he knew and the medieval literature that he taught. By contrast, Shippey's later book, *J.R.R. Tolkien: Author of the Century*, looks at *LOTR* in its twentieth-century literary context.

With the diachronic–synchronic distinction in mind the following are some recommendations, and suggestions (since the field is wide) for the next stage of reading and study. The essential first task is to read some of the medieval literature that Tolkien was steeped in. A companion piece then would be the book *The Keys to Middle-earth* by Stuart Lee and Elizabeth Solopova. To follow further in Tolkien's footsteps there is a good wide selection of medieval writers in Treharne, with the bonus of a translation on the facing page. It makes sense for readers to use parallel texts in order to see the words that the medieval writer actually used rather than only their modern translated equivalents. As for the literary background, there are many reliable introductions, including Magennis and O'Donoghue for Old English, Turville-Petre for Middle English, and North/Allard and O'Donoghue for Old Norse. For learning the original languages, an activity that was dear to Tolkien's heart, see the introductions to Old English by Atherton or Baker, or McCully/Hilles, on Middle English by Burrow and Turville-Petre, while for Old Norse, E.V. Gordon's textbook is still available; as far as convenient dictionaries are concerned there is Clark Hall for Old English and Zoëga for Old Norse. For English dialects there are, for example, the essays edited by David Britain or the books by James and Lesley Milroy; Philip Durkin provides a valuable general guide to etymology, while Cameron and Gelling cover place names, and Gilliver, Jackson and Mugglestone explore lexicography and the *OED*. For writers and movements contemporary to Tolkien in the 1920s and 1930s a good survey is Fimi, and more generally such guides as Drabble or Sanders. Oxford and Cambridge Companions and Introductions form a useful port of call for major writers of the late nineteenth and early twentieth centuries; for example, Sandra Kemp *et al.* on Edwardian fiction or Pericles Lewis on modernism. For children's literature see Cook, Grenby and Pearson. Finally, *Tolkien Companion*, ed. Stuart Lee (Wiley-Blackwell, forthcoming), aims to provide full coverage of all the themes and interests that Tolkien covered in his creative and academic writing.

Agøy, Nils Avar, 'The Christian Tolkien: A Response to Ronald Hutton', in Paul E. Kerry, *The Ring and the Cross: Christianiy and the Lord of the Rings* (Madison NJ and Plymouth: Fairley Dickinson University Press, 2011), 71–89.

Alderson, Brian, ed., *The Red Fairy Book, Collected by Andrew Lang* (Harmondsworth: Kestrel, 1976).

Anderson, Douglas A., '"An industrial little devil": E.V. Gordon as Friend and Collaborator with Tolkien', in Jane Chance, ed., *Tolkien the Medievalist* (London: Routledge, 2003), 15–25.

————, ed., *The Annotated Hobbit*, 2nd edn (London: HarperCollins, 2003).

Anonymous, *The Saga of King Hrolf Kraki*, trans. Jesse L. Byock (London: Penguin, 1998).

Armitage, Simon, *Sir Gawain and the Green Knight* (London: Faber and Faber, 2007).

Artamonova, Maria, 'Writing for an Anglo-Saxon Audience in the Twentieth Century: J.R.R. Tolkien's Old English Chronicles', in David Clark and Nicholas Perkins, eds,

Anglo-Saxon Culture and the Modern Imagination (Cambridge: D.S. Brewer, 2010), 71–88.

Atherton, Mark, *Complete Old English* (London: Hodder and Stoughton, 2010).

————, 'Priming the Poets: The Making of Henry Sweet's *Anglo-Saxon Reader*', in David Clark and Nicholas Perkins, eds, *Anglo-Saxon Culture and the Modern Imagination* (Cambridge: D.S. Brewer, 2010), 31–49.

Auden, W.H., 'The Quest Hero', in R.A. Zimbardo and N.D. Isaacs, *Understanding The Lord of the Rings* (Boston: Houghton Mifflin, 2004), 31–51 (orig. publ. 1962).

Avery, Gillian, 'Introduction and Notes' to E. Nesbit, *Five Children and It* (New York: Penguin, 2005).

Babington Smith, Constance, *John Masefield: A Life* (Oxford: Oxford University Press, 1978).

Baker, Peter S., *Introduction to Old English*, 2nd edition (Oxford: Blackwell, 2007).

Barfield, Owen, *Poetic Diction: A Study in Meaning* (London: Faber and Gwyer, 1928).

Barron, W.R.J., ed., *Sir Gawain and the Green Knight* (Manchester: Manchester University Press, 1974).

Benson, Larry D., ed., *The Riverside Chaucer*, 3rd edition (Oxford: Oxford University Press, 1988).

Birzer, Bradley J., *J.R.R. Tolkien's Sanctifying Myth: Understanding Middle-earth* (Wilmington DE: ISI Books, 2003).

————, 'The Last Battle as a Johannine Raganrök: Tolkien and the Universal', in Paul E. Kerry, *The Ring and the Cross: Christianity and the Lord of the Rings* (Madison NJ and Plymouth: Fairley Dickinson University Press, 2011), 259–80.

Blackham, Robert S., *The Roots of Tolkien's Middle-earth* (Stroud: Tempus, 2006).

Blair, John, *Anglo-Saxon England: A Very Short Introduction* (Oxford: Oxford University Press, 2000).

Blake, Norman, *The English Language in Medieval Literature* (London: Methuen, 1977).

Blythe, Ronald, *Akenfield: Portrait of an English Village* (London: Penguin, 1972).

Boccaccio, Giovanni, *The Decameron*, trans. G.H. McWilliam (London: Penguin, 2003)

Bradley, Henry, *The Making of English* (London: Macmillan, 1904).

Bradley, S.A.J., trans., *Anglo-Saxon Poetry* (London: Everyman, 1995).

Brewer, Derek S., '*The Lord of the Rings* as Romance', in Mary Salu and Robert T. Farrell, eds, *J.R.R. Tolkien: Scholar and Story Teller* (Ithaca NY and London: Cornell University Press, 1979), 249–64.

———— and Jonathan Gibson, eds, *A Companion to the* Gawain-*poet* (Cambridge: D.S. Brewer, 1997).

Briggs, Katherine M., *The Fairies in English Tradition and Literature* (London: Bellew, 1989) (orig. publ. 1967).

Britain, David, *Language in the British Isles* (Cambridge: Cambridge University Press, 2007).

Brogan, Hugh, 'Tolkien's Great War', in Gillian Avery and Julia Briggs, eds, *Children and their Books: A Celebration of the Work of Iona and Peter Opie* (Oxford: Clarendon Press, 1989), 351–67.

Burns, Marjorie, *Perilous Realms: Celtic and Norse in Tolkien's Middle-earth* (Toronto ON: University of Toronto Press, 2005).

Burrow, J.A. and T. Turville-Petre, *A Book of Middle English* (Oxford: Blackwell, 1992).

Byock, Jesse L., trans., *The Saga of King Hrolf Kraki* (London: Penguin, 1998).

Caldecott, Stratford, *Secret Fire: The Spiritual Vision of J.R.R. Tolkien* (London: Darton, Longman and Todd, 2003).

_____ and Thomas Honegger, *Tolkien's* The Lord of the Rings: *Sources of Inspiration* (Zurich and Jena: Walking Tree Publishers, 2008).

Cameron, Kenneth, *English Place Names*, new edition (London: Batsford, 1996).

Cannon, Christopher, *Middle English Literature* (Cambridge: Polity Press, 2008).

Carpenter, Humphrey, *J.R.R. Tolkien: A Biography* (London: George Allen & Unwin, 1977).

_____, *The Inklings: C.S. Lewis, J.R.R. Tolkien, Charles Williams and their Friends* (London: HarperCollins, 2006).

Chance, Jane, ed., *Tolkien the Medievalist* (London: Routledge, 2003).

_____, *Tolkien and the Invention of Myth: A Reader* (Lexington: University Press of Kentucky, 2004).

_____ and Alfred K. Siewers, *Tolkien's Modern Middle Ages* (New York: Palgrave Macmillan, 2005).

Christensen, Bonniejean, 'Gollum's Character Transformation in *The Hobbit*', in Jared Lobdell, ed., *A Tolkien Compass*, 2nd edition (Chicago IL: Open Court, 2003), 7–26.

Clark, David and Nicholas Perkins, eds, *Anglo-Saxon Culture and the Modern Imagination* (Cambridge: D.S. Brewer, 2010).

Clark, George and Daniel Timmons, eds, *J.R.R. Tolkien and his Literary Resonances* (Westport CT: Greenwood Press, 2000).

Clark Hall, J.R., trans., *Beowulf and the Finnesburg Fragment* (London: George Allen & Unwin, 1940).

_____, *A Concise Anglo-Saxon Dictionary* (Toronto ON and London: University of Toronto Press reprint, 2000).

Cook, Elizabeth, *The Ordinary and the Fabulous: An Introduction to Myths, Legends and Fairy Tales*, 2nd edition (Cambridge: Cambridge University Press, 1976).

Croft, Janet Brennan, *War and the Works of J.R.R. Tolkien* (Westport CT and London: Praeger, 2004).

_____, 'Walter E. Haigh, Author of *A New Glossary of the Dialect of the Huddersfield District*', *Tolkien Studies*, 4 (2007), 184–8.

Crompton, Richmal, *William and the Moon Rocket* (London: Macmillan, 1991) (orig. publ. London: Newnes, 1954).

Crystal, David, *The Stories of English* (London: Penguin, 2004).

Curry, Patrick, *Defending Middle-earth* (London: HarperCollins, 1998).

Dickerson, Matthew T. and Jonathan D. Evans, *Ents, Elves, and Eriador: The Environmental Vision of J.R.R. Tolkien* (Lexington: University Press of Kentucky, 2006).

Dorson, Richard M., *The British Folklorists: A History* (London and New York: Routledge, 1968).

Drabble, Margaret, *The Oxford Companion to English Literature* (Oxford and New York: Oxford University Press, 1998).

Dronke, Ursula, ed., *The Poetic Edda Volume II: Mythological Poems* (Oxford: Clarendon Press, 1997).

Dunsany, Lord, *The Book of Wonder* (London: William Heinemann, 1912).

————, *The King of Elfland's Daughter* (London: Gollancz, 2001) (orig. publ. London and New York: G.P. Putnam's Sons, 1924).

————, *The Blessing of Pan* (London and New York: G.P. Putnam's Sons, 1927).

Durkin, Philip, *The Oxford Guide to Etymology* (Oxford: Oxford University Press, 2009).

Durrell, Lawrence, 'Landscape and Character', in *Spirit of Place: Letters and Essays on Travel*, ed. Alan G. Thomas (London: Faber and Faber, 1969), 156–63.

Eaglestone, Robert, *Reading* The Lord of the Rings: *New Writings on Tolkien's Classic* (London: Continuum, 2006).

Ekwall, Eilert, *English Place-Names in -ing* (London: Milford, 1923).

————, *English River-names* (Oxford: Clarendon Press, 1928).

Eliot, T.S., *Selected Prose of T.S. Eliot*, ed. Frank Kermode (London: Faber and Faber, 1975).

Fimi, Dimitra, *Tolkien, Race and Cultural History: From Fairies to Hobbits* (London: Palgrave Macmillan, 2009).

Flieger, Verlyn, *Splintered Light: Logos and Language in Tolkien's World*, 2nd edition (Kent OH: Kent State University Press, 2002).

————, '"There would always be a fairy-tale": J.R.R. Tolkien and the Folklore Controversy', in Jane Chance (ed.), *Tolkien the Medievalist* (London: Routledge, 2003), 26–35.

————, *Interrupted Music: The Making of Tolkien's Mythology* (Kent OH: Kent State University Press, 2005).

———— and Carl F. Hostetter, *Tolkien's Legendarium: Essays on the History of Middle-earth* (Westport CT: Greenwood Press, 2000).

Fulk, R.D., ed. and trans., *The Beowulf Manuscript* (Cambridge MA and London: Harvard University Press, 2010).

Fussell, Paul, *The Great War and Modern Memory* (Oxford: Oxford University Press, 1977).

Garbowski, Christopher, *Recovery and Transcendence for the Contemporary Mythmaker: The Spiritual Dimension in the Works of J.R.R. Tolkien*, 2nd edition (Zurich: Walking Tree Publishers, 2004).

Gardner, Angela, ed., *Black and White Ogre Country: The Lost Tales of Hilary Tolkien* (Moreton-in-Marsh: ADC Publications, 2009).

Garner, Alan, *The Voice that Thunders: Essays and Lectures* (London: The Harvil Press, 1997).

Garth, John, *Tolkien and the Great War: The Threshold of Middle-earth* (London: HarperCollins, 2004).

Gelling, Margaret, *The Place-names of Oxfordshire* (Cambridge: Cambridge University Press, 1953–54).

————, *Place-names in the Landscape* (London: Dent, 1984).

Gilliver, Peter, Jeremy Marshall and Edmund Weiner, *The Ring of Words: Tolkien and the Oxford English Dictionary* (Oxford: Oxford University Press, 2006).

Glyer, Diana P., *The Company they Keep: C.S. Lewis and J.R.R. Tolkien as Writers in Community* (Kent OH: Kent State University Press, 2007).

Godden, Malcolm and Michael Lapidge, *The Cambridge Companion to Old English Literature* (Cambridge: Cambridge University Press, 1991).

Gordon, Eric V., *An Introduction to Old Norse* (Oxford: Clarendon Press, 1927).

_____ and A.R. Taylor, *An Introduction to Old Norse*, 2nd edition (Oxford: Clarendon Press, 1957).

_____ and J.R.R. Tolkien (eds), *Sir Gawain and the Green Knight* (Oxford: Clarendon Press, 1925).

Gordon, Ida L., ed., *Pearl* (Oxford: Clarendon Press, 1953).

Grahame, Kenneth, 'The Reluctant Dragon', in *Dream Days* (London: Bodley Head, 1978) (orig. publ. 1898).

_____, *The Wind in the Willows* (London: Methuen, 1908).

Graves, Robert, *Fairies and Fusiliers* (London: Heinemann, 1917).

_____, *Goodbye to All That* (London: Penguin, 2000) (orig. publ. London: Jonathan Cape, 1929).

_____, *The White Goddess: A Historical Grammar of Poetic Myth*, 3rd edition (London: Faber and Faber, 1952).

Grenby, M.O., *The Cambridge Companion to Children's Literature* (Cambridge: Cambridge University Press, 2009).

Grimm, Jacob, and Wilhelm Grimm, *Selected Tales*, ed. and trans. David Luke (Harmondsworth: Penguin, 1982).

Haigh, Walter E., *A New Glossary of the Dialect of the Huddersfield District* (London: Oxford University Press and Humphrey Milford, 1928).

Halliwell, J.O., *The Nursery Rhymes of England*, 5th edition (London, 1853; reprinted London: Bodley Head, 1970).

Hamer, Richard, ed. and trans., *A Choice of Anglo-Saxon Verse* (London: Faber and Faber, 1970).

Hammond, Wayne G., with the assistance of Douglas A. Anderson, *J.R.R. Tolkien: A Descriptive Bibliography* (Winchester: St Paul's Bibliographies, 1993).

_____ and Christina Scull, *J.R.R. Tolkien: Artist and Illustrator* (London: HarperCollins, 1998).

_____ and Christina Scull, *The Lord of the Rings: A Reader's Companion* (London: HarperCollins, 2008).

Hardy, Thomas, *Under the Greenwood Tree*, or *The Mellstock Quire: A Rural Painting of the Dutch School* (London: Penguin, 1985) (orig. publ. 1872).

Hart, Rachel, 'Tolkien, St Andrews, and Dragons', in Trevor Hart and Ivan Khovacs, eds, *Tree of Tales: Tolkien, Literature, and Theology* (Waco, TX; Baylor University Press, 2007), 1–11.

Heaney, Seamus, *Beowulf* (London: Faber and Faber, 1999).

Hogg, Richard M., *The Cambridge History of the English Language. Volume I. The Beginnings to 1066* (Cambridge: Cambridge University Press, 1992).

Honegger, Thomas, 'The Passing of the Elves and the Arrival of Modernity: Tolkien's "Mythical Method"', in Thomas Honegger and Frank Weinreich, eds, *Tolkien and Modernity* (Zurich: Walking Tree Publishers, 2006), vol. 2, 213–32.

Hopkins, Gerard Manley, *Poems and Prose*, ed. W.H. Gardner (Harmondsworth: Penguin, 1953).

Horobin, Simon, 'J.R.R. Tolkien as a Philologist: A Reconsideration of the Northernisms in Chaucer's Reeve's Tale', *English Studies*, 82 (2001), 97–105.

_____, *An Introduction to Middle English* (Edinburgh: Edinburgh University Press, 2002).

_____, *Chaucer's Language* (Basingstoke: Palgrave Macmillan, 2007).

Hostetter, Carl F., 'Over Middle-earth Sent unto Men: On the Philological Origins of Tolkien's Eärendel Myth', *Mythlore* 17, no. 3, whole no. 65 (spring, 1991), 5–10.

Hunt, Margaret, *Grimm's Household Tales*, 2 vols (London: G. Bell and Sons, 1884).

Hutchisson, James M., *The Rise of Sinclair Lewis 1920–1930* (University Park: University of Pennsylvania Press, 1996).

Hutton, Ronald, 'The Pagan Tolkien', in Paul E. Kerry, *The Ring and the Cross: Christianity and the Lord of the Rings* (Madison NJ and Plymouth: Fairley Dickinson University Press, 2011), 57–70.

_____, 'Can We Still Have a Pagan Tolkien', in Paul E. Kerry, *The Ring and the Cross: Christianity and the Lord of the Rings* (Madison NJ and Plymouth: Fairley Dickinson University Press, 2011), 90–105.

Jack, George, ed., *Beowulf: A Student Edition* (Oxford: Clarendon Press, 1994).

Jackson, Howard, *Lexicography: An Introduction* (London: Routledge, 2002).

Johnson, David F. and Elaine Treharne, *Readings in Medieval Texts: Interpreting Old and Middle English Literature* (Oxford: Oxford University Press, 2005).

Johnson, George Burke, 'The Poetry of J.R.R. Tolkien', *Mankato State University Studies*, 2 (February 1967), 63–75.

Jones, David, *In Parenthesis* (London: Faber and Faber, 1963).

Kemp, Sandra, Charlotte Mitchell and David Trotter, *Edwardian Fiction* (Oxford and New York: Oxford University Press, 1997).

Kipling, Rudyard, *Puck of Pook's Hill* and *Rewards and Fairies*, ed. Donald Mackenzie (Oxford: Oxford University Press, 1993) (orig. publ. 1906 and 1910).

Lang, Andrew, *The Red Fairy Book* (London: Longmans, Green & Co., 1890).

_____, 'Edward Burnett Tylor', in W.H.R. Rivers, ed., *Anthropological Essays Presented to Edward Burnett Tylor* (Oxford: Clarendon Press, 1907), 1–15.

Lapidge, Michael, John Blair, Simon Keynes and Donald Scragg, eds, *The Blackwell Encyclopedia of Anglo-Saxon England* (Oxford: Blackwell, 1999).

_____ and Malcom Godden, *The Cambridge Companion to Old English Literature* (Cambridge: Cambridge University Press, 1991).

Larrington, Carolyne, trans., *The Poetic Edda* (Oxford: Oxford University Press, 1996).

Lazo, Andrew, 'Gathered round Northern Fires: The Imaginative Impact of the Kolbítar', in Jane Chance, ed., *Tolkien and the Invention of Myth: A Reader* (Lexington: United Press of Kentucky, 2004), 191–226.

Lee, Stuart and Elizabeth Solopova, *The Keys of Middle-earth: Discovering Medieval Literature through the Fiction of J.R.R. Tolkien* (Basingstoke: Palgrave Macmillan, 2005).

Lewis, Alex, 'The Lost Heart of the Little Kingdom', in *Leaves from the Tree: J.R.R. Tolkien's Shorter Fiction* (London: Tolkien Society, 1991), 33–44.

Lewis, C.S., *Rehabilitations and Other Essays* (London: Oxford University Press, 1939).

————, 'On Stories', *Essays Presented to Charles Williams* (London: Oxford University Press, 1947), 90–105.

————, *The Voyage of the Dawntreader* (Harmondsworth: Penguin, 1965) (orig. publ. 1952).

————, *An Experiment in Criticism* (Cambridge: Cambridge University Press, 1961).

————, *The Discarded Image: An Introduction to Medieval and Renaissance Literature* (Cambridge: Cambridge University Press, 1964).

————, *All My Road before Me: The Diary of C.S. Lewis 1922–27*, ed. Walter Hooper (London: Harper Collins, 1991).

Lewis, Pericles, *The Cambridge Introduction to Modernism* (Cambridge: Cambridge University Press, 2007).

Lewis, Sinclair, *Babbitt* (New York: Harcourt and London: Jonathan Cape, 1922).

Lofting, Hugh, *Doctor Dolittle: Being the History of his Peculiar Life at Home, and Astonishing Adventures in Foreign Parts* (London: Jonathan Cape, 1922).

Lönnrot, Elias, *The Kalevala*, trans. Keith Bosley (Oxford: Oxford University Press, 1999).

Lucas, John, 'The Sunlight on the Garden', in Carola M. Kaplan and Anne B. Simpson, eds, *Seeing Double: Revisioning Edwardian and Modernist Literature* (London: Macmillan, 1996), 59–77.

MacCarthy, Fiona, *William Morris* (London: Faber and Faber, 1994).

MacDonald, George, *At the Back of the North Wind* (London: Dent, 1956) (orig. publ. 1868).

————, *The Complete Fairy Tales*, ed. U.C. Knoepflmacher (London: Penguin, 1999).

Magennis, Hugh, *The Cambridge Introduction to Anglo-Saxon Literature* (Cambridge: Cambridge University Press, 2011).

Marks, Emerson R., *Taming the Chaos: English Poetic Diction Theory since the Renaissance* (Detroit MI: Wayne State University Press, 1998).

Masefield, John, *Collected Poems* (London: Heinemann, 1938).

Mathews, Richard, *Fantasy: The Liberation of the Imagination* (New York and London: Routledge, 2002).

McCully, Chris and Sharon Hilles, *The Earliest English: An Introduction to Old English* (Harlow: Pearson Education, 2005).

Milbank, Alison, *Chesterton and Tolkien as Theologians: The Fantasy of the Real* (London and New York: T&T Clark, 2007).

Milroy, James and Lesley Milroy, *Authority in Language: Investigating Standard English*, 3rd edition (London: Routledge, 1999).

_____ and Lesley Milroy, eds, *Real English: The Grammar of English Dialects in the British Isles* (London: Longman, 1993).

Morpurgo Davies, Anna, *Nineteenth-Century Linguistics* (London: Longmans, 1992).

Morris, William, *The Roots of the Mountains* (London: George Prior, 1979) (orig. publ. London: Reeves and Turner, 1890).

_____, *News from Nowhere*, reprinted in *Selected Writings* (London: Nonesuch Press, 1946) (orig. publ. 1890).

_____, *The Well at the World's End* (New York: Ballantine, 1970) (orig. publ. 1896).

Morton, Andrew H., *Tolkien's Bag End* (Studley, Warwickshire: Brewin Books, 2009).

_____ and John Hayes, *Tolkien's Gedling: The Birth of a Legend* (Studley, Warwickshire: Brewin Books, 2008).

Mugglestone, Lynda, *Talking Proper: The Rise of Accent as Social Symbol* (Oxford: Oxford University Press, 2003).

Müller, Friedrich Max, 'Comparative Mythology', in *Chips from a German Workshop* new edition, vol. 4 (London: Longmans, Green & Co. 1856/95), 1–154.

_____, *Lectures on the Science of Language*: *First Series* (London: Longman, Green, Longman and Roberts, 1861; reprinted London: Routledge/Thoemmes, 1994).

_____, *Lectures on the Science of Language*: *Second Series* (London: Longman, Green, Longman, Roberts and Green, 1864; reprinted London: Routledge/Thoemmes, 1994).

Murphy, G. Ronald, *The Owl, The Raven, and the Dove: The Religious Meaning of the Grimms' Magic Fairy Tales* (Oxford: Oxford University Press, 2000).

Nesbit, Edith, *Five Children and It* (London: T. Fisher Unwin, 1902).

North, Richard and Jo Allard, *Beowulf and Other Stories: A New Introduction to Old English, Old Icelandic and Anglo-Norman Literatures* (Harlow: Pearson Education, 2007).

A Northern Venture, Verses by Members of the Leeds University English School Association (Leeds: At the Swan Press, 1923).

O'Donoghue, Heather, *Old Norse-Icelandic Literature: A Short Introduction* (Oxford: Blackwell, 2004).

Opie, Iona and Peter Opie, *The Oxford Dictionary of Nursery Rhymes*, 2nd edition (Oxford: Oxford University Press, 1997).

Orchard, Andy, *A Critical Companion to Beowulf* (Cambridge: D.S. Brewer, 2003).

Oser, Lee, *The Return of Christian Humanism: Chesterton, Eliot, Tolkien, and the Romance of History* (Columbia and London: University of Missouri Press, 2007).

Pearson, Lucy, *Children's Literature* (London: York, 2011).

Pennant, Thomas, *A Tour in Scotland*, 4th edition (London: Benjamin White, 1776) (orig. publ. 1769).

Phelpstead, Carl, *Tolkien and Wales. Language, Literature and Identity* (Cardiff: University of Wales Press, 2011).

Poe, Harry Lee and James Ray Veneman, *The Inklings of Oxford: C.S. Lewis, J.R.R. Tolkien and their Friends* (Grand Rapids MI: Zondervan, 2009).

Porter, John, ed. and trans., *Anglo-Saxon Riddles* (Hockwold-cum-Wilton: Anglo-Saxon Books, 2003).

Pulsiano, Phillip and Elaine Treharne, *A Companion to Anglo-Saxon Literature* (Oxford: Blackwell, 2001).

Purkiss, Diane, *Troublesome Things: A History of Fairies and Fairy Stories* (London: Allen Lane, 2000).

Quigley, Hugh, *Passchendaele and the Somme: A Diary of 1917* (London: Methuen, 1928).

Rateliff, John D., *The History of the Hobbit. Part One: Mr Baggins* (London: Harper Collins, 2007).

Rauer, Christine, *Beowulf and the Dragon: Parallels and Analogues* (Cambridge and New York: Boydell and Brewer, 2000).

Robins, R.H., *A Short History of Linguistics*, 4th edition (London: Longman, 1997).

Robinson, Jeremy Mark, *J.R.R. Tolkien: The Books, the Films, the Whole Cultural Phenomenon. Including a Scene-by-Scene Analysis of the 2001–2003 Lord of the Rings Films* (Maidstone: Crecent Moon, 2008).

Rutledge, Fleming, 'Prologue: *The Hobbit*', in *The Battle for Middle-earth* (Grand Rapids MI and Cambridge: William B. Eerdmans, 2004), 21–45.

Sammons, Martha C., *War of the Fantasy Worlds. C.S. Lewis and J.R.R. Tolkien on Art and Imagination* (Santa Barbara CA and Oxford: Praeger, 2010).

Sanders, Andrew, *The Short Oxford History of English Literature*, 3rd edition (Oxford: Oxford University Press, 2004).

Schlobin, Roger C., 'The Monsters are Talismans and Transgressions: Tolkien and *Sir Gawain and the Green Knight*', in George Clark and Daniel Timmons, eds, *J.R.R. Tolkien and his Literary Resonances* (Westport CT: Greenwood Press, 2000), 71–81.

Scull, Christina, 'Dragons from Andrew Lang's Retelling of Sigurd to Tolkien's Chrysophylax', in *Leaves from the Tree: J.R.R. Tolkien's Shorter Fiction* (London: Tolkien Society, 1991), 49–62.

_____ and Wayne G. Hammond, *The J.R.R. Tolkien Companion and Guide: Chronology* (London: Harper Collins, 2006).

_____ and Wayne G. Hammond, *The J.R.R. Tolkien Companion and Guide: Reader's Guide* (London: HarperCollins, 2006).

Segal, Robert A., 'Myth as Primitive Philosophy: The Case of E.B. Tylor', in Kevin Schilbrack, ed., *Thinking through Myths: Philosophical Perspectives* (London and New York: Routledge, 2002), 18–45.

Shippey, Tom, *The Road to Middle-earth* (London: George Allen & Unwin, 1982, 2nd edition (London: Grafton, 1992).

_____, 'Orcs, Wraiths, Wights: Tolkien's Images of Evil', in George Clark and Daniel Timmons, eds, *J.R.R. Tolkien and his Literary Resonances* (Westport CT: Greenwood Press, 2000), 183–198.

_____, *J.R.R. Tolkien: Author of the Century* (London: HarperCollins, 2000).

Silkin, Jon, ed., *The Penguin Book of First World War Poetry*, 2nd edition (Harmondsworth: Penguin, 1981).

Simpson, Jaqueline, *British Dragons* (London: B.T. Batsford, 1980).

Sisam, Kenneth, *Fourteenth-Century Verse and Prose* (Oxford: Clarendon Press, 1978) (orig. publ. 1921).

Smith, Albert Hugh, *The Merry Shire: Poems in the Yorkshire Dialect* (Leeds: At the Swan Press, 1923).

_____, *The Place-names of the North Riding of Yorkshire* (Cambridge: Cambridge University Press, 1928).

_____, *English Place-Name Elements*, 2 vols (Cambridge: Cambridge University Press, 1970).

Smith, Geoffrey Bache, *A Spring Harvest* (London: Erskine Macdonald, 1918).

Smith, Ross, 'Fitting Sense to Sound: Linguistic Aesthetics and Phono-semantics in the Work of J.R.R. Tolkien', *Tolkien Studies*, 3 (2006), 1–21.

Stray, Christopher, *Classics Transformed: Schools, Universities, and Society in England, 1830–1960* (Oxford: Clarendon Press, 1998).

Sturluson, Snorri, *Edda*, trans. Anthony Faulkes (London: J.M. Dent, 1987).

Sweet, Henry, *An Anglo-Saxon Reader in Prose and Verse*, 8th revised edition (Oxford: Clarendon Press, 1908) (orig. publ. 1876).

_____, 'Some of the Sources of the Anglo-Saxon Chronicle', *Englische Studien*, 2 (1879), 310–12.

_____, *An Anglo-Saxon Primer* (Oxford: Clarendon Press, 1882).

_____, *A New English Grammar. Logical and Historical. Part I* (Oxford: Clarendon Press, 1960) (orig. publ. 1891).

_____, *First Steps in Anglo-Saxon* (Oxford: Clarendon Press, 1897).

_____, *A New English Grammar. Part II* (Oxford: Clarendon Press, 1898).

Taylor, Paul B. and W.H. Auden, trans., *The Elder Edda* (London: Faber and Faber, 1973).

Thomas, Edward, 'Winter Music', in *Light and Twilight* (London: Duckworth, 1911), 69–95.

_____, *Norse Tales* (Oxford: Clarendon Press, 1912).

_____, *The Annotated Collected Poems*, ed. Edna Longley (Tarset, Northumberland: Bloodaxe Books, 2008).

Thomas, Paul Edmund, 'Some of Tolkien's Narrators', in Verlyn Flieger and Carl F. Hostetter, eds, *Tolkien's Legendarium: Essays on the History of Middle-earth* (Westport CT: Greenwood Press, 2000), 161–81.

Thompson, Francis, *Poems*, ed. Brigid M. Boardman (London and New York: Continuum, 2001).

Tolkien, Christopher, ed., *The Saga of King Heidrek the Wise* (London: Thomas Nelson, 1960).

_____, *Pictures by J.R.R. Tolkien* (London: George Allen & Unwin, 1979).

Tolkien, Hilary, *Black and White Ogre Country*, ed. Angela Gardner (Moreton-in-Marsh: ADC Publications, 2009).

Tolkien, J.R.R., 'The Happy Mariners', in *The Stapeldon Magazine*, 5 (December 1919–June 1922), 69–70.

————, *A Middle English Vocabulary* (Oxford: Clarendon Press, 1922); printed in Kenneth Sisam, ed., *Fourteenth-Century Verse and Prose* (Oxford: Clarendon Press, 1978), 293–454.

————, 'Henry Bradley, 3 Dec. 1845–23 May 1923', *The Bulletin of the Modern Humanities Association* (October, 1923), 4–5.

————, 'The Cat and the Fiddle: A Nursery Rhyme Undone and its Scandalous Secret Unlocked', the new poem heading the issue in *Yorkshire Poetry* 2, no. 19 (20 October 1923), pp. 1–3. Revised version published as 'The Man in the Moon Stayed up too Late', in Tolkien, *Adventures of Tom Bombadil*.

————, 'Philology: General Works', in *The Year's Work in English Studies*, vol. 4 (1923), ed. Sidney Lee and F.S. Boas (Oxford: Oxford University Press, 1924), 20–44.

———— (writing as K. Bagpuize), 'Progress in Bimble Town', *Oxford Magazine*, 50, no. 1 (15 October 1931), 22.

————, 'The Adventures of Tom Bombadil', *Oxford Magazine*, vol. 52, no. 13 (15 February 1934), 464–5; reprinted in Wayne G. Hammond and Christina Scull, *The Lord of the Rings: A Reader's Companion* (London: HarperCollins, 2008), 124–7; a later version of the poem appeared in Tolkien, *The Adventures of Tom Bombadil*.

————, 'Chaucer as Philologist: *The Reeve's Tale*', *Transactions of the Philological Society* (1934), 1–70.

————, 'The Dragon's Visit', *Oxford Magazine*, vol. 55, no. 11 (4 February 1937), 342; reprinted in Anderson, *The Annotated Hobbit*, 335–7.

————, *The Hobbit*, 1st edition (London: George Allen & Unwin, 1937).

————, 'Prefatory Remarks', in John R. Clarke Hall, trans., *Beowulf and the Finnesburg Fragment* (London: George Allen & Unwin, 1940).

————, *The Hobbit*, 2nd edition (London: George Allen & Unwin, 1951).

————, *The Fellowship of the Ring*, Part I of *The Lord of the Rings* (London: George Allen & Unwin, 1954).

————, *The Two Towers*, Part II of *The Lord of the Rings* (London: George Allen & Unwin, 1954).

————, *The Return of the King*, Part III of *The Lord of the Rings* (London: George Allen & Unwin, 1955).

————, *The Adventures of Tom Bombadil and Other Verses from the Red Book* (London: George Allen & Unwin, 1962).

———— trans., *Sir Gawain and the Green Knight, Pearl, and Sir Orfeo* (London: George Allen & Unwin, 1975).

————, *The Silmarillion*, ed. Christopher Tolkien (London: George Allen & Unwin, 1977).

_____, 'Valedictory Address', in Mary Salu and Robert T. Farrell, eds, *J.R.R. Tolkien: Scholar and Story Teller* (Ithaca NY and London: Cornell University Press, 1979), 16–32.

_____, *Unfinished Tales of Númenor and Middle-Earth*, ed. Christopher Tolkien (London: George Allen & Unwin, 1980).

_____, *The Letters of J.R.R. Tolkien*, ed. Humphrey Carpenter (London: George Allen & Unwin, 1981).

_____, *The Monsters and the Critics and Other Essays*, ed. Christopher Tolkien (London: George Allen & Unwin, 1983).

_____, *The Book of Lost Tales, Part I*, ed. Christopher Tolkien, *The History of Middle-earth, I* (London: George Allen & Unwin, 1983).

_____, *The Book of Lost Tales, Part II*, ed. Christopher Tolkien, *The History of Middle-earth, II* (London: George Allen & Unwin, 1984).

_____, *The Shaping of Middle-earth*, ed. Christopher Tolkien, *The History of Middle-earth, IV* (London: HarperCollins, 2002) (orig. publ. London: George Allen & Unwin, 1986).

_____, *The Return of the Shadow*, ed. Christopher Tolkien, *The History of Middle-earth, VI* (London: HarperCollins, 2002) (orig. publ. London: Unwin Hyman, 1988).

_____, *Roverandom*, ed. Christina Scull and Wayne G. Hammond (London: HarperCollins, 1998).

_____, 'The Lonely Isle', in John Garth, *Tolkien and the Great War: The Threshold of Middle-earth* (London: HarperCollins, 2004), 145.

_____, *Letters from Father Christmas*, ed. Baillie Tolkien (London: HarperCollins, 2004).

_____, *On Fairy-stories*, expanded edition, ed. Verlyn Flieger and Douglas A. Anderson (London: HarperCollins, 2008).

_____, *The Legend of Sigurd and Gudrún*, ed. Christopher Tolkien (London: HarperCollins, 2010).

_____, '"The Story of Kullervo" and Essays on *Kalevala*', ed. Verlyn Flieger, *Tolkien Studies*, 7 (2010), 211–78.

Tolkien, Priscilla, ed., *The Tolkien Family Album* (London: Harper Collins, 1992).

Tolley, Clive, 'Old English Influence on *The Lord of the Rings*', in Richard North and Joe Allard, eds, *Beowulf and Other Stories* (Edinburgh: Pearson, 2007), 38–62.

Treharne, Elaine, ed., *Old and Middle English c.890–c.1450: An Anthology*, 3rd edition (Oxford: Blackwell, 2010).

Trudgill, Peter, *The Dialects of England*, 2nd edition (Oxford, Blackwell, 1999).

Turner, Allan, *Translating Tolkien: Philological Elements in The Lord of the Rings* (Frankfurt am Main and Oxford: Peter Lang, 2005).

Turville-Petre, Thorlac, *Reading Middle English Literature* (Oxford: Blackwell, 2007).

Tylor, Edward Burnett, *Primitive Culture*, 2 vols (London: Murray, 1871).

_____, *Anthropology: An Introduction to the Study of Man and Civilisation* (London: Macmillan, 1881).

Vaninskaya, Anna, 'Tolkien: A Man of his Time?', in Frank Weinreich and Thomas Honegger, *Tolkien and Modernity*, 2 vols (Zurich: Walking Tree Publishers, 2006), vol. 1, 1–30.

Waithe, Marcus, *William Morris's Utopia of Strangers: Victorian Medievalism and the Ideal of Hospitality* (Cambridge: D.S. Brewer, 2006).

Walker, Steve, *The Power of Tolkien's Prose: Middle-Earth's Magical Style* (Basingstoke: Palgrave Macmillan, 2009).

Walsh, Chris, '"From Mind to Mind": Robert Browning and J.R.R. Tolkien', *Inaugural and Professorial Lectures, 2005* (Chester: Chester Academic Press, 2007).

Wawn, Andrew, *The Vikings and the Victorians: Inventing the Old North 19th-Century Britain* (Woodbridge: D.S. Brewer, 2000).

Whittingham, Elizabeth A., *The Evolution of Tolkien's Mythology: A Study of the History of Middle-earth* (Jefferson NC and London: McFarland, 2008).

Wilkinson, Loren, 'Tolkien and the Surrendering of Power', in Trevor Hart and Ivan Khovacs, eds, *Tree of Tales: Tolkien, Literature, and Theology* (Waco TX: Baylor University Press, 2007), 71–83.

Wright, Elizabeth, *Rustic Speech and Folk-Lore* (London: Oxford University Press, 1913).

Wright, Joseph, *The English Dialect Dictionary*, 6 vols (London: Henry Frowde, 1898–1905).

Wyke Smith, E.A., *The Marvellous Land of Snergs* (London: Ernest Benn, 1927).

Yorke, Barbara, *The Anglo-Saxons* (Stroud: Sutton, 1999).

Zoëga, Geir T., *A Concise Dictionary of Old Icelandic* (Oxford: Benediction Classics, 2010) (orig. publ. Oxford: Clarendon Press, 1910).

Zytaruk, George J. and James T. Boulton, eds, *The Letters of D.H. Lawrence. Volume II. June 1913–October 1916* (Cambridge: Cambridge University Press, 1981).

Index

Words in languages other than modern English are shown in bold; specialised modern English words and concepts are given in inverted commas. References to names in Tolkien's fiction are selective only.